The Geometric Supposer:

What is it a Case of?

TECHNOLOGY IN EDUCATION SERIES

Edited by
Raymond S. Nickerson

The Geometric Supposer:

What is it a Case of?

Edited by

Judah L. Schwartz
Harvard Graduate School of Education

Michal Yerushalmy
The University of Haifa

Beth Wilson
Education Development Center, Inc.
Newton, Massachusetts

LAWRENCE ERLBAUM ASSOCIATES, PUBLISHERS
1993   Hillsdale, New Jersey   Hove and London

Copyright © 1993 by Lawrence Erlbaum Associates, Inc.
All rights reserved. No part of this book may be reproduced in
any form, by photostat, microform, retrieval system, or any other
means, without the prior written permission of the publisher.

Lawrence Erlbaum Associates, Inc., Publishers
365 Broadway
Hillsdale, New Jersey 07642

Library of Congress Cataloging-in-Publication Data

The geometric supposer : what is it a case of? / edited by Judah
  Schwartz
      p.   cm. — (Technology and education series)
    Includes bibliographical references and index.
    ISBN 0-8058-0720-9
    1. Geometry—Study and teaching. 2. Geometry—Computer-assisted
instruction. I. Schwartz, Judah L., 1934-   II. Yerushalmy, Michal.
III. Wilson, Beth. IV. Series.
QA462.G42   1993
516′.0071 — dc20   92-20461
                                                       CIP

Books published by Lawrence Erlbaum Associates are printed on acid-free
paper, and their bindings are chosen for strength and durability.

Printed in the United States of America
10 9 8 7 6 5 4 3 2 1

Contents

PART III: PROBLEMS OF TEACHING

PART IV: PROBLEMS OF IMPLEMENTATION

Introduction: The Many Faces of Educational Innovation

Judah L. Schwartz
Massachusetts Institute of Technology and
Harvard Graduate School of Education

Many undertakings in life turn out to be substantially more complex than we imagined them to be at the outset. So it has been with the Geometric Supposer, an educational innovation that has had an important impact on mathematics education in the last half decade. Developing and using the Supposer as an educational tool has forced us to face and think about many unexpected entailments and consequences of our work.

All innovations in education must maintain contact with their philosophical and ideological roots, and we have constantly had to question our own behavior with students and teachers. Because students' learning and attitudes are important dimensions of the effect of an innovation, we found ourselves attending carefully to these matters as well. Similarly, teachers' teaching (and learning) and attitudes are important in analyzing the effect of an educational innovation. Finally, those who seek to produce educational innovation must face the problems of implementing the innovation in the settings for which it was designed. All of these issues have concerned us as we have endeavored to bring about change in a particular area of mathematics education.

This volume is an attempt to bring together in one place a collection of reports on the Supposer that address this range of concerns. Because of their diversity, it is not likely that a reader would, in the normal course of events, encounter this variety of reports on a single innovation within the covers of a single volume.

We believe this volume is of interest to mathematics educators who wish to learn more about learning and teaching geometry. At the same time, we want to address an even wider audience. We believe that aspects of the story we have to tell are central to the concerns of a broad audience of teachers of all subjects at all levels as well as to cognitive scientists, educational administrators, school board members, and, of course, people interested in educational technology. In fact, we invite our readers, in the spirit of the Supposer, to read this volume with the following question in mind: "What is this story a case of?"

We think the Supposer experience is a wonderfully optimistic story about mathematics education. We hope that our readers agree. We hope that you see the same melding of concern for content, potential of educational technology, and celebration of the diversity of individual students and teachers and classroom settings that we see. We hope you ask yourselves, as we ask ourselves, "Can we do this sort of thing in other areas of mathematics education?" We hope you ask, with us, "Is this a model that can be instantiated beyond mathematics education?" We do not claim to have anything but the most partial of answers to these questions. Nevertheless, we think the answers to these questions have important consequences for all who are connected with education, and to the extent we believe we have answered them reasonably, we present what we have found. We do this tentatively and in full realization that what we have learned should be regarded by others as suggestive rather than definitive.

This volume has four sections. The first contains two chapters intended to introduce the reader to the Supposer. The first of these chapters is by Judah L. Schwartz, professor of Engineering Science and Education at MIT and co-director of the Educational Technology Center at the Harvard Graduate School of Education. Schwartz describes the work that Michal Yerushalmy and he did in developing the Supposer, independently at first and then at the Education Development Center. The chapter is idiosyncratic in tone and content, reflecting the fact that innovations often grow out of the obsessions of individuals.

In the second introductory chapter, Beth Wilson attempts to convey to the reader something of the ambiance of a Supposer classroom. She opens with a classroom vignette to illustrate the kinds of problems students explore, the sorts of displays they see on the computer screen, and the flavor of the interactions that take place. Wilson goes on to discuss changes for teachers and students in the way they think about geometry, about technology, and about teaching and learning. Although the discussion focuses on the Supposer innovation, it raises more general questions of how any innovation affects those in classrooms.

The second section of the volume is concerned with problems of learning. Michal Yerushalmy and Daniel Chazan, in their chapter on overcoming visual obstacles in the learning of geometry, focus on how cognitive difficulties can be uncovered and ameliorated. The idea of obstacles to the learning of a subject is a recurring theme in all of education, and it manifests itself in an especially interesting way in the learning of geometry. Yerushalmy and Chazan are concerned with the particularity of geometric diagrams and the generality of the constructs they are surrogates for. They report on students' growing ability to take a flexible approach to diagrams, coming to see them as models that may have particular attributes not shared by other members of the classes to which they belong. Yerushalmy is one of the co-developers of the Geometric Supposer and is currently on the faculty of the School of Education of the University of Haifa in Israel. Chazan was a secondary school mathematics teacher while he completed his doctoral research. He is currently on the faculty of the School of Education at Michigan State University.

The next chapter in this section is by Michal Yerushalmy and deals with the problem of generalization. The theme of particularity and generality is universal in education. Indeed, one might say that students who learn to raise on their own initiative the question, "What is this a case of?" have been successfully educated. In this chapter, Yerushalmy discusses the distinctions and relationships among generalization, induction, and conjecture. After reviewing the literature in this area, she goes on to present, from studies of students using the Supposer, data on students' generalizations, inductions, and conjectures. And in a preview of the next section of this book, she points to the importance for the student of having teachers model the use of inductive strategies.

As a bridge between the section of the volume that focuses on learning and the one that focuses on teaching, we include a chapter of a somewhat unusual nature. This chapter was written jointly by Chip Healy, a 10th-grade math teacher in Los Angeles, and his students. The chapter captures the richness and the idiosyncrasy of the voices and concerns of both teacher and students. In our role as editors, we have chosen to leave this rambling richness of language and concerns and not try to prune the text until only those parts pertinent to the learning and teaching of geometry remained. In this kaleidoscope of reflections of adolescent students and their deeply committed teacher, it is possible to discern a variety of themes that characterize life in the urban high schools of today. Healy, trying to address the pedagogic challenge of engaging a group of young adolescents whose primary concerns were far from geometry, got them to understand by direct experience what is meant by building an intellectual discipline. They invented and devised new constructs, considering each one gravely before including it in the growing compendium that became the geometry book they wrote. All in all, it was a rich and complicated year in that geometry classroom, with many kinds of results. Certainly among the best of these outcomes was that a substantial number of youngsters began to reflect deeply on the true nature of learning in general and their own learning in particular.

The third section of the volume deals with the problems of teaching with educational innovations. This section opens with a chapter by Chazan on the instructional implications of a study of students' understanding of the nature and role of proof. The study reveals that students possess a variety of misconceptions about the nature of formal proof in geometry in particular and in mathematics in general. Needless to say, one must shape instruction to take these misconceptions into account. This is, of course, a particular case of a phenomenon that goes well beyond geometry. All innovations in education, if observed closely and reflected upon, have implications for teachers and instructional practice.

In the next chapter of this section, Michal Yerushalmy, Daniel Chazan, and Myles Gordon, vice-president of the Education Development Center, look closely at the art and craft of posing interesting problems. They present guidelines for formulating inquiry problems that leave room for student initiative and creativity. They go on to discuss a variety of problems and analyze them from the point of view of the kind of problem, its size and scope, and the demands it places on a student's ability and background. Here too, we see an instance of an instructional problem that goes beyond geometry. Teachers in all subjects are regularly faced with the need to challenge their students in ways that stretch them and evoke the best creative efforts they can make.

In the next chapter, Magdalene Lampert, professor of mathematics education at Michigan State University writes about teachers' thinking about students' thinking about geometry. She reports on a study that probed teachers' views of how using the Supposer had changed the way they teach geometry. She explores their thinking about subject matter and about the role of induction and their own role in teaching and learning. Lampert goes on to discuss instructional sequences, the implications of teaching without right answers, collaborative learning among peers and between teachers and students, as well as the question of who is responsible for student learning. The concerns addressed in this chapter, although prompted by a study of a particular innovation in a particular subject, are common to teachers in all subjects.

The final chapter in this section of the volume is an autobiographical statement by Richard Houde, now associate superintendent of the Weston, Massachusetts schools. Houde was a classroom teacher who worked closely with Schwartz and Yerushalmy during the course of the development of the Supposer. Houde writes the autobiographical statement from the journal notes he kept during the period of the development of the Supposer. The chapter tells the story of how the Supposer helped to change one teacher's thinking about geometry and teaching and how it contributed to his professional growth.

The last section of the volume deals with problems of the implementation and dissemination of educational innovations. The chapter by Martha Stone Wiske, co-director of the Educational Technology Center at the Harvard Graduate School of Education, and Richard Houde examines efforts of a group of secondary school geometry teachers to shift their instruction toward guided inquiry with the use of the Supposer. The chapter focuses on the evolution of teachers' concerns, especially the curricular and pedagogical dilemmas they faced during their second year with this approach. They analyze themes that are likely to reappear whenever teachers try to move away from traditional instruction toward guided inquiry, concluding with an analysis of the implications of their findings for the support teachers need as they try to change.

The next chapter in this section, by Mark Driscoll and Grace Kelemanik of the Education Development Center, describes the use of the Supposer by teachers involved in the Urban Mathematics Collaborative. This Ford Foundation funded collaborative is a consortium of math teachers in the major urban centers of the country who exchange insights and experiences on the teaching of mathematics and support one another in a variety of professional ways. The chapter draws on the experience of two particular teachers and discusses the attempts of the collaborative to provide needed supports to these teachers. In contrast to the treatment of this theme in earlier chapters, here we learn about problems of implementation in a world of teachers and schools far removed from the designers of the innovation and the first-generation teachers.

In the last chapter of the volume, Myles Gordon steps back and takes a longer look at the Supposer experience. He finds there is good news and other news. The good news is that both students' and teachers' mathematical behavior grows more sophisticated as they gain experience with the Supposer and with guided inquiry and that their attitudes toward the subject improve. In addition, there seem to be real and lasting changes in students' learning behaviors and teachers' teaching behaviors. The other news is that innovations like the Supposer produce new demands that are not easily answered and dilemmas that are not readily resolved. In analyzing the implications of these findings, Gordon calls for a shift in thinking on the part of a wide range of concerned clienteles, from the parents of the children in each class to the Congress of the United States.

In summary, we have attempted in this volume to bring together a range of viewpoints and perspectives on an innovation in mathematics education. We hope that the spectrum of interacting themes in the Supposer story enlightens readers' efforts to improve education in whatever subject, at whatever level, and in whatever setting they are working.

INTRODUCING THE READER
TO THE SUPPOSER

1 A Personal View of the Supposer: Reflections on Particularities and Generalities in Educational Reform

Judah L. Schwartz
*Massachusetts Institute of Technology and
Harvard Graduate School of Education*

A BIT OF BACKGROUND—HOW THE SUPPOSER CAME TO BE

In many respects the last 5 or 6 years have been for me the most exciting years of a professional career that began nearly 35 years ago. During this latter period I have been fortunate enough to be intimately involved with the development and implementation of an important innovation in the teaching of mathematics, a series of computer software environments collectively known as The Geometric Supposer.

My experiences with the Geometric Supposer over the past 5 years or so have led me to consider a wide range of issues bearing on the enterprise of education. The broadest of these issues concerns the desiderata of an education for citizenship in a democratic society. Some of the more focused issues concern the nature of geometry as a field of mathematics and ways of teaching the subject to students whose interest in and talent for it vary. In this chapter, I shall sketch the story of my experience with the Supposer and the range and substance of the educational issues that I was forced to confront in trying to make sense of the experience.

In the mid-1960s, while on the research staff of the Lawrence Radiation Laboratory in California, two colleagues and I developed a series of computer-generated motion picture films that depicted graphically the collisions of subatomic particles as described by the formal mathematical machinery of quantum mechanics. I became interested in the potential of the computer to make accessible representations of spatial and temporal phenomena whose natural distance and time scales lay well outside the ken of human sensory apparatus. My colleagues and I pursued these efforts for a while but soon concluded that the true utility of computers to help people with mathematical abstraction would lie in the interactivity and control that the soon-to-come microcomputer would offer.

Shortly thereafter I left California and joined the staff of the Education Research Center at the Massachusetts Institute of Technology (MIT). There I met and was profoundly influenced by the late Jerrold R. Zacharias. He taught me much about education as it is and as it might be, and I like to believe that he would be comfortable with the view of education that I have evolved. He was fond of saying, "Children are different from one another and schools should make them more so." That phrase captures succinctly the essence of an educational philosophy that has among its central tenets a deep respect for diversity. Professor Zacharias also taught me the importance of the endless frontier of knowledge-making as a core activity of schools and the people in them at all levels. He taught me that education must always have a subject matter and that subject matter content, with all of its nuance and subtlety, is central to the educational enterprise. Finally, he taught me that ultimately we must each assume authority and responsibility for our own learning and that schools ought to help us do that.

Largely as a result of Professor Zacharias' influence, I decided to leave behind my research in physics and to direct my professional activity toward educational reform. In the context of a series of federally and foundation supported projects, I worked on science curriculum development, the nature of undergraduate education, and alternative assessment methods for instruction and accountability.

In the late 1970s and early 1980s, I taught a course entitled "The Intelligent Eye and the Intelligible Image" in the now defunct Division for Study and Research in Education (DSRE) at MIT. The central theme of the course was an examination of the variety of visual representations of abstractions that human beings fashion for themselves and of how they help make sense of the not always perceptible concepts that are central to their theories about the world around them.

Each time I taught the course, I became puzzled once again by a seemingly inescapable paradox that accompanied the use of images, that is, that the images formulated to aid in understanding and analysis of the abstract are, of necessity, particular. Indeed, they are often far more particular than the abstractions they are intended to help us understand. I observed that people were frequently distracted by the artifactual and incidental properties of the images they used, often going so far as to make inferences about the referent of the image on the basis of the incidental properties of the image itself.

It seemed to me this conundrum raised by the image course had implications for all of education. I found echoes of this theme wherever I looked. One studies the great 19th-century Russian novels, not for their particularity, but rather for the generality of their message about the human condition. One studies history, not for facts and dates, but rather to understand how the lessons of the past might be used to understand and shape the present and the future. It was, however, in the context of the world of visual images that I found the theme of the particular and the general most compelling.

I taught the image course every other semester. In the alternating semesters I taught a course on "Microcomputers in Education." Microcomputers were then beginning to spread rapidly throughout the society in general and schools in particular. Having spent a good deal of time 10 years earlier trying to understand the roles computers might usefully play in education, I was attracted to the problem once again, suspecting that the new microcomputer technology might offer opportunities that the mainframe technology of the prior decade was incapable of. Having decided to learn more about what could be done, I did what most academics do under such circumstances: I offered a course in the subject.

At the beginning of one of my microcomputer semesters, a young Israeli woman by the name of Michal Yerushalmy asked me whether she could audit my course. She had a strong background in mathematics and computer science and had been a high school mathematics teacher for nearly a decade. The prospect of having such a bright and knowledgeable person in the room was inviting, and I readily agreed to her request.

When Michal came to me only a few weeks later and asked me to suggest an interesting microcomputer project for her, I saw in her request a possible confluence of my interests in both images and microcomputers. The graphical capabilities of the microcomputers of that time were limited to not much more than the simple shapes of school geometry. Limitations notwithstanding, that would do as an arena to explore the recurring puzzle of my other course, that is, the question of the particularity of images. I explained my continuing image paradox to Michal, and we quickly worked out the core notions that underlay the design of what was to become the first of the Geometric Supposers.

Thus began an intellectual odyssey that changed my life. Over the succeeding years, I have been forced to learn a great deal about things I had previously grasped only dimly. I have learned a great deal about geometry and about the possibilities and constraints of small personal computers. I have also learned a great deal about the nature and the process of educational change in this country and about the institutional channels that either promote or impede such change.

There was a time in the late 1950s and through most of the 1960s when the federal government provided important leadership and resources for educational reform. These efforts focused on, but were not confined to, curriculum reform. When I first turned to full-time education reform, most of my efforts were supported by people I felt to be forward looking and imaginative program officers in the federal agencies with which I dealt. In time, however, this federal role came under attack from several sources both in and out of government. As a consequence, the federal leadership fragmented, and its coherence dissipated. There seemed to be a growing disinclination to support bold education reform efforts that questioned cherished assumptions or that had the potential to reconceptualize a subject area and the way it was taught and learned. Unfortunately, in my view, this fragmentation and absence of bold vision continues to this day to characterize federal efforts in educational reform.

Because of my growing pessimism about the possibility of federal support for major change in education, I began to look for other channels through which I could play a constructive role in the process of educational reform. My previous experiences with another potential lever on the educational system, namely the traditional educational publishers, had been discouraging. Specifically, I had spent a good deal of time over the previous several years working with Jerrold Zacharias and others at Education Development Center formulating alternative approaches to the problem of educational assessment. Although we had succeeded in devising new ways of thinking about the issues that were not fraught with the intellectual malnourishment of psychometrics, we were unable to persuade publishers to change their practice. As nearly as I could tell, the driving impetus of the country's educational publishers was return on investment not American education. I concluded that despite their capability, they were not likely to provide a channel for the kind of positive educational impact on our schools that I believed and continue to believe is necessary.

Thus, I was in a fog of disillusionment about the possibilities of radical change in American education. Our schools were educating only a small fraction of our youngsters even tolerably well, and the majority of our population was poorly served by an educational system that gave lip service to diversity but had little in the way of structure or practice to enhance and promote it. At a time when our country most needed to move boldly to rethink the content and structure of schooling so that it could better serve a broader population, federal leadership failed. School systems were still relying on the traditional educational publishers and the intellectually bankrupt psychometric tradition for assessment to serve both societal and instructional needs. At about this time, the personal computer appeared on the scene and began to spread rapidly throughout the schools. The more I explored the device and the kinds of probing and questioning that good software made it possible for teachers and students to do, the more I became convinced that the microcomputer revolution might provide a qualitatively new kind of lever on the educational system — a sort of Trojan horse by which one could dramatically reshape what happens in schools. The experience of the last several years with the Geometric Supposers has persuaded me of the merit of this view.

SOME OBSERVATIONS ABOUT MATHEMATICS (AND SOME OTHER SUBJECTS) IN SCHOOLS

For the most part, the mathematics taught in the primary and secondary schools is the mathematics already made by other people. Were schools to teach language in the same way, students would be asked to learn a play by Shakespeare, an essay by Emerson, and a short story by Hemingway, but never asked to write prose of their own. In mathematics, by contrast, we seem willing to say that intellectuality lies in the ability to analyze and criticize rather than to create and invent.

I believe that students have a right to be challenged to create in every field they study in school. Further, I believe that in a society committed to the celebration of the diversity of individuals, schools have the obligation to challenge students to create in every field they ask students to learn. In some subject areas, students, their parents, and society have come to expect schools to offer the challenge of creating. In mathematics this is rarely the case.

In practice, this means that the teaching of youngsters to analyze and criticize, while important and necessary, is not sufficient. Students must also be challenged to invent and create. Schools must become more than institutions for the analysis and the transmission of the known. They must become, and we must come to think of them as, institutions in which students and teachers regularly make new knowledge.

I believe that challenging students to create is more than an obligation of schools and the people who run them. I believe that creating is a deep human need and that each of us is capable of doing so. To be sure, different people are creative in different domains and the fulfillment of the individual lies in part in finding those domains in which he or she can be inventive and creative.

I believe that it is important to challenge students to create not only for ideological reasons but also for pragmatic ones. Ultimately, one understands best that which one is most invested in. What better way for youngsters to be invested in a subject than to explore it driven by their own curiosity and, indeed, to invent some of it themselves?

The importance of this issue goes well beyond the need to give individual youngsters the richest possible educational opportunity. There has long been a gap between the rhetoric and the practice of our society. For most of our history, our society has succeeded in educating well only the thinnest sliver of the elite. Even the better educated of our students rarely succeed in developing an interest in and a talent for the quantitative arts. For most of our history, this practice was pragmatically, if not morally, adequate, but this quantitative infirmity that has traditionally characterized even the best educated and well-bred of our society, leaves a great deal to be desired in an era that makes increasingly complex and quantitative demands on both the analytic and synthetic abilities of our leaders. We are now faced with the practical need to change the way we educate to more nearly coincide with the way we describe ourselves to ourselves and to others.

I do not minimize the complexity and difficulty of implementing this point of view. Nor do I minimize the difficulty that society will have in accommodating a successful outcome of such an effort. Students who challenge easily and skillfully, who question received wisdom, who are willing, eager, and able to invent new formulations of old questions, as well as to formulate new questions, are not likely to be docile members of society.

INVENTION IN MATHEMATICS

For the sake of specificity, I limit the discussion of the problem of challenging students to create and invent in the domain of mathematics.

Given the difficulty teachers have in teaching mathematics and students have in learning mathematics, one might think this a hopelessly quixotic goal, one that stands little chance of being realized. Before rejecting the goal, however, it is worth exploring what the essence of creativity in mathematics might be and whether its realization is so utterly unreasonable.

I assert that the essence of mathematical creativity lies in the making and exploring of mathematical conjectures. By mathematical conjecture, I mean a proposition about a hitherto unsuspected relationship thought to hold among two or more mathematical objects.

What then is a mathematical object? A mathematical object is a formally defined construct such as a number, a shape, a vector, a matrix, a function, etc. In general, for each mathematical object there are one or more defined mathematical operations that can be carried out on the object and that can transform it in some way.

Suppose that the essence of mathematical creativity is the making and exploring of mathematical conjectures. Why have such activities not been a serious part of mathematics teaching and learning in the schools? I suggest that this sort of conjecturing is difficult to carry out without suitable tools and that only very recently have such tools begun to come into widespread use. Adequate tools make the trouble associated with the making and exploring of conjectures manageable. If people don't have the tools, they are unlikely to engage in the activity.

INTELLECTUAL INVENTION AND THE PERSONAL COMPUTER

It is now possible to bring together the three strands of discussion on the table. The first of these strands is the potential of the microcomputer to penetrate the classrooms of the country without the heavy hand of an inertia-ridden governmental establishment for educational research and development or the self-serving efforts of the educational publishing industry. The second strand is the right and need of every student to be challenged to create and invent in every subject area that he or she is asked to study, although we have limited our discussion here to creation and invention in mathematics. The third strand deals with the central role of the making and exploring of conjectures in intellectual invention in general and in mathematical invention in particular.

I see these three strands coming together in the design of certain types of attractive and engaging microcomputer software. I believe that appropriately designed microcomputer software can provide environments in which users, be they students or teachers, can explore an intellectual domain. If such software environments reduce the difficulties and provide rich tools for exploring the domain, those who have access to such environments are more likely to pursue such exploration.

Mathematics is peculiarly appropriate to the creation of exploratory environments that offer a rich set of tools for making conjectures. Such environments can display quickly the results of a conjecture. Using such environments as *intellectual mirrors,* users can probe their own understanding of a domain as well as devise new relationships among the objects of the domain. It becomes inviting and engaging in such environments to think inductively and to explore one's inductive notions. Similarly, the software environment and its tools invite users to generalize their thinking and to examine the range of validity of those generalizations. The mental acts of thinking inductively and generalizing are at the heart of what mathematics students ought to learn to do. I assert that appropriately designed software environments can help reach that goal.

I believe that the Geometric Supposer instantiates these possibilities well. It can, and is, permeating the mathematics classrooms of the country, providing an environment in which it is easier than it previously was to challenge youngsters to create and invent. It is, in my view, the paradigmatic intellectual mirror software.

THE SUPPOSER AS INTELLECTUAL MIRROR

The human cognitive apparatus seems to need the external aide of drawings and diagrams to think about spatial and visual matters. Yet as soon as one moves to answer that need by making or providing diagrams to be used in the learning of geometry, for example, one runs the risk of defeating one's own purposes.

Here is the heart of the matter. Consider, for example, the class of shapes that are called regular polygons. One can construct a regular 3-gon, a regular 17-gon, a regular (any particular number)-gon, but one cannot construct a regular N-gon. Similarly, one can construct *any* particular triangle, but one cannot construct a triangle that is any triangle. If one constructs a diagram of a triangle, then aside from the size of the triangle, there is only one such triangle. (This is in sharp contrast to the situation in algebra where a notation system allows one to write $F(x) = mx + b$ to denote any linear function.) The geometry one wishes to learn, teach, and make does not deal with the properties of particular shapes but rather with the properties of classes of shapes. How does one resolve this seeming conflict between the cognitive need for diagrams and images on the one hand and the necessarily particular and specific nature of those diagrams on the other?

Suppose that starting with a particular triangle, one makes a construction and discovers that in this case some interesting property obtains. Clearly, one wishes to know whether or not this interesting property obtains for other triangles as well. One can view the construction made on the original triangle ABC as a procedure that takes the three points in the plane ABC as its argument. If the environment is such that the procedure is executed in terms of a manageably small number of elemental procedures, then it is possible to capture the steps of the procedure. The captured procedure can then be repeated on any other triplet of points A'B'C' in the plane.

Although this repetition of the procedure is clearly incapable of proving anything, it can lead to added or lessened conviction that the property observed to be true in the particular case is indeed generally true. Both the psychological and logistical costs of making and exploring the conjecture are thus dramatically reduced. By allowing students to capture their procedures and to explore the effect of these procedures on other members of the same class of shapes, the Supposer directly confronts them with the question, "What is this construction a case of?" The Supposer is thus a tool for exploring particularity with an eye toward the problem of generality. No claim is made that the Supposer necessarily induces users to greater degrees of generalization. But it does provide the setting and the occasion.

WHY THE SUPPOSER IS THE WAY IT IS – SOME PEDAGOGICAL CONSIDERATIONS

Having described the central idea that drove the making of the Supposers, that is, the visual conundrum of the complementarity and conflict of the particular and the general, I think it is important to describe something of the larger software surround within which this problem is engaged.

First of all, a few observations about the overall design of the Supposer are in order. I believe it is important for educational software to make the intellectual content of a domain appealing and engaging. The Supposer has no cover story designed to sugar-coat the mathematics.

I also believe that in the long run, youngsters must learn to pose, as well as solve, problems. In my view the best way to do this is to allow them to practice posing problems in an environment that makes it inviting to pose problems and explore potential solutions. Thus, the Supposer does not pose problems for the user. I think that is best done by discussion among students and teachers.

Let us turn now to a more detailed look at some of the design issues the Supposer raised for Michal and me. Two facilities characterize the Supposer. The first of these is a construction facility, and the second is a facility to operate on and manage the constructions one has made.

The construction facility of the Supposer environment for triangles, for example, contains such primitive operations as the ability to draw medians, altitudes, angle bisectors, and perpendicular and parallel lines, as well as the ability to label intersections, subdivide segments into N ($N = 2$ to 8), reflect both points and lines in lines, and place random points inside, outside, or on a triangle defined by any 3 points on the screen.

The facility to operate on and manage constructions includes the ability to measure angles, lengths, distances, and areas, as well as the ability to rescale the construction, clear the construction, and most important of all, repeat the construction on a new primitive shape, that is, a new triangle, quadrilateral, and son on.

The design of the construction facility was not intuitively obvious to us. Indeed, it took a fair amount of time for us to understand two important issues — the problem of making the primitive operations of the software environment too simple and the problem of making them too complex. In addition we had to come to realize that we were building a pedagogical tool for learning, teaching, and making plane geometry, not a Computer-Aided Design (CAD) system.

Let me expand on these problems a bit. The mathematically trained person is likely to fall prey to a temptation to conceive of the primitive construction operations of a computer environment in geometry as the ability to make straight lines and arcs of circles. After all, is it not possible to derive all of Euclidean geometry from these simple and elegant beginnings? It is, of course, but at a price. The price is the tediousness of the task. If a user of the software must make an elaborate series of straight line and circular arc constructions in order to draw a median or an angle bisector, that user is unlikely to explore playfully the properties of geometric constructions that are rife with medians and angle bisectors.

The reader will no doubt object to this point, arguing that in a computer environment it should be possible to capture a series of commands and define them as a *macro,* that is, to create and name a composite command that consists of the sequence of commands that have been captured. In fact, is this not what the Supposer itself does? If it were possible to construct macros, then the user would not have to undergo a painful repetition of intermediate constructions to arrive at a perpendicular bisector or a median.

This point is logically correct. Nevertheless, there are two reasons for the lack of macros in the microcomputer versions of the Geometric Supposers. The first reason has to do with the amount of computer memory that microcomputers in schools could be presumed to have. We tried to design the software to be usable with the hardware that was to be found in classrooms. The second reason for the lack of macros is pedagogical. Building and naming a procedure as a way of extending a language is a subtle and delicate idea. Although it is a very important idea and one that is certainly worth learning, it seems not to be an easy idea for many people to grasp. One needs only to look at the many widely used spreadsheet and word processing programs in which powerful macro facilities are present and unused. We felt that it would be unwise to confound the problem of learning geometry with another set of important ideas about formulating and naming procedures. Before leaving this point, I must confess my impatience for the day when procedural thinking will have so broadly permeated the way we think and the way we train youngsters to think that the design of future Supposer-like software environments can incorporate such ideas in a natural and obvious way.

Having argued against making the primitive operations of the software environment too simple, let me now discuss the problem of making them too complex. It seems to me there are several good reasons to avoid too great a degree of complexity in the primitive operations available in a software environment. The first of these reasons is simply that complexity of primitive operations conflicts directly with ease of use. The more bells and whistles present in a piece of software, the less obvious its operation is to the naive user and the longer it takes to learn to use the program to accomplish useful work. It is a source of some pride that the Supposers seem to require no computer background or experience of the user. They do, of course, require some geometrical knowledge of the user, but that, we believe, is as it should be.

A second reason for not making the primitive operations of the environment too complex is pedagogical: The software should provide an environment in which the user can formulate an extended line of argument. If the primitive operations provided the user by the software allow for complex ideas to be instantiated instantly with no hint of their internal structure and composition, it is likely that intellectual opportunities will be lost. For example, suppose there were a primitive operation that allowed the user to construct with a single command the three medians of a triangle. A user, in those circumstances, is unlikely to wonder about the fact that the medians of a triangle are concurrent.

Yet another reason for not making the primitive operations of a software environment too complex is to avoid a trap that Michal and I fell into early on. We managed to extricate ourselves from the trap before we were embarrassed into doing so by a community of users, but there is little guarantee of being so fortunate. In an early version of one of the Supposers, in addition to including a primitive operation that allowed the user to subdivide a segment into N segments of equal length, we included a primitive that allowed the user to subdivide an angle into N angles of equal measure. The subdivision of an angle into an arbitrary number of equal angles is not a construction that can be made using the primitive Euclidean construction tools, that is, straight edge and compass. We had lost sight of the primacy of Euclidean geometry and were seduced by the capabilities of the environment. If we had left such a primitive in place, we would have crippled the ability of the Supposers to serve as an environment for the making and exploring of conjectures about Euclidean geometry.

Finally, it is important to make a clean distinction between a tool like the Geometric Supposer and a CAD system. It is not difficult to imagine a CAD system that would incorporate the features of the Geometric Supposer among many other capabilities. Would such a system be a more appropriate tool for the geometry classroom? I believe not. CAD systems, no matter how elegant, enable users to manipulate spatial constructs in order to design specific objects. They address fundamentally synthetic ends. The implicit agenda of the Supposer, and one that it seems to address well, is to seduce the user into addressing analytic ends: wondering, conjecturing, and finally proving things about the general categories to which the spatial objects manipulated in the program belong.

WHAT HAPPENS WITH THE SUPPOSER AND WHAT DOES IT IMPLY?

There is a great deal more to the Supposer story. Much of it deals with such issues as designing good problems, training teachers, matching software and hardware resources to teachers and student needs, and attitudes of teachers and students. In addition, there are problems of pedagogic style and learning style. There are issues of administrative support for innovation and the expectations a school system has for its teachers and students. Subsequent chapters by others address these questions. Here I turn to a brief summary of some of the more important outcomes of the Supposer story.

The facility for making and exploring conjectures, which the Geometric Supposers provide, is leading to extraordinary changes in the learning and teaching of geometry in the United States. These include:

1. Students' and teachers' realization that it is not possible for any single person to know all of plane geometry because the process of inventing plane geometry is an unending one.

2. Changes in the roles of teachers and students in the classroom. Teachers have become more willing to listen to the mathematical formulations of their students. Students have become more willing to take intellectual risks.

3. Students coming to understand deeply and for themselves the need for formal proof in mathematics. I believe this is a result of using an environment in which the value of demonstration as a way of knowing is cheapened because of its ease.

4. Teachers thinking of themselves as people who continue to learn the subject they are teaching. In my view this is a necessary, albeit insufficient, condition for being a good teacher.

5. Students (and teachers) understanding that mathematics is not a spectator sport, but an intellectual pursuit that all can engage in.

These are wonderful and encouraging signs. My encouragement goes beyond the teaching and learning of geometry. I find the theme of the particular and the general to be, in large measure, a metaphor for all of education. Unfortunately, both teachers and students find it difficult to keep such an exalted theme in mind in the face of pressures and demands from many sources. If we can make the task somewhat simpler by providing curricular environments that support the making and exploring of conjectures about the general based on the ability to manipulate the particular, then we have contributed in a material way to the problem of improving education.

But making and exploring conjectures requires more than having curricular materials and environments that make these activities simple and engaging. It also requires a mind set on the part of the teacher and the students that this sort of activity is productive. They must believe in the productivity of exploration and synthesis, both in the short term as a way of preparing for the next assessment instrument the school board or the state education agency will subject them to and in the long term as a way of teaching people to reflect and invent as well as analyze and critique.

Belief in the importance of exploration and synthesis is necessary but not sufficient for this view of an educational future to take hold. Making classrooms into places where knowledge is created has implications for the way teachers practice their craft and implications for the way teachers-to-be are taught to practice. Perhaps foremost among these is a shift in teachers' view of themselves toward becoming continuing learners and makers of the subject matter they teach.

Schools are more than collections of classrooms. They are small communities of parents, teachers, administrators, and students. All the members of these communities must come to share a changed view of the kind of institution school might be. As they do so, they will inevitably begin to shift their notions of excellent and desirable performance, not only on the part of students but also on the parts of teachers, administrators, and even parents.

The implications of this sort of change go beyond the individual school and the community that surrounds it. If this vision of an educational future is to take hold and flourish, then the view of school as a conduit for the transmission of the knowledge of the past is insufficient. No matter how fashionable the notion of school as transmission line may currently be among governmental education officials and university professors who write popular books lamenting what they regard as the parlous state of American education, one must not succumb to the idea that it is sufficient to prove a theorem but not invent one or recite a poem but not compose one.

2 The Geometric Supposer in the Classroom

Beth Wilson
Education Development Center

Gary Simon, a mathematics teacher at Cambridge Rindge and Latin High School, meets his geometry class in the computer lab approximately two of five mornings each week. He hands students a problem as they come in to take their places, individually or in pairs, at one of the dozen computers in the room. The Supposer is already booted in the machines, so they get right to work on Simon's instructions:

> Draw triangle ABC. Connect the midpoints of two sides of the triangle (midsegment). Connect one of the midpoints with the nonadjacent vertex of the triangle. State as many conjectures as you can about the relationships among the points, segments, angles, and triangles.

Consulting each other in pairs or working alone, students use the Supposer to construct this figure on their screens (see Fig. 2.1). In no time, they move on to the business of making measurements, looking for patterns, forming conjectures, and making more constructions to test them.

Soon, a student working alone begins to wave his hand and call out, "Mr. Simon, come look at this. I think I've found something." Simon, however, is at the other end of the lab, talking with another pair of students. As the excited discoverer continues to wave, his classmate leans over, "Tell *me* what you've found." Unlike most mathematics teachers, Simon permits — even encourages — such exchanges: The two trade comments, questions, ooohs and aaahs; then both appear satisfied and move on to more constructions and conjectures.

Toward the end of the class, Simon summons everyone's attention as he

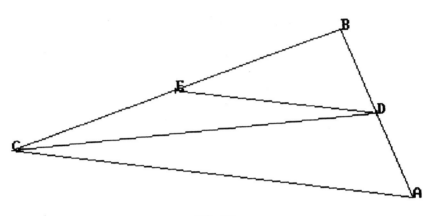

FIG. 2.1.

explains the homework assignment. "List the data you gathered today, including measurements and diagrams. Then write down at least two conjectures based on your data."

A few diehards continue to work at the computers even after the bell rings. "Don't you have another class?" inquires Simon, gratified by their enthusiasm but doubtful their next teacher will feel the same way. He's also eager for a few moments alone: teaching this way – guiding students along their own paths of inquiry – is fraught with surprises and dilemmas, even for seasoned teachers like him.

THE GEOMETRIC SUPPOSER: THE SOFTWARE AND THE INNOVATION

The Geometric Supposer is a piece of educational software. It comes on four floppy disks (one each for circles, triangles, and quadrilaterals, and a fourth introductory program called the Geometric Presupposer), and it allows students to make geometric constructions of the sort created with a straightedge and compass. It also provides a facility to measure angles, areas, and line segments and to perform arithmetic operations on these numerical data. The software remembers a construction as a procedure and allows the user to repeat the construction on another geometric figure of the same sort, either a random one or one defined by the user. Thus the software enables students and teachers to gather geometric data, observe patterns in visual and numerical data, and test conjectures about geometry. Instead of starting with postulates and proofs, students can start with the "stuff" of geometry and follow their own intuitions and hunches in the search for laws and theorems.

Because of this capability, the Geometric Supposer software makes it possible for the Geometric Supposer innovation to happen — makes it possible but in no way guarantees it. Those familiar with traditional geometry instruction recognize immediately how radically Gary Simon's approach differs from the way the subject is usually taught. Geometry is usually touted as the course in which students are introduced to deductive reasoning and in which they learn to think logically, both in mathematics and in general. Mathematicians, including mathematics teachers, appreciate the elegant simplicity of the Euclidian system that can produce a whole system of mathematics from just a few axioms and definitions. Students typically write two-column proofs in which they must construct a series of logical steps that lead from the information that is given to the conclusion to be proved. Once a statement is proved, it becomes a theorem and can be used to prove other statements encountered later.

In practice, however, students typically accept the truth of geometric statements because their teachers or textbooks say they are true. When teachers assign proofs, as Magdalene Lampert points out in this volume, there is never any question that what needs to be proved can and will be proved. Not surprisingly, students often wonder why they should bother to prove what they and their teachers already know to be true. Thus, they may learn what their teachers, textbooks, and tests require them to know about proofs and how to write them, most acquire little appreciation or respect for the important role of proof in mathematics.

Although the Supposer can be used in traditional instruction with a teacher lecturing and using the computer as a sort of electronic blackboard for whole-class demonstrations, it lends itself readily to a more open-ended approach. It offers teachers the opportunity to bring inductive learning back into the geometry curriculum. Students generate and examine large quantities of visual information, using it as a basis for conjectures and generalizations. They learn the value of working from data, but they also learn that only a proof can turn a conjecture into a theorem.

Most of the Supposer work described in this volume took place in the context of a guided inquiry approach to teaching and learning in which teachers tried to cultivate student exploration and problem solving. Introducing problems much the way Gary Simon did in the vignette at the beginning of this chapter, they encourage students to work on them alone or in pairs at the Supposer. Later, teachers lead discussions to help students synthesize their findings in relationship to the teacher's instructional goals and the standard geometry curriculum.

Reports from the classroom suggest that the process and the results of guided inquiry with the Supposer are exciting and brimming with challenges. Using the Supposer as part of a guided inquiry approach sets in motion certain significant shifts in thinking concerning subject matter, classroom organization, assessment, and what it means to be a teacher or a learner.

FROM THE TEACHER'S PERSPECTIVE

One feature of traditional geometry instruction is that teachers exert almost total control over what is taught. They decide what to cover in their presentations and what to assign in their texts. Because they mostly assign problems that ask students to prove theorems that have already been discovered rather than problems that encourage students to create mathematics through open-ended explorations, teachers can anticipate what will be discussed during a given lesson and can brush up on that aspect of the subject matter in preparation.

With the Supposer, all of that changes. Given the opportunity to explore problems on their own, students find relationships, invent ideas, or raise questions teachers had not intended to deal with for another semester. Occasionally student inquiry leads beyond the bounds of the teacher's own knowledge of the domain. To teach effectively using this open-ended approach, teachers need a thorough knowledge of geometry, a deep understanding of the processes of deductive and inductive reasoning, and experience with integrating these two ways of thinking to do mathematics. Teachers need to know how to model, present, and encourage such thinking. They need the confidence to bounce back quickly when carefully planned lessons fall flat. And not incidentally, they need familiarity and fluency with the software, its facilities, and menus. Sometimes that means time to practice with it in private before taking it into the classroom.

Teaching geometry inductively with the Supposer also requires teachers to take on a different role, to organize the classroom differently, and to help students learn new ways of thinking and behaving. Besides presenting problems, providing guidance as students work on the problems, and helping students synthesize their findings, they must nurture a classroom culture in which students take a more active role in their own learning and in which teachers relinquish some of the authority they are used to holding.

Many teachers find themselves flexing pedagogical muscles they never knew they had. For some, it is a new experience to admit to students that they don't know something—and to turn those moments from occasions of embarrassing ignorance to opportunities to credit student ingenuity, reinforce the idea that the classroom is a community of learners, and model productive ways to behave when one does not know something.

Running a Supposer lab session presents its own challenges: how to monitor whether students are working productively, how to facilitate collaboration while ensuring that each individual takes responsibility for his or her own learning, and so on. Orchestrating a productive discussion after a lab session takes great care: How should students share their findings with one another? How can their ideas be linked to the regular curriculum? Most mathematics teachers have little experience as discussion leaders and feel uneasy in the role.

Furthermore, teachers face dilemmas about how to evaluate student work on these open-ended problems. Accustomed to the relatively cut-and-dried process of correcting proofs, they may feel overwhelmed by the grab bag of homework papers that result from a single Supposer assignment. Putting in the extra hours, working the bugs out of new grading systems, and facing the uncertainty about whether students are learning enough all require commitment. In this volume, the chapters by Martha Stone Wiske and Richard Houde and by Houde, provide a rich and detailed examination of how teachers change as they work with the Supposer in their classrooms.

FROM THE STUDENT'S PERSPECTIVE

Regardless of rhetoric about the satisfaction of discovering knowledge for oneself, many students have thoroughly internalized the school's unwritten definition of learning as ingesting information that teachers present and repeating it back—often without understanding it—in papers, tests, and reports. Accustomed to having knowledge doled out to them via lectures and textbooks, students may feel that teachers who ask them to become active in their own learning are shirkers, foisting their responsibility to teach onto the shoulders of their students. The Supposer provides a wonderful vehicle for students making their first forays into this kind of self-motivated learning. Because the tool is easy to use and invites exploration, it maximizes the chance that students will feel successful and minimizes the burden on teachers to legitimatize inquiry as a route to knowledge.

Of course, some students take to the change like ducks to water, relishing the chance to follow their own instincts and be more active learners: "This is more parallel to the way I learn. I like learning from experience or from seeing what other people have done. You're doing stuff yourself so you're rediscovering stuff. It's really your own learning." Others feel lost without a clear structure and the security of a right answer: "You have to get a conjecture out of nowhere!" Such students need more help to learn specific inquiry skills and to learn the patience and persistence needed for self-directed learning. They need teachers who can tailor instruction to their needs, knowing when to provide guidance and structure and when to withdraw it.

In addition, few students are accustomed to working collaboratively with peers, as they frequently must do in the computer lab, solving problems and preparing reports together. In fact, such collaboration is taboo in most traditional classes. To make the shift, students need skillful teachers who can help them to maintain their own individual work ethic and acquire the communication skills needed for healthy cooperative work. In this volume, the chapter by Charles (Chip) Healy presents a rich range of student reactions and suggests how those reactions evolve with time and experience.

THE GEOMETRIC SUPPOSER: A LEVER FOR CHANGE

Traditional instruction in geometry and other subjects can tend subtly to pit teachers and students against one another: Teachers and textbooks have the knowledge, and students must vie to obtain it. The usual chalk-and-talk methods of instruction sometimes produce learning that lasts long enough to pass the final exam or the SAT but seldom runs deep enough for students to retain it, build on it, or apply it to solve problems. A completely student-directed approach, on the other hand, might lead to helter-skelter and unproductive explorations.

Guided inquiry with the Supposer is a hybrid that represents the best features of both traditional and unstructured instruction. It offers teachers new opportunities to facilitate student inquiry and promote conceptual change. It alters teachers' role but retains their status as the crucial link between the characteristics of students, the demands of the curriculum, and the power of the technology. Moving from lecturing to coaching and consulting with students on problems, most teachers find they have more contact with students, not less. Given a supportive context, this new way of teaching and learning places teachers and students on the same side and give them a rich and powerful set of tools with which to become codiscoverers of knowledge.

II | PROBLEMS OF LEARNING

3 Overcoming Visual Obstacles With the Aid of the Supposer

Michal Yerushalmy
The University of Haifa

Daniel Chazan
Michigan State University

Diagrams are one of the most common ways to represent and communicate geometrical knowledge. Yet, despite the benefits of diagrams, researchers have pointed out that they also present "obstacles children have to overcome in learning about geometry" (Bishop, 1986, p. 150). Presmeg (1986a, 1986b) called these obstacles "difficulties experienced by visualizers," whereas Hoz (1981) described the "rigidity" that arises when students' conceptions are limited by the use of diagrams or mental images. These obstacles can be grouped around three themes: diagrams are particular; common usage confuses certain standard diagrams with the classes of objects to which they belong; and a single diagram is often viewed in different ways.

THE PARTICULARITY OF DIAGRAMS

In most cases in a high school geometry class, diagrams are intended as models. They are meant to be understood as representing a class of objects, or as Rissland (1977) put it, they are supposed to "contain the essence of a situation" (p. 56). Nevertheless, every diagram has characteristics that are individual and not representative of the class. For example, Rissland pointed out that the following triangle ABC (see Fig. 3.1) that is meant to represent all triangles "is by no means a universally valid representation since it does not depict obtuse angles" (p. 58).

Schwartz (1988) called this "the type-token problem" or "the peril of the particular."

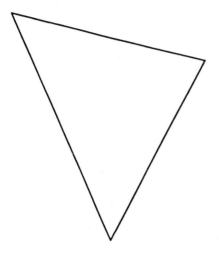

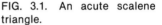

FIG. 3.1. An acute scalene triangle.

Presmeg (1986a) indicated that this obstacle causes students to be trapped by "the one-case concreteness of an image or diagram [which] may tie thought to irrelevant details, or may even introduce false data" (p. 44). For example, some of her students assumed that lines were parallel if they looked parallel. The particularity of diagrams is also related to students' difficulties with loci (Schoenfeld, 1986), for by definition a locus is a collection of points; it can be thought of as the result of the superposition of many diagrams or as alterations to a single diagram. When describing a locus, one must transcend the particular diagram and describe the path that a particular element of the diagram would trace out were some characteristic of the original diagram to be changed continuously.

STANDARD DIAGRAMS AS MODELS

If students learn a definition only when examining standard diagrams, the particularity of diagrams can lead to another obstacle: "An image of a standard figure (diagram) may induce inflexible thinking which prevents the recognition of a concept in a non-standard diagram" (Presmeg 1986a, p. 298). Students' definitions may include an irrelevant characteristic of the standard diagram, causing difficulties in creating or interpreting diagrams. Hershkovitz (1987, Hershkovitz, Bruckeimer, & Vinner, 1987) presented evidence of this kind of obstacle. Interestingly, teachers and students were unwilling to draw the exterior altitudes for obtuse triangles. They drew only interior diagonals from the vertices of concave polygons. They were much better at recognizing right triangles in an upright position than when the

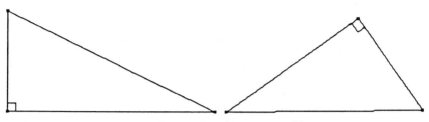

FIG. 3.2   Standard and on top positions.

right angle was at the top (see Fig. 3.2), and were much better at recognizing isosceles triangles standing on their base, than ones that were rotated (see Fig. 3.3).

INABILITY TO SEE A DIAGRAM IN DIFFERENT WAYS

Gestalt psychologists have identified diagrams and pictures that some people are able to reorganize and see in different ways (see Fig. 3.4).

As Bishop (1986) pointed out, psychologists often test spatial ability by designing tests (see Fig. 3.5) like "the classic test of embedded figures . . . where a simple figure, like A, must be identified in a more complex figure, like B" (p. 152).[1]

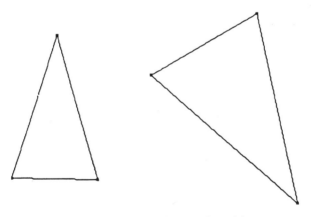

FIG. 3.3   Standard and rotated positions.

---

[1]A further indication of the perceived connection between problems of this sort and intellectual maturity is their central role in Feurstein's Instrumental Enrichment program. Examples of this sort of exercise for his students are "Organization of Dots" and "Analytic Perception" (Feurstein, Rand, Hoftman, & Miller, 1980). For similar reasons, problems of this sort frequently appear in books like Jim Fixx's *Games for the Superintellegent*.

FIG. 3.4. A picture which can be seen in different ways.

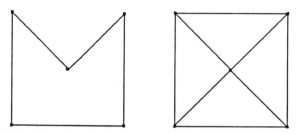

FIG. 3.5. Figures A and B from Bishop, 1986, p. 152.

Hofstadter (1980) considered this sort of reorganization, sometimes called *figure-ground reversal,* to be a central aspect of mathematical creativity. Max Wertheimer (1945) provided examples of situations where students are asked to do this sort of reorganization in high school geometry.[2]

Unfortunately, the ability to attend selectively and sequentially to parts and wholes does not come easily for many students. According to Hoffer's (1981) formulation, the van Hiele stages, a scheme to describe the development of the student's understanding of geometry, suggest that at Level 1 (Recognition) "the student . . . recognizes a shape as a whole" (p. 13). It is only at Level 2 (Analysis) that the student can focus on parts of a diagram and analyze properties of figures. As Hoz (1981) also pointed out, in geometry many students are unable to see a diagram in different ways. For example, in Fig. 3.6, students may not be able to see AD as a side of triangles ABD and ACD, because it is seen only as the height of the triangle ABC. (This difficulty is related to the concept of *functional fixedness* as defined by Anderson, 1985, p. 224.)

These three obstacles are part of the impetus to create The Geometric Supposer (Schwartz & Yerushalmy, 1985–1988),which attempts to reduce

---

[2]See Greeno (1983) for an attempt to teach a part/whole reorganization scheme to help students solve one of the problems mentioned by Wertheimer.

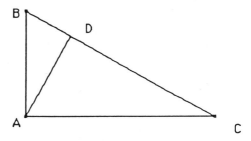

FIG. 3.6. Right triangle with altitude from right angle vertex.

students' dependence on single diagrams presented in their geometry texts as models for classes of diagrams.[3] Since the 1983–1984 school year, use of the Supposer has been integrated throughout typical year-long Euclidean geometry courses in public high schools to support a style of teaching that includes laboratory sessions where students investigate empirically the characteristics of geometric constructions. In a lab session, students are typically given a problem and asked to (a) record numerical and visual information gleaned from using the Supposer, (b) formulate conjectures about this data, (c) offer arguments or proofs to support the conjectures, and (d) note any other relevant thoughts, questions, or concerns (for an elaborated description of the approach to teaching with the Supposer used in these studies, see Chazan & Houde, 1989, or Yerushalmy, Chazan, Gordon, & Houde, 1987).

This pedagogical approach has been used in American public high school Euclidean geometry courses since the 1983–1984 school year. The research summarized in this chapter began the following year. Some of this research compares Supposer and non-Supposer classes for a full year: in 1984–1985, two Boston-area Supposer classes and a comparison class (Yerushalmy, 1986); in 1985–1986 three Boston-area Supposer classes and three comparison classes (Yerushalmy et al., 1987). Other year-long studies are not comparative. In Israel in 1987–1988, two eighth-grade (Yerushalmy,1991) and one ninth-grade (Yerushalmy & Mann, 1988) Supposer classes were studied. Finally, some of the research studies smaller instructional units (typically about 1 month in duration): In 1986–1987, four Boston-area Supposer classes used a unit on similarity (Chazan, 1988) and two used a unit on deductive proof; in 1987–1988, five Boston-area Supposer classrooms used a unit on proof (Chazan, 1989).

This chapter presents an analysis of excerpts from student papers, augmented where possible by classroom observations and statistical results collected during these research projects. In the early projects, both the participating teachers and researchers felt that one of the important

---

[3]Geometry textbooks rarely include two diagrams to illustrate a single problem. Indeed, in most texts a single diagram is used for two problems.

differences between students learning with the Supposer and students these individuals had taught previously involved students' use of diagrams (Yerushalmy et al., 1987). This feeling led to an examination of the collected sources of data for confirmation or disconfirmation. Thus, the analysis was post hoc arising from interpretations of the collected data and experience.

The main source of data collected in these early exploratory studies was student papers; there were no clinical interviews. Student papers were chosen as the main source of data because of a commitment to focus the classroom research on students' classroom behavior. Fortunately, analysis revealed that this commitment did not hamper the investigation of students' use of diagrams. The structure of the student lab papers used in these projects allowed for the collection of sufficient information to document in rich detail the products resulting from student exploration that shed light on students' problem-solving strategies. Although this source of data does not support a detailed reconstruction of students' cognitive processes, the collected material suggests that the Supposer helped students surmount the diagram-related obstacles. Parts of the subsequent research studies are designed to examine explicitly certain aspects of students' use of diagrams.

This chapter integrates the findings of all the studies that relate to students' use of diagrams. It reports statistical results, classrooms observations, and material excerpted from students' papers. Though some of the studies are designed to compare students using the Supposer to students not using the Supposer, the presented analysis is not always explicitly comparative. In the earlier qualitative examination of students' papers, there was no control group; the students in the noncomputer classrooms did not explore inquiry problems. The noncomparative evidence is presented in this chapter to provide a sense of the richness of the behaviors that were observed in the Supposer classrooms and to argue that some of the students using the Supposer overcame obstacles to geometric learning that many students in previous research projects or in traditional classroom settings do not overcome. This evidence is not presented to argue that all Supposer students overcame these obstacles (an unrealistic goal!) or that on average students using the Supposer overcame these obstacles more readily than students in traditional instruction (though the later studies make this point statistically).

THE RESOURCES OF A TEACHING AND LEARNING TOOL

The Supposer was created to aid students in conjecturing and thus to enable teachers to use students' conjecturing to teach high school geometry. The software facilitates the process of making and testing conjectures by generating requested numerical and visual empirical information about geometrical constructions specified by users. Students using this tool are presented with large amounts of visual information, that is, more than in traditional classes. To appreciate this visual information, it is crucial that they overcome the obstacles associated with diagrams. Some of the Supposer's options are explicitly designed to help them do so. This section analyzes how the Supposer's options accomplish this goal; it begins by examining options separately and then discusses the way the options interact. This analysis is difficult, because it requires isolating specific software options from the whole, when in reality the impact of the software is the combination of all the options. For the ease of the reader, all concrete examples of the workings of options are described as implemented in the Supposer Triangles program for the Apple II + computer as opposed to a more recent IBM PC version. The Apple version of the Supposer was the one used by the classes in the research described in this chapter, though they used the Quadrilaterals and Circles programs in addition to the Triangles one.

Choosing an Initial Shape

The Supposer makes the classification of shapes into types a salient aspect of students' learning. For example, when using the Triangles program, from the first key press the user must specify the triangle that is the initial shape. The user chooses to work on a RIGHT, ACUTE scalene, OBTUSE scalene, ISOSCELES, EQUILATERAL, or YOUR OWN triangle. When the user chooses one of the predefined categories, the Supposer challenges the notion of a standard triangle by presenting a random triangle of that kind (random size and where possible random relationship between sides and angles) in a random orientation. For example, the five isosceles triangles in Fig. 3.7 demonstrate that the base of an isosceles triangle does not have to be horizontal. Moreover, because computers boot separately, each screen shows a visibly different triangle. Students in a computer lab or classroom are confronted with the fact that their diagram is not the only diagram that can result from the procedure described in a particular problem.

The Supposer also allows the user to test conjectures by creating extreme cases that are candidates for counterexamples. If the user does not choose one of the predefined categories, he or she can exercise options to control the creation of the initial shapes by specifying the size of the sides and angles.

Construction Tools

By providing construction tools that reduce the mechanical difficulty of creating accurate Euclidean geometrical constructions, the Supposer makes

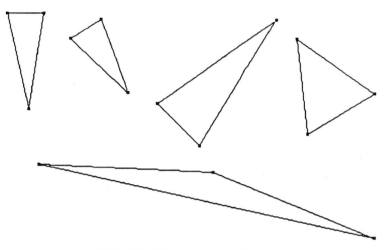

FIG. 3.7.   Five isosceles triangles.

it possible to teach and learn based on large quantities of visual information. The Supposer does not simply provide an electronic straightedge and compass. Instead the DRAW, LABEL, and ERASE menus include construction tools, like MEDIAN that can be constructed with compass and straightedge. These construction tools allow the user to create any Euclidean construction quickly and simply without allowing non-Euclidean constructions.

Furthermore, in the Supposer's menu-driven environment, the user specifies the desired construction by choosing a menu item and using correct, formal geometric language to describe, without ambiguity, where the construction is to be carried out. For example, in the Triangles program, to create a MEDIAN the user must specify the triangle in which and the vertex from which the median is to be drawn. There are other ways to create a software environment to do the same task. For example, the user could indicate points, segments, circles, and lines by using a mouse or pointers (as in the CABRI Geometre software, Laboratoire Structures Discretes et Didactique, 1988). The precise identification demanded by the Supposer requires that the user pay attention to the diagram and its labels. The labels help the user remember the properties of the different points. This is also relevant to the REPEAT option described later.

The format of the construction tools has other ramifications. For example, within this format, it is not possible to make a mathematically incorrect geometric construction, although it is possible to get an unexpected diagram without making an incorrect key press. If the user has an incorrect, or limited, mental model of a geometric concept, then a correct construction may be surprising. For example, a student might think that a median bisects the vertex angle in addition to the opposite side. For a student with this conception, the diagram in Fig. 3.8 might be a surprise.

Repeating Procedures

The Supposer includes a REPEAT option that also contributes to the ease of the creation of visual information by reducing the construction burden even further. Because the user has unambiguously specified the constructions in formal, geometric language, the Supposer captures all the constructions carried out on an initial triangle as a procedure. In the Triangles program, the REPEAT option allows the user to try this procedure on a NEW or PREVIOUS initial triangle. The option to repeat on a previous initial triangle allows the user to move back and forth between four diagrams that result from carrying out the procedure on different initial triangles. Beyond the ease with which diagrams can be created, however, this option allows users to test their mental images across many cases (freeing users from single diagrams) and to track characteristics of a construction that are invariant from triangle to triangle. For example, a user draws all three medians in a triangle. Noticing that the three medians are concurrent in this triangle, the user wonders whether this is true for other triangles. The REPEAT option makes it easy to explore this possibility and thus lead to a general conjecture that might be proven deductively.

Interactions

The combination of the classification scheme for the predefined types of shapes and the REPEAT option offers the user natural comparison criteria for figures. For the Triangles program the user might ask: What features of the diagrams are invariant when the procedure is repeated within and among categories of triangles? The YOUR OWN option for creating initial

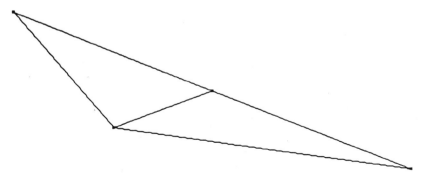

FIG. 3.8. A median that is clearly not an angle bisector.

shapes also combines nicely with the REPEAT option to allow users to create (invent) their own class of shapes, for example, the class of triangles whose sides are consecutive numbers (5,6,7; 6,7,8). Furthermore, this option is used in a sophisticated manner by users who want their diagrams to be dynamic. If a user has a variable in mind, for example, the measure of the largest angle in a triangle, the YOUR OWN and REPEAT options are used to create a set of initial triangles that animate the construction in a systematic manner. The user tracks the changes in the diagrams resulting from a procedure in which the largest angle of the triangle is incremented.

Complementary Design Choices

The Supposer has many options not directly connected with visual information, such as the measurement utilities. Within these are small design choices that complement the options described so far by helping the user work with visual information. First, when a procedure is repeated on a new initial triangle, the procedure is carried out one construction at a time. The user must press the space bar to continue. This feature helps the user keep track of the procedure and focus on critical aspects of the resulting diagrams. Second, an ERASE facility allows the user to simplify a diagram and focus on a key part. Third, a SCALE utility allows the user to work on the largest diagram that fits on the screen and includes all of the points in the construction. By toggling back and forth between this OPTIMAL diagram and the diagram in the ORIGINAL scale, the user focuses on specific areas of interest or on the whole diagram.

It is extremely important to emphasize that the Supposer does not stand alone; it is part of an approach to teaching geometry that is used by teachers as they see fit and that includes problems and projects for students. The students' work with the software is a part of the course, not the whole. Therefore, as important or even more important than the software itself is how its use is integrated into the course and how teachers make use of the capabilities the software provides. Any discussion of the resources of the tool must indicate how these resources are used in the classroom.

THE EVIDENCE

Although research suggests that visual obstacles are not overcome by traditional instruction (Hoz, 1981), evidence from the Supposer classes indicates the success of the Supposer as a pedagogical tool to help students overcome the obstacles to geometric understanding associated with diagrams. This section begins with two short descriptions, chosen for their extreme nature, of Supposer students' work when they began their studies.

These descriptions establish that some of the Supposer students in the studies had some of the diagram-related difficulties mentioned in the research literature. The remainder of the section presents evidence these students later overcame the visual obstacles.

Blocked by Obstacles

During October 1985, three classes were presented with the following problem. Part A of the problem was intended to serve as an enticing puzzle to rouse student interest in the general problem presented in Part B (see Fig. 3.9).

> Part A: In a triangle ABC [The intention is any triangle; it does not matter which one], ED is parallel to GF and IH. Also AD is parallel to EF and GH. Construct this drawing without using the parallel option in the Supposer. Describe your method.

> Part B: Given any triangle ABC [The intention is that no matter which one you try your method should work], derive at least three different methods to construct parallel lines without using the parallel option in the Supposer. You do not need to produce the same diagram as above!

Notice that although the diagram for Part A looks like a right triangle, the written description specifies only which lines are parallel, not the particular type of initial triangle ABC. The diagram is used as a model or an example, not as an accurate drawing. The triangle in the diagram, although it looks

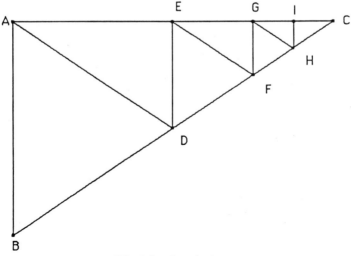

FIG. 3.9.   One instance.

like a right triangle, is a representation of the general case, "a triangle." Any diagram conforming to the written description and displaying the zig-zag pattern of the diagram is a solution for Part A.

In October, students interpreted this diagram as part of the specification of the desired construction. Because the triangle in the diagram looked like a right triangle, they made their triangles right triangles. Furthermore, they wanted their drawing to be an exact replica of the triangle on the page. They rejected some right triangles because their orientation did not match the orientation of the triangle in the picture. In other cases, before starting the construction, students rotated their paper to line up their triangle on paper with the image on the screen. One pair of students had a solution and were only a scale change away from recognizing it when they rejected their diagram, because it did not resemble the sample closely enough. Students had this difficulty, because they saw the diagram not as a model but as a particular case.

For another beginning geometry student, the image of a standard diagram overrode what she saw with the Supposer. The class was discussing the definition of an altitude. As reported in Yerushalmy et al. (1987), after discussing altitudes in acute triangles, the discussion turned to obtuse triangles:

> One student presented the drawing in Fig. 3.10 as evidence to support her definition. She claimed that her drawing was an accurate copy from the screen of the Supposer. Her definition of an altitude was "a line in a triangle that makes ninety degrees." (p. 22)

In constructing her definition of an altitude, she used the standard horizontal and vertical position of perpendicular lines and saw all three altitudes as perpendicular to the horizontal side, even though that was not how they really looked (see Fig. 3.11).

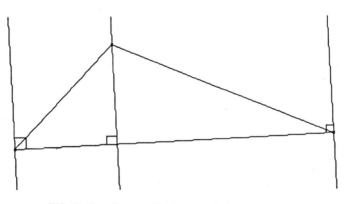

FIG. 3.10.   Three altitudes: a student's image.

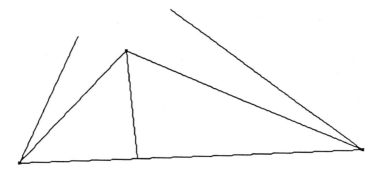

FIG. 3.11. Three altitudes: the actual drawing.

Overcoming the Obstacles

As their work with the Supposer progressed, the students began to show that they had overcome the obstacles that diagrams pose for geometrical understanding. An initial indication that diagrams had taken on increased importance for Supposer students came from a 1984-1985 study of two Supposer classes and one comparison class (Yerushalmy, 1986). Statistical results from a generalization test given at the end of the year indicated differences between the Supposer and non-Supposer students. Most of the non-Supposer students (about 80%) did not use diagrams on the pre/ posttests, whereas on the posttest, "Diagrams seemed to accompany the thinking process of Group A (Supposer) students. . . . One [Supposer] student, who in the pretest used only verbal answers, in the post-test used diagrams to answer all three problems. . . . There were numerous free-hand drawings" (Yerushalmy, 1986, pp. 95–96).

Research in two eighth-grade Israeli Supposer classrooms, using an instrument developed and normed by Hershkovitz (1987; Hershkovitz et al., 1987), provides further confirmation. Supposer students are less often confused by diagrams that are in a nonstandard orientation. Of the Supposer students, 90.2% successfully drew the altitudes in right triangles of different orientations, as opposed to 28% in Hershkovitz et al.'s study of 129 eighth graders (1987, p. 22); 87.7% of the Supposer students successfully drew altitudes in obtuse triangles of different orientations, as opposed to 38% for Hershkovitz et al.'s nondisadvantaged students and 28% for their complete sample (p. 24; the Supposer research is reported in Yerushalmy, 1991). The remainder of this section presents three other kinds of evidence that Supposer students overcame the obstacles associated with diagrams.

Working with Sequences of Pictures

One indication of growth in Supposer students' approach to diagrams is that they stopped identifying whole classes of figures with single diagrams

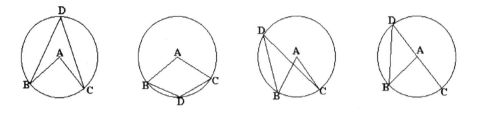

BC is a minor arc of circle A and D is a point on the circle.

1. Make a drawing that looks like #1 and state a conjecture about the relationship between m BC and m BDC.

2. Make a drawing like #2, #3, and #4 and check that the data supports your conjecture.

3. In *one case* you will find that the data *does not* support your conjecture. Can you find a reasonable explanation for this? Can you *restate* the problem so that this case "works"?

4. Give a proof of your conjecture. (Hint: Join D to A and extend the segment DA, so as to form exterior angles for DAB and DAC.)

FIG 3.12.   A circles problem.

(members of the class). Instead, students worked with many diagrams, saw them as instances of a single class, and were able to abstract the features that characterize the class, leaving behind the particular, non-characteristic aspects of the individual diagrams. In some cases, in class or at the computer, when students saw a series of diagrams representing a class of figures, they envisioned an order, or progression, having an animated, dynamic quality. For example, when given the problem as shown in Fig. 3.12, students saw the four pictures not as separate cases but as different pictures of the same situation. In their words, "The point D is moving on the circle."

Many students in the Supposer classes imputed movement to diagrams, treated individual diagrams as snapshots of a process occurring to one underlying configuration, and thought of those snapshots as a class of figures with common characteristics.[4] Beyond seeing movement in a set of simultaneously presented diagrams of members of the same class, as in the previous example, students saw such movement in examples produced sequentially by the Supposer, created their own displays to show others what they had seen, and, when working without the computer on a single member of a class, were even able to imagine other members of that class and build arguments on this basis.

For example, when students in one class were asked to draw the three

[4]We chose to take all of the remaining examples under this heading from the work of one class to indicate that these phenomena occurred frequently.

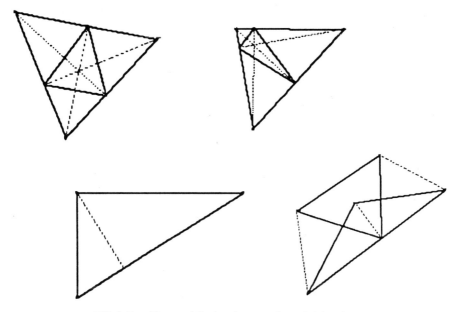

FIG.3.13. Three altitudes in a series of triangles.

altitudes of a triangle and to connect the feet of the altitudes, they recorded the diagrams that represent the repetition of this construction on different types of initial triangles in order of the largest angle in the triangle from acute through right to obtuse (see Fig 3.13).

One pair conjectured that "in a right triangle, if you draw the altitudes, then the center triangle disappears" (Yerushalmy, Chazan, Gordon, & Houde, 1986, p. 188). To support their argument that "it (the triangle) disappears because the altitude is the leg" (p. 188), the students drew the following (see Fig. 3.14):

Note that their conjecture uses the active verb "disappears" to refer to the triangle that is visible when the construction is made on nonright triangles and that the order of their presentation of the diagrams suggests the movement they describe. Furthermore, their statement indicates that the right triangle diagram is a member of the class of diagrams where "you draw

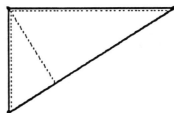

FIG. 3.14. A student's explanation: why the triangle disappears.

the altitudes." This particular member of the class has a unique characteristic: "the center triangle disappears."

In the previous example, the structure of the software (the REPEAT
option and the classification scheme for triangles) and possibly the demands
of the problem helped students treat the different diagrams as members of
the same class. Yet, there were also instances of students using their own
schemes to create classes of diagrams (the REPEAT option in combination
with the YOUR OWN option, as described previously with regard to the
class of triangles whose sides have lengths that are consecutive numbers).
For example, students in another class were asked to construct a triangle by
connecting the midpoints of the sides of another triangle and to investigate
the ratio between the radii of the circles circumscribed around each of the
two triangles (see Fig. 3.15).

A pair of students (possibly by mistake) decided to investigate the
relationship between the radii of the circumscribed and inscribed circles of
triangles (see Fig. 3.16).

In their exploration, they created a sequence of diagrams (see Fig. 3.17)
and conjectured that "the triangles with the largest angles have the largest
radius ratio (taking the radius of the circumscribed circle / the radius of the
inscribed circle). Triangles like the equilateral with all congruent angles
have the smallest ratio (2)."

It is important to note that neither the problem nor the software
suggested to students how to see these diagrams as a sequence. The students
themselves decided to focus on the size of the largest angle as the crucial
variable. They explored a relationship that interested them systematically by
examining a series of specific members of a class of diagrams.

All of this work with sequences of pictures seemed to have a favorable
impact on students' views of individual diagrams. Students were able to

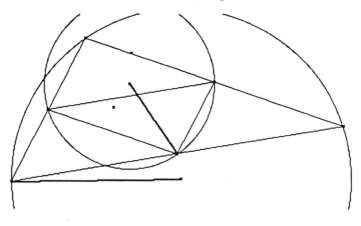

FIG. 3.15. Radii of two circumscribed circles.

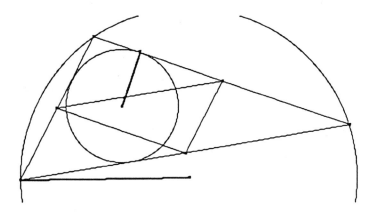

FIG. 3.16.   Radii of one circumscribed and one inscribed circle.

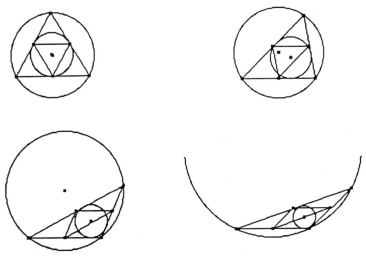

FIG. 3.17.   Getting smaller and smaller.

treat a single diagram as a model for a whole class of diagrams and, at the same time, to understand that such models may include characteristics not shared by all members of the set. They were able to imagine other members of the set to see if a characteristic seemed common to all. For example, Yerushalmy et al. (1987) reported:

The class was working with a drawing (see Fig. 3.18) that included two parallel lines, BC and EF. The students were not told that the lines were parallel, had not yet conjectured that they were, and, with the knowledge they had, could not prove that these lines were parallel. It was however a legitimate and

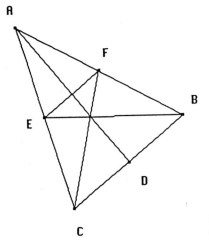

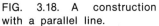

FIG. 3.18. A construction with a parallel line.

verifiable conjecture. AD was an altitude and thus perpendicular to BC. One student argued that AD was also perpendicular to EF, implying that EF and BC were parallel, but not mentioning that fact. Another students argued that "it doesn't work if EF is tilted." In other words, it doesn't work if EF is not parallel to BC. This assertion was not based on the way the diagram looked. The student was manipulating the diagram and considering an alternative in her "mind's eye." (pp. 15–16)

Clearly, this student understood that a diagram may include characteristics not shared by all members of the class and did not identify the particular diagram with the class of diagrams constructed by the procedure. In addition, this student was able to envision mentally other possible configurations of the diagram.

Reorganizing the Visual Field

When presenting his heuristics for understanding a problem, Polya (1945/1973) suggested:

Consider your problem from various sides. Emphasize different parts, examine different details, examine the same details repeatedly, but in different ways, combine the details differently, approach them from different sides. Try to see some new meaning in each detail, some new interpretation of the whole. (p. 34)

In geometry, this exhortation for flexibility translates into the ability to examine a diagram from various sides and in different ways. Supposer students' approach to individual diagrams was flexible in the way that Polya described; they were able to see and focus on different parts of individual diagrams. Test results, classroom observation, and students' papers indicate that they were willing and able to change their point of view. Some students even created systematic strategies for using the software or for recording conjectures to help change their focus in examining a diagram.

The results of a comparison of Supposer and non-Supposer students on a pencil and paper test to evaluate students' conjecturing ability suggest that Supposer students are more likely to write conjectures based on a change in their view of the diagram (Yerushalmy et al. 1987). In a problem that presents a right triangle with semicircles on each side (see Fig. 3.19), Supposer students made conjectures about equality of lengths, the arclengths of the semicircles, and the measures of the central angles in the circles as compared to their arcs.

Beyond this quantitative evidence, many incidents from classroom observations make it clear that students using the Supposer are able to move from an examination of certain parts of a diagram to a focus on other parts or the whole. Some of these observations are especially convincing, because the students looked at the diagrams differently from the way their teachers intended them to, making it clear that the new view had come about without explicit teacher intervention. For example, a teacher in the similarity study (Chazan, 1988) used a problem geared towards students' difficulties with right triangles with the altitude drawn from the right angle. Students were asked to draw a right triangle with its interior altitude and then to reflect that altitude over each of the two legs resulting in a shape like the one in Fig.3.20.

As the teacher had hoped, students were able to focus on different parts of the diagram, recognize the five triangles present, and imagine lifting

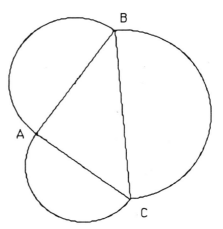

FIG. 3.19. Semicircles added
by Supposer students.

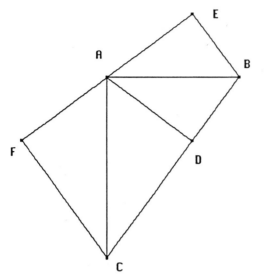

FIG. 3.20. A right trapezoid.

them off the diagram and rotating them in order to identify their correspondence. The students conjectured that all five triangles (BAC, AFC,
AEB, ADB, ADC) were similar. In addition, many students focused on
aspects of the diagram that the teacher had not considered and produced
conjectures that surprised her. Some students focused on the outer segments
of the diagram and conjectured that the outside shape was a right trapezoid,
whereas others focused on one vertex (not even a closed shape) and
conjectured that angles FAC, CAB, and BAE made a straight line. Both of
these conjectures are based on selective attention to the details of the
diagram; the students focused on a part of the diagram and lifted it from its
context.

Careful examination of student papers reveals that some students had
formalized strategies to present their view of a diagram to others and to help
themselves look at diagrams differently. For example, students were asked
to draw all three angle bisectors in an isosceles triangle and label the point
of intersection (see Fig. 3.21).

A pair of students turned in the diagrams in Fig. 3.22 to accompany their
conjectures and proofs.

These students were able to look at the diagram flexibly, focus on
different parts of the diagram, and see some parts of the diagram as
elements in different shapes. By making these diagrams separately from
their recording of the initial diagram, these students indicated which part of
the diagram they were focussing on and presented their conjectures clearly
for their teacher. They were even able to isolate parts of the diagram that do
not share the same orientation as their initial diagram.

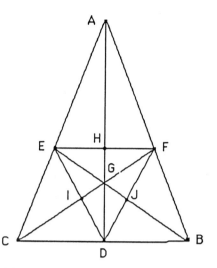

FIG. 3.21.   Three angle bisectors in an isosceles triangle.

Although the students whose work appears in Fig. 3.22 used *peeling away* strategies,[5] other students in their class used *building up* strategies. This type of strategy was first noticed when one pair of students worked differently from the rest of the class. Instead of completing the whole construction and then repeating the construction on different initial triangles, these students first added one new element to their triangle, made conjectures, and when necessary repeated the construction before going on to the next step of the construction. They explained that this method enabled them to see things that they might otherwise miss as they examined the figure anew after each additional step. Their method is remarkable also for its emphasis on the process of making the construction rather than on the final product, the completed diagram. Figure 3.23 shows a student paper in which a different pair of students from this class used both peeling away and building up strategies. These strategies indicate an attention to the parts of a construction and the ability to communicate this focus to others. They recorded the five-step process by which their diagram was constructed and accompanied their proof with a "close-up of triangle DEF."

This example also indicates that members of the class considered these two strategies useful for communication and that their use spread beyond their originators.

Adding Auxiliary Lines

Students who add auxiliary lines to diagrams indicate by their action that for them diagrams are not an untouchable, final product. Instead, diagrams

---

[5]See Anderson (1980) for the distinction between taking apart and peeling apart decomposition approaches.

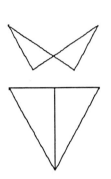
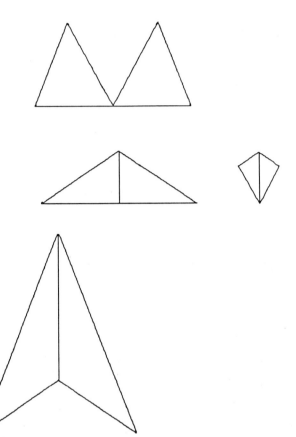

FIG. 3.22.   Parts of the original diagram.

are to be investigated; they are the result of a process that can be added to or changed. Polya (1945/1973) presented several problem situations in which the construction and use of auxiliary lines indicates an understanding, or learning, of geometry that transcends having been merely taught geometry. In Polya's view, adding auxiliary lines helps the problem solver access prior knowledge. "Having recollected a formerly solved related problem and wishing to use it for our present one, we must often ask: Should we introduce some auxiliary element in order to make its use possible? (p. 47). Yet, auxiliary lines have another function, a creative one. Adding an auxiliary line, and focusing on parts of the diagram that include this new line, generates new insights into the diagram, yielding both questions and conjectures.

Supposer students used auxiliary lines both on and off the computer in service of proof and to create new conjectures. Supposer students also used the addition of auxiliary lines to repeat a procedure first carried out on the

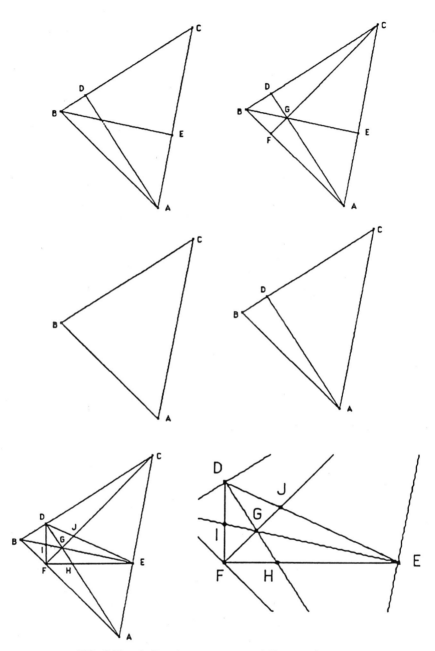

FIG. 3.23. A five-step process and then a close-up.

initial shape with shapes created subsequently. This repetition has a dynamic quality that exemplifies the potentially unfinished quality that diagrams had for these students.

Using auxiliary lines in order to make use of prior knowledge is a behavior that Supposer students displayed at the end of the year on a paper-and-pencil task (not Supposer-related) that asked them to analyze an unfamiliar geometrical situation and find arguments in support of a given statement. As part of a test on proof skills, both Supposer and non-Supposer students were asked to provide arguments explaining why an unfamiliar statement, "In a regular 8-gon the sum of the 8 exterior angles is 360 degrees," is true. The Supposer students used auxiliary lines to look for previously learned connected facts. "Statistical analysis of the test showed that students in the inductive (Supposer) class used analysis by diagram (adding auxiliary lines) as their main tool for reaching a convincing argument significantly more often than students in the traditional (non-Supposer) class" (Yerushalmy, 1986, p. 191; see pp. 191–194 for four individual cases of Supposer students' addition of auxiliary lines). A similar test was given other Supposer and non-Supposer students the next year with similar results (Yerushalmy et al., 1987). Figure 3.24 shows five examples of Supposer students' auxiliary lines all taken from the test papers in that study.

This use of auxiliary lines did not appear out of the blue at the end of the year but was observed throughout the second half of the course in Supposer classes (after students had been introduced to deductive proof). Frequently, the episodes of adding auxiliary lines occurred in the computer lab as students looked for supporting arguments for conjectures they had developed from their empirical work (for a full exposition of such an example, see Yerushalmy, 1986, pp. 203–205).

In the examples in Fig. 3.25 and 3.26, Supposer students developed creative, irregular, or surprising conjectures after adding auxiliary constructions *of their own initiative.*[6] They used auxiliary lines in this way with the Supposer and on end-of-the-year paper-and-pencil tasks. The first example occurred in response to the following problem:

Divide the sides of a square ABCD into three equal parts and form quadrilateral EGIK as shown in Fig. 3.25:

Compare ABCD and EGIK with respect to areas, perimeters, and lengths of the sides. State your conjectures.

---

[6]It is important to emphasize once again that the Supposer is only a tool that, in this case, makes it easy to draw auxiliary lines. Students' motivation to produce conjectures and to add auxiliary lines in the service of this goal is a function of the student and the environment (teacher, class mates, etc.). In a class that is a community of learners who appreciate good new ideas, students have reason to use auxiliary lines to make conjectures.

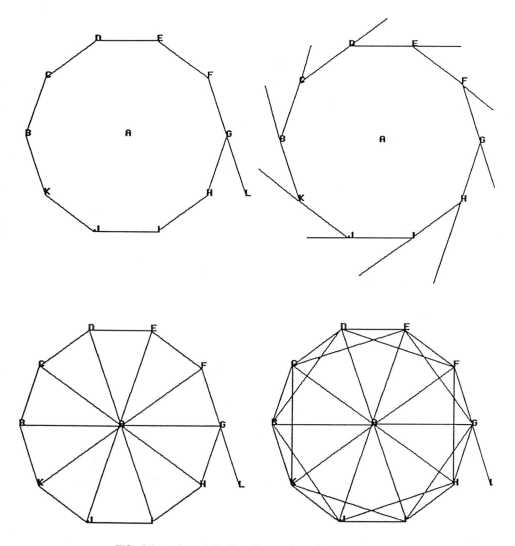

FIG. 3.24. An original and a series of auxiliary lines.

Although the problem has an explicit goal, the teacher in this classroom also wanted students to explore their diagrams more broadly and make as many interesting conjectures as they could. One student was not sure whether it was okay to add auxiliary lines. Before adding the diagonals of the original square to the assigned construction, she asked her teacher's permission and explained that she thought the diagonals might lead to interesting conjectures. After adding the diagonals, she marked the points of intersection of the diagonals with the inside quadrilateral, investigated the resulting

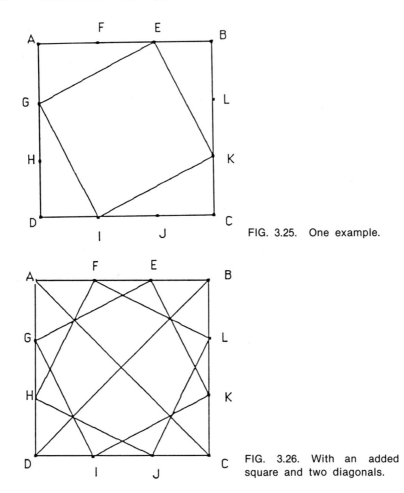

FIG. 3.25. One example.

FIG. 3.26. With an added square and two diagonals.

diagram, and conjectured that the diagonals split the sides of the inside quadrilateral into two pieces whose lengths are in a 1:2 ratio. She continued to add to the construction, connected the unconnected subdivisions of the outside square (to make quadrilateral EGIK out of segments EG, GI, IK, and KE), and noted that the diagonals pass through the points where the two inside quadrilaterals meet.

Diagrams were not finished products for this student. They could be added to and continued by making auxiliary lines. Furthermore, this student was able to use the added constructions to develop new and interesting conjectures about her diagram.

Like Supposer students' use of auxiliary lines to help prove a statement, their use of auxiliary lines to form conjectures also transferred to paper-and-pencil tasks. For example, on a test of conjecturing ability, Supposer students (there was no comparison group) added auxiliary lines to help them make conjectures. In a class of 20 students, for one problem, there were eight different ways of adding auxiliary lines to the given diagram (see Fig. 3.27).

Some of the added lines were almost trivial (figure 3.27, top right), whereas others led to sophisticated ideas. One student (Fig. 3.27, bottom left) conjectured: "There are an infinite number of lines going through the

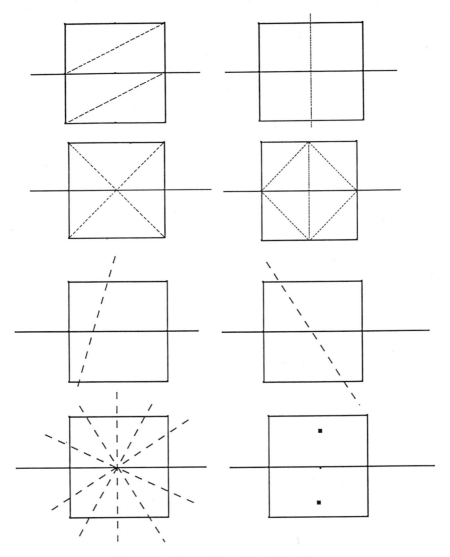

FIG. 3.27. Eight different auxiliary lines.

center of a square, and as they come closer to the one parallel line their length decreases until it reaches the length of the side of the square." Another student (Fig. 3.27, top left) preferred to draw other segments, different in their geometric nature from the given line.

Thus, in addition to being useful to help prove assertions, students found the use of auxiliary lines to be a helpful strategy for thinking creatively and flexibly, for creating new and interesting conjectures. Adding auxiliary lines and focusing on the relationship between these new lines and the original lines suggested new conjectures and questions. Finally, Supposer students also added auxiliary lines to create dynamic movement in a single diagram, to repeat a process in their diagrams.

When students worked on the connecting the feet of the altitude problem mentioned earlier, many students continued the construction by drawing the altitudes in the smaller triangle (created by joining the feet of the altitudes of the original one) and joining the feet of these altitudes to create a third triangle (see Fig. 3.28).

During the class discussion of the problem, one student came to the board and showed how he had created the third triangle. Two students in the back of the room got into an argument over whether this process could be repeated forever. One student said, "There wouldn't be room (to continue this process forever)." The other responded, "You could always scale change (a reference to a menu option on the Supposer) and make more room." This argument was taken up again by the class when exploring a problem that asked students to connect the midpoints of the three sides of a triangle. Again, some students had connected the midpoints of the newly created inner triangle. This time, however, a characteristic of the drawing

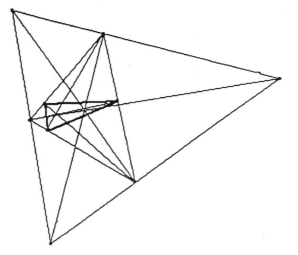

FIG. 3.28. The continuation of a construction process.

stayed constant as the process was repeated. "It's like DEF becomes ABC and HIJ is the same shape in different size. The angles are the same and the sides are different." The repetition of a construction in this way was not supported by the software, but students undertook it nevertheless by adding auxiliary lines.

CONCLUSION

Other classes don't go into as much detail as we do . . . We really go in-depth. Other people, they just know what they (medians) are and what they do. I think we are more familiar with them. (Taken from a year-end interview with a Supposer student, reported in Yerushalmy et al., 1987, p. 47)

I believe that these students did get more out of their Geometry class than they would have done in a traditional class . . . (Taken from a year-end evaluation by a Supposer teacher, reported in Yerushalmy et al., 1987, p. 40.)

When evaluating the effect of an educational innovation, it is important to use appropriate standards and to test for the goals that the innovation has set out to accomplish. One important goal of the Supposer intervention is to help students use diagrams effectively. This chapter has assessed student learning outcomes and evaluated this one aspect of students' geometrical abilities. It has presented research evidence to support the sentiments expressed above by Supposer students and teachers.

The evidence indicates that students using the Supposer understand diagrams and their limitations better than students in traditional classrooms portrayed in the research literature. They overcome the three diagram-related learning obstacles that traditionally beset students; their approach to diagrams is flexible, not rigid. Specifically, they are able to treat a single diagram as a model for a whole class of diagrams and simultaneously are aware that such models have characteristics not shared by all members of the class. They focus on different parts of a diagram and do not consider a diagram as a finished product. They add auxiliary lines to diagrams and are able to carry out dynamic processes on diagrams.

The material presented in this chapter also demonstrates that the Supposer students in these studies have acquired important and powerful problem-solving strategies for analyzing problems, conjecturing, and proving. One of the difficulties in analyzing a problem is that the givens are not always specified explicitly. For example, sometimes a diagram intended as a model, yet unaccompanied by a written description, is provided to specify the goal of a task, Such a use of a particular instance is difficult for students (See Chapter 7 in this volume). Students in this study are adept at analyzing such diagrams and imagining other members of the set that help them understand the problems' goals. They are not trapped by the particularity of the given diagram. Another skill related to diagrams that enhances students' ability to analyze problems is the ability to draw a geometrical construction stage by stage, observing and analyzing the additional properties of each new element.

When given problems to analyze, the students in this study are willing and able to focus on different parts of diagrams, look for nonstandard diagrams, and add auxiliary lines to diagrams in order to derive conjectures. They are also adept at creating and examining sequences of related diagrams. Their use of these abilities led to many interesting, novel conjectures. Finally, the skills in working with diagrams are also helpful to these students when proving their conjectures. They are able to abstract the variant and invariant aspects of the set of objects in series of diagrams and to use auxiliary lines and their ability to focus on parts of diagrams to derive proofs.

One Final Note

The experience reported in this chapter and the research literature on visualization make it clear that when creating software tools that include a visual representation to aid student inquiry, it is extremely important to understand the obstacles that students experience when working with visual representations and to design the software to help students overcome these obstacles. The experiences described in this chapter also suggest that when such software is designed with these visual obstacles in mind, students overcome obstacles to using visual representations and make good use of these representations in their learning and conjecture-making. This conclusion encourages the creation of, and experimentation with, software tools that include a visual representation to aid student conjecturing in other fields of mathematics.

ACKNOWLEDGMENTS

The preparation of this paper was supported in part by the National Academy of Education's Spencer Fellowship program.

A version of this paper appears in *Educational Studies in Mathematics*, 1990 vol. 21.

REFERENCES

Anderson, J. (1980). *Cognitive psychology and its implications.* San Francisco: Freeman.
Bishop, A. J. (1986). What are some obstacles to learning geometry? In Robert Morris (Ed.), *Studies in mathematics education: Vol. 5. The teaching of geometry* (pp. 141–159). Paris: UNESCO.

Chazan, D. (1988). *Similarity: Exploring the understanding of a geometric concept.* (Tech. Rep. No. 88-15). Cambridge, MA: Harvard Graduate School of Education, Educational Technology Center.

Chazan, D. (1989). *Ways of knowing: High school students' conceptions of mathematical proof.* Unpublished doctoral dissertation, Harvard Graduate School of Education, Cambridge, MA.

Chazan, D. & Houde, R. (1989). *How to use conjecturing and microcomputers to teach high school geometry.* Reston, VA: National Council of Teachers of Mathematics.

Feurstein, R., Rand, Y., Hoffman, M. B., & Miller, R. (1980). *Instrumental Enrichment.* University Park, MD: University Park Press.

Fixx, J. (1972). *Games for the superintelligent.* New York: Fawcett.

Greeno, J. (1983). Conceptual entities. In D. Gentner & A. Stevens (Eds.), *Mental models* (pp. 227–252). Hillsdale, NJ: Lawrence Erlbaum Associates.

Hershkovitz, R. (1987). The acquisition of concepts and misconceptions in basic geometry — or when "A little learning is a dangerous thing." In J. Novak (Ed.), *Proceedings of the Second International Seminar on Misconceptions and Educational Strategies in Science and Mathematics.* Ithica, NY: Cornell University.

Hershkovitz, R., Bruckheimer, M. & Vinner, S. (1987). Activities with teachers based on cognitive research. In C. R. Hirsch & M. J. Zweng (Eds.), *The secondary school mathematics curriculum* (pp. 222 – 235). Reston, VA: National Council of Teachers of Mathematics.

Hoffer, A. (1981). Geometry is more than proof. *Mathematics Teacher, 74*(1), 11–18.

Hofstadter, D. (1980). *Godel, Escher, Bach: An eternal golden braid.* New York: Vintage.

Hoz, R. (1981). The effects of rigidity on school geometry learning. *Educational Studies in Mathematics, 12,* 171–190.

Laboratoire Structures Discretes et Didactique. (1988). *Cabri Geometre.* Grenoble, France: Universite Joseph Fourier.

Polya, G. (1973). *How to solve it.* Princeton, NJ: Princeton University Press. (Original work published 1945)

Presmeg, N. (1986a). Visualization and mathematical giftedness. *Educational Studies in Mathematics,17,* 297–311.

Presmeg, N. (1986b). Visualization in high-school mathematics. *For the learning of mathematics,6,* 42–46.

Rissland (Michener), E. (1977). *Epistemology, Representation, Understanding, and Interactive Exploration of Mathematical Theories.* Unpublished doctoral dissertation, Massachusetts Institute for Technology, Cambridge, MA.

Schoenfeld, A. (1986). On having and using geometric knowledge. In J. Hiebert (Ed.), *Conceptual and procural knowledge: The case of mathematics.* Hillsdale, NJ: Lawrence Erlbaum Associates.

Schwartz, J. L. (1988). The power and peril of the particular: Thoughts on a role for microcomputers in science and mathematics education. *Machine-Mediated Learning, 1*(4), 345

Schwartz, J. L. & Yerushalmy, M. (1985-1988). *The Geometric Supposer.* Pleasantville, NY: Sunburst.

Wertheimer, M. (1945). *Productive thinking.* New York: Harper.

Yerushalmy, M. (1986). *Induction and generalization: An experiment in teaching and learning high school geometry.* Unpublished doctoral dissertation, Harvard Graduate School of Education, Cambridge, MA.

Yerushalmy, M. (1991). Enhancing acquisition of basic geometrical concepts with the use of the Geometric Supposer. *Journal of Educational Computing Research, 7,*(4), 407–420.

Yerushalmy, M., Chazan, D., & Gordon, M. (1988). *Posing problems: One aspect of bringing inquiry into classrooms* (Tech. Rep. No. 88-21). Cambridge, MA: Harvard Graduate School of Education, Educational Technology Center.

Yerushalmy, M., Chazan, D., Gordon, M., & Houde, R. (1986). Microcomputer assisted instruction in geometry: A preliminary report. In G. Lappan & R. Even (Eds.), *Proceedings of the Eighth Annual Meeting of the North American Chapter of the Internation Group for the Psychology of Mathematics Education* (pp. 181–186). East Lansing, MI.

Yerushalmy, M., Chazan, D., Gordon, M., & Houde, R. (1987). *Guided inquiry and technology: A year-long study of children and teachers using the Geometric Supposer* (Tech. Rep. No. 88-6). Cambridge, MA: Harvard Graduate School of Education, Educational Technology Center.

Yerushalmy, M., & Maman, H. (1988). *The Supposer as the base for a whole group exploration.* (Tech. Rep. No. 9). Haifa, Israel: Haifa University, School of Education.

4 Generalization in Geometry

Michal Yerushalmy
The University of Haifa

GENERALIZATION, INDUCTION, AND CONJECTURING: A THEORETICAL PERSPECTIVE

A major obstacle in teaching plausible reasoning skills is the confusion among the terms *generalization, induction,* and *conjecturing.* First, generalization is a label for both a process and the products of this process: The process of generalization creates a generalization. This confusion is compounded by the custom of labeling the product of induction as a generalization as well. Conjectures can be developed through both induction and generalization. Second, the words generalization (in its process meaning) and induction are often used interchangeably. For example, "A further simplification can be accomplished by replacing a term in the formula by a variable, thus generalizing the formula and allowing an induction on the new variable's position in the formula" (Cohen & Feigenbaum, 1982, p. 108). Third, induction is sometimes thought of as the opposite of deduction. Any reasoning process that does not proceed by deduction is thus considered to proceed by induction. In this chapter I seek a sharper, more concise definition, beginning with a discussion of commonalities and differences between the processes of generalization and induction.

Conjecturing and Conjectures

People reach conclusions by many processes. One of them is conjecturing, whereby one offers a statement that one thinks may be true, though at the time one doesn't know for sure. Such a statement is a conjecture. Calling a

57

statement a conjecture, or saying that it results from a person's conjecturing, implies no particular process of creation. A conjecture can result from explanation, belief, experience, deductive proof, or generalization (see Fig. 4.1).

Geometric conjectures have three key parts: the relationship described in the conjecture, the set of objects for which the relationship holds, and the quantifier that determines the members of the set of objects for which the relationship holds. Sometimes one or more of these parts is not explicitly stated but is understood.

Generalization And Induction

Generalizations are a particular kind of conjecture, created by reasoning from the specific to the general. The processes of generalization and induction are methods for creating generalizations, a type of conjecture. Neither is a process for deriving definite knowledge. In both, the end result is a statement whose truth is unknown at the time it is made. In induction, the generalization is created from the examination of instances or examples. As an instance or a set of instances is examined, certain properties are identified. The given example is then taken as a member of a larger set and its properties are imputed to the larger set. Thus, in induction, a generalization is induced from examples. Generalization, on the other hand, is a process acted out on a statement (either a conjecture or a proven statement). "We say that one description, A, is more general than another description, B, if A applies in all of the situations in which B applies and then some more" (Cohen & Feigenbaum, 1982, p. 365). Thus, in generalization, a more specific statement becomes a more general statement. Such generali-

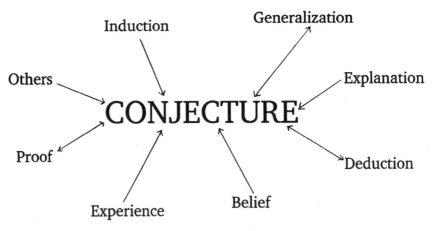

FIG. 4.1. Objects and relations within inductive learning.

zation can be effected in many ways. New words can be substituted for words currently in the statement, or the accepted meanings of the words in the statement can be changed. Kline (1980) suggested that one way to generalize a relationship is to change a constant to a variable: "The conic sections of ellipse, parabola, and hyperbola are represented algebraically by equations of the second degree. A few curves represented by equations of the third degree are useful for applications. Generalization jumps at once to curves whose equations are of the nth degree . . . " (p. 283). Polya (1973/1945) suggested "Generalization is passing from consideration of a given set of objects to that of a larger set, containing the given one" (p. 12). Thus, a second way to generalize a given statement, is to change its set of objects to a more general set. The last way to effect a generalization is to change the definition of the words in a statement. As Kitcher (1983) suggested, "Generalization is [can be] a process in which the language of mathematics is extended. Prior constraints on the usage of expressions are relaxed, so as to advance our understanding of entities previously discussed" (p. 212).

It is important to note at this stage that not all changes in a statement are generalizations of it. For example, the statement, "A median in a triangle splits the triangle into two parts of equal area," is not generalized by the substitution, "An angle bisector in a triangle splits the triangle into two parts whose area is proportionate to the pieces cut off on the base." The second is a transformation of the first but not a generalization of it.

Furthermore, there are situations in which the distinction is difficult to apply. First, when a numerical aspect of a statement is generalized, the word *induction* seems to be an appropriate, or natural, description of the process (see the quote from Cohen, cited earlier). In this view, the initial statement is one example, and any statement that substitutes a different numerical value is another example. The general statement is then reached by examining the specific cases. Second, in situations when a diagram and a particular statement are given, it is difficult to know whether the person addressing the problem is working from the example or from the statement. To draw conclusions in such a case, one must infer what is taking place in the mind of the conjecturer. Despite these difficulties, it is valuable to distinguish among the different ways generalizations are created. In induction, the generalization is derived from the observations of examples. In generalization, examples may be checked, but the game of creating a generalization can be played without recourse to empirical experience. Although the differentiation is crucial, the terminology may vary. For example, Holland, Holyoak, Nisbett, & Thagard (1986) use the term *condition-simplifying generalization* for generalization of statements (ideas) and *instance-based generalization* for generalization from examples.

Finally, it is necessary to clarify the distinction between generalization by

induction and mathematical induction. Mathematical induction is a procedure, not a process. Not a part of Polya's (1962) plausible reasoning, it is "a
demonstrative procedure often useful in verifying mathematical conjectures
at which we arrived" (p. 112). Both mathematical induction and induction
as described above operate on examples. In mathematical induction these
examples are statements that can be envisioned as members of a sequence of
statements that can be ordered in the same way the natural numbers can be
ordered.

OBSTACLES TO FORMING GENERALIZATIONS IN MATHEMATICS

Do learners encounter any difficulties in forming conjectures? Nickerson,
Perkins, and Smith (1985) argued that the ability to test theories seems to be
more prevalent than the ability to construct them: "Deductive and analytical
skills are more common, we suspect, than is the ability to generate useful
hypotheses, or to impose structure on data that are not related in an obvious
way" (p. 50).

In this section I present evidence that the lack of this ability and the habit
of educating mathematics students to test hypotheses deductively rather
than to generate hypotheses create obstacles to understanding and manipulating mathematics. I review various reasons for overgeneralization in
mathematics, such as use of an insufficient set of examples, prevalent
concept images and beliefs, and the tendency to reject negative examples.

Matz (1982) studied errors occurring in high school algebra problem
solving. Matz found that the errors resulted from reasonable attempts to
generalize previous knowledge into a new situation. The attempts were
viewed as reasonable steps because in all cases they involved rules that had
worked appropriately in other examples. Matz identified many errors
caused by the generalization of linear decompositions on expressions that
cannot be decomposed linearly. The errors occur when the student observes
no differences in the structures of the expressions and therefore assumes
that the known rule can adequately serve for new examples.

Difficulties similar to these algebraic overgeneralizations were observed
by Nickerson et al. (1985), who concluded that people usually limit their
hypothesis space to oversimplified situations instead of considering all
possible hypotheses that can be formed from a sample. They also pointed
out that people tend to create an hypothesis that relates any two factors X
and Y by observing only the cases in which both are valid, while ignoring
the other three possible types of cases.

In algebra, as identified by Matz, students create a model in which it is
possible to generalize properties and rules for any number, when actually

the original rules are formed for special numbers such as the identity numbers. A similar finding underlies the work of Burton and Brown in their research on false algorithms of computations (Burton, 1982). Their work assumes that bugs in number computations result from false generalization of rules. Both studies conclude that the ability to extend rules using correct generalization techniques is a major characteristic of mathematical competence.

Rissland (1977) studied obstacles to understanding mathematical processes that involve the use of representation by diagrams. Rissland found that although diagrams are supposed "to contain the essence of a situation" (p. 56), every diagram has a large number of characteristics that are individual and not representative of the class. In most cases for high school geometry students, diagrams are intended as models (Yerushalmy & Chazan, in press), but because people usually sample upon availability and mostly from memory, the models or the standard diagrams serve as the sample for generalization and bias its results.

Another aspect of false generalizations in geometry is presented in the research on misconceptions by Hershkovitz, Bruckheimer, and Vinner (1987), whose findings suggest that the beliefs and the concept images that students carry dominate reality. Consequently, students do not look for negative cases or nonexamples of a concept and easily generalize perception into wrong concept or definition. The literature points to the problems of confirmation and availability as possible causes of such behavior. People usually look for examples that confirm their hypothesis and ignore negative cases (Anderson, 1985). The confirmation paradox is known as a bias of inductive reasoning, both in creating samples and in forming conjectures. Holland et al. (1986) found that a belief in a specific hypothesis usually leads to sampling towards the confirmation of the hypothesis. No special effort is made to find disconfirming evidence. When a noninstance occurs spontaneously, it is ignored in order to allow confirmation.

THE ROLE OF THE SUPPOSER

The Supposer (Schwartz & Yerushalmy, 1985–1988) is a tool that generates numerical and visual information about geometrical constructions specified by users. It was created to aid students in conjecturing and thus enable teachers to use students' conjecturing to teach high school geometry. It facilitates the process of conjecture making by providing students with empirical information to create and test conjectures. Nevertheless, to appreciate the data, students must overcome the obstacles associated with inductive reasoning, some of which were just outlined.

The Supposer was designed to focus and direct users' attention by providing certain options and not others and by making some things easy to do while making others difficult or impossible. For the sake of the current analysis specific software options must be isolated from the whole, whereas in reality the impact of the software is the combined impact of all of the options. Therefore, the analysis begins with separate options and then discusses the way the options interact.

Choosing an Initial Shape: Built in Categories for Sampling

One important aspect of the design of the Supposer is the way triangles (or any other polygon) are classified (see Appendix at end of book). When using the Triangles program, the user must specify the triangle that is the initial shape. The user chooses to work on a RIGHT, ACUTE scalene, OBTUSE scalene, ISOSCELES, EQUILATERAL, or YOUR OWN triangle. If the user chooses one of the predefined categories, a random triangle of that kind (random size and where possible random relationship between sides and angles) appears on the screen in a random orientation. This characteristic of the tool challenges students' misconceptions about shapes. For example, the diagrams in Fig. 4.2 demonstrate that the base of an isosceles triangle does not have to be horizontal.

If the user does not choose one of the predefined categories, he or she controls the creation of the initial triangles using YOUR OWN option. This characteristic of the Supposer allows the user the freedom to test conjectures by creating extreme cases that are candidates for counter examples.

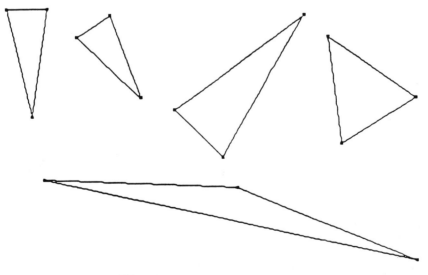

FIG. 4.2.   Five Isosceles Triangles.

Construction Tools: Availability of Visual Information

After choosing the initial shape, the user uses the Supposer's construction tools to produce a geometrical construction. These tools allow the user to create any Euclidean construction quickly and simply without allowing non-Euclidean constructions and provide primitives, like median, that are less primitive than pure compass and straightedge construction. By reducing the overhead for creating accurate geometrical constructions, this aspect of the software makes it possible to teach and learn based on large quantities of visual information.

Repeating on a Process

In the Supposer's menu-driven environment, the user specifies the desired construction by choosing a menu item and using correct, formal geometric language to describe, without ambiguity, where the construction is to be carried out. Because the user has unambiguously specified the constructions in formal, geometric language, the Supposer captures, as a procedure, all of the constructions carried out on an initial triangle. The REPEAT option allows the user to try this procedure on a new or previous initial shape, thus reducing the construction burden even further. This option allows the user to test his or her mental image in many cases (freeing the user from the single diagram) and to track characteristics of a construction that are invariant from shape to shape. For example, a user draws all three medians in a triangle. Noticing that the three medians are concurrent in this triangle, he or she wonders whether this is true for other triangles. The REPEAT option makes it easy to test this conjecture. The combination of the classification scheme for the predefined types of triangles and the REPEAT option creates natural comparison criteria for the user: What features of the construction are invariant when the procedure is repeated within and among categories of triangles?

Numerical Information

Within the Supposer, numbers are used in two ways: in measurements and in constructions that request specification of length, size of angle, and so on. Within each of the two uses, the numbers have two meanings: numbers that present on-screen measurements and numbers that present a geometric property by ratios. Here are two examples to clarify this distinction:

Numerical input within constructions option:

Figure 4.3 presents a construction of a parallel segment in the length of six screen units. When repeating the same construction on a different

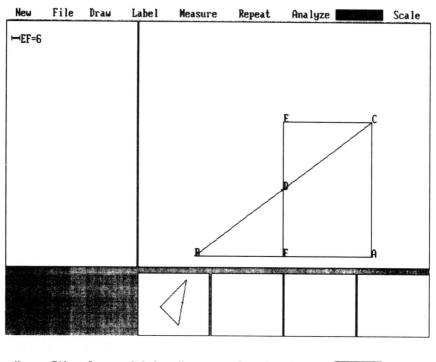

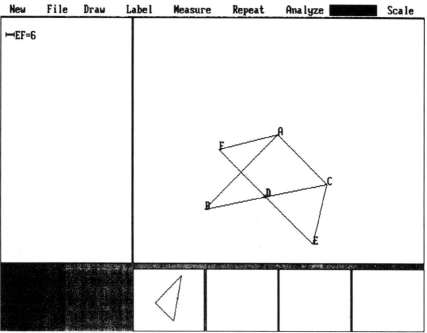

FIG. 4.3. Construction while using an absolute length (EF =6 units).

triangle (Fig. 4.3a) or even when re-scaling the diagram (Fig. 4.3b), the construction looks geometrically different.

Thus, if one focuses on the local and irrelevant property of concrete length, the shape of the construction changes its properties. In Fig. 4.4, the length of the parallel line is specified by a related measure to the side AB (AB/EF = 1). Doing so maintains the geometric properties while varying the initial shape. Numerical output within measurements option:

In the construction of two intersecting medians (see Fig. 4.5), the measurement of each segment varies, but the ratio between pairs of segments is constant.

Thus, the availability of a binary operation calculator within the Supposer supports the generalizations derived from measurements.

Finally, it must be emphasized, here as in other chapters, that the Supposer does not stand alone; it is part of an approach to teaching geometry. The students' work with the software is a part of the course, not the whole. Therefore, as important or even more important than the software itself is how its use is integrated into the course and how teachers make use of the capabilities the software provides.

THE NATURE OF THE SUPPOSER STUDIES

The Supposer has been used in American public high school Euclidian geometry courses since the 1983–1984 school year. Research began the following year. This chapter draws on data from the same studies discussed in the previous chapter on students' learning to overcome visual obstacles in geometry. All the studies were conducted in the Boston area or in Israel from 1984 through 1988. The data sources for all the studies were classroom observations, students' written works, and tests to evaluate their generalization skill. In a few cases I collected and recorded the teachers' as well as students' perspectives about the work.

Classroom Observations

Each class was observed at least once a week during the whole period of learning. The observers wrote reports on the class following each visit. These reports were reviewed regularly by a team of teachers and researchers, then clarified or elaborated by the observers. The main theme in the classroom descriptions is the difficulty students experienced making conjectures and the response of the teachers to these difficulties.

Student Supposer Work

All written student work on Supposer problems was collected. The work was either checked weekly or collected and left for the researcher after the period of the study.

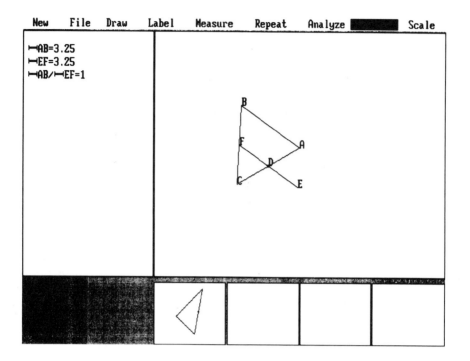

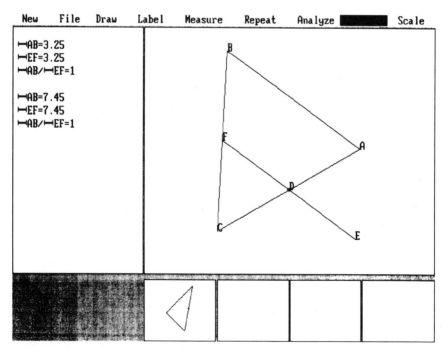

FIG. 4.4. Construction while using a relative length (EF = AB).

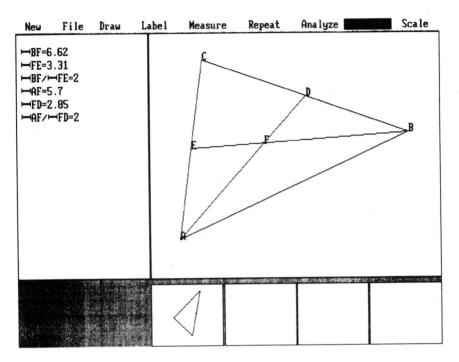

FIG. 4.5. Conservation of a Geometric Property.

Conjecture Tests (Yerushalmy Chazan, & Gordon, 1987)

A pretest and a posttest were designed to assess students' ability to make conjectures or general statements (see Yerushalmy, 1986, for complete details). The tests present students with problems that are composed of a statement and diagram(s) that illustrate the statement. Problems on the tests are posed as data formulations and abstract formulations. In data formulations, the statements contain data and are designed to provide insight into students' ability to generalize based on given instances. In the abstract formulations, the statements are designed to provide insights into students' ability to derive plausible categories for generalizations. The tests ask students to "write significant connected statements" in response to the problem. Although it is important to note what students consider to be "significant" and "connected" statements, the variable of greatest interest is the level of generality of the conjectures that students generate. These tests were administered to experimental and comparison classes. Chi-square analyses were performed to check for significant differences between the groups. The differences found were then interpreted in light of all other types of data reported earlier.

Argument Test (Yerushalmy et al., 1987)

Designed to assess students' ability to produce proofs for true statements (see Yerushalmy, 1986, for details), this test presents three problems with two true statements accompanied by diagrams. It asks students to provide arguments or support for whichever statement they find more convincing.

DEVELOPMENT OF GENERALIZATION SKILLS

These studies show that beginners in geometry face difficulties in trying to integrate inductive reasoning into their work. They become trapped in a standard diagram (Yerushalmy & Chazan, in press) and therefore provide limited types of diagrams in their samples. They collect irrelevant numbers of examples, and often their examples are related to a narrow subset of the data, whereas the conclusion related to the full range of the set. At times they use a fixed quantity of examples in a fixed order no matter what the problem is. The order is sometimes one that a friend or the teacher recommended as a useful method. At other times it is the order of the appearance of elements in the Supposer menu (right triangle, acute, obtuse, etc.). From the first month of the course, students' papers always provided three examples to confirm true conjectures as well as to contradict false conjectures! Low scores on the conjectures pretest reflect their very limited generalization ability.

In this section I describe students' actions within three major processes of generalizations. The first is the ability to develop and identify categories for generalization, in other words, to invent a situation that is more general than a given situation. The second is the ability to form a coherent sample of instances. The third is the ability to induce generality from a sample of instances, that is, form a conjecture by induction.

Generalizations of Ideas: Forming Categories to Generalize

> (Student 1) You have to get conjectures out of nowhere. I don't know. What do you think? (Student 2) You have to start it all on your own. She [the teacher] will give us a little something. The sheets that we work on will say a little something. We have to come up with everything. That's what we're supposed to do. We're not complaining. It's just a little hard sometimes. Maybe we are complaining (Yerushalmy et al., 1987, p. 43).

This quotation from an interview with two Supposer students expresses the difficulty they faced in what is assumed to be the most complex type of generalization: generalizing an idea. Surprisingly, a frequent finding is that students are able to reach a higher level of generalization on this type of task. Results of one year's posttests indicate that "students seem less inhibited in their generalizations and experience greater freedom of thought when the question is posed abstractly. Their conjectures are more general" (Yerushalmy et al., 1987, p. 132). Students in the comparison classes produce conjectures of a slightly higher level on generalization problems than on induction problems. The conjectures of the Supposer classes are at even higher levels, however. The difference on the level variable between the responses of the experimental and comparison classes is significant for both two of three questions. Supposer students are 31 times more likely than comparison students to produce a generalization above Level One (see Yerushalmy et al., 1987, p. 57).

In 1987–1988, two Supposer groups (with different teachers) reached the highest level of generalization on an abstract formulation problem. There are, however, significant differences in favor of the group that was formally taught strategies for generalization. Because, as mentioned earlier, it is more difficult with abstract questions such as those in the test to determine the level and the cause for the generality of the conjectures produced, I concentrate on evidence gathered in classroom observations, lab work, and students' papers to clarify how students generalize ideas.

Using the "What if Not" Strategy. Supposer students are more able and nimble in changing the focus of the given statements in the conjecture tests (Yerushalmy et al., 1987), regardless of the type of teaching intervention. Accordingly, I designed an experiment to assess the impact of direct teaching on the formation of generalizations. I taught one of two comparable Supposer groups (ninth graders) to produce generalizations and to analyze geometric ideas through posing questions about each of the statements' attributes. At the end of the learning period a significant difference was obtained between the two groups in their ability to generalize (for more details see Yerushalmy & Maman, 1988). The teacher in the experimental group used a strategy of problem posing rather than problem solving. She chose to do it in a way suggested by Brown and Walter (1983) that they called the "what if not" strategy. Using this strategy, one generalizes by relaxing conditions within a problem, asking, for example, "What if this condition (restriction) does not exist?" Figure 4.6 illustrates schematically the progression of geometric themes discussed and worked on in this class using the Supposer, following the "what if not" strategy. When asked to conjecture about a different geometrical subject while working independently, these students used the strategy modelled by their teacher and formulated many interesting questions and conjectures.

On the generalization posttest students tended to make changes using the

The inequality of sides lengths in a triangle

not sides

Inequalities: distances of a point inside a triangle to sides and vertices

Inequalities: distances of a point outside a triangle to sides and vertices

Inequalities: medians, midsegments & sides

Inequalities between elements: median, angle bisector and altitude from common vertex

not inequality

Properties of medians, angle bisectors, altitudes

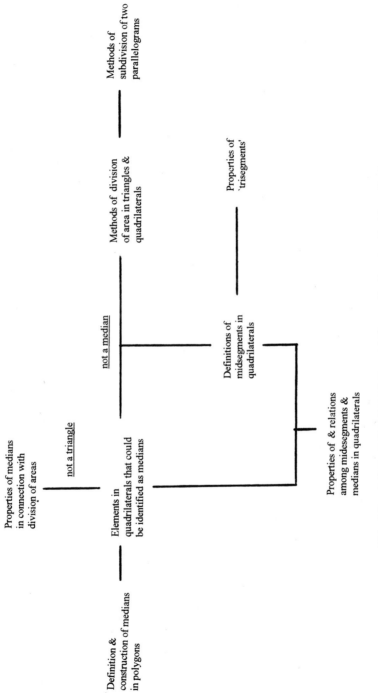

FIG. 4.6. A Schematic Description of Generalization by Problem Posing.

Definition &
construction of medians
in polygons

Properties of medians
in connection with
division of areas

not a triangle

Elements in
quadrilaterals that could
be identified as medians

not a median

Methods of division
of area in triangles &
quadrilaterals

Methods of
subdivision of two
parallelograms

Definitions of
midsegments in
quadrilaterals

Properties of
'trisegments'

Properties of & relations
among midesegments &
medians in quadrilaterals

"what if not" strategy (without actually using the Supposer) in order to generalize abstract formulation statements. Their changes were unexpected.

Here is an example from their work on this given statement in the posttest (Yerushalmy & Maman, 1988, Appendix 4, p. 39): "The two altitudes constructed from the heel of an anglebisector are of equal length." The given situation was new for them (they had not been formally taught about anglebisectors), and the categories for generalization served as a method to analyze the role of each attribute. Through their questions they isolated each component of the statement: the anglebisector, the heel, the altitudes, etc.

> Will the two medians or the two anglebisectors constructed from the heel of the anglebisector be equal? Will the construction of altitudes from the heel of the median make two equal lengths? If we draw altitudes from any point on the anglebisector will they be of equal length?

Students developed the ability to perceive a geometric idea as a versatile entity that could be changed or identified as a case of a class. This notion helped them to master the impact of each component of a statement using the "what if not" strategy.

Generalizations by Forming a Sequence from an Instance. Similar growth was found in the ability of Supposer students to generalize a statement by observing a diagram as one of a sequence of diagrams. Analysis of the visual development of Supposer students (See Yerushalmy & Chazan in this volume) suggests two trends for forming directions for generalization from a single diagram. One trend is that the structure of the software (The REPEAT option and the classification scheme of the chosen shapes) motivates students to choose one of the built-in classifications as a direction for a generalization. In such cases students usually generalized a phenomenon over various types of shapes. The second trend goes far beyond the cases in the first. I often found students using their own schemes to create classes of diagrams from a given single statement and a diagram. For example, students in one study were asked to explore the relationship between the sum of the distances from a random point to the sides of a parallelogram and the perimeter of a parallelogram. They focused on the measure of one of the four interior angles that dictates the measures of the remaining three interior angles. They investigated the relationship between the angle and the ratio between the sum of the lengths of the distances and the perimeter and produced the diagrams shown in Figure 4.7.

Through analysis of the measurements they concluded that when the parallelogram is closer to a rectangle, the sum of two distances is closer to the length of a side. Later they were able to formalize their observation into

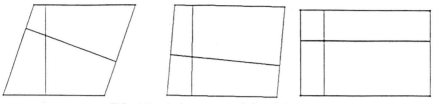

FIG. 4.7. A Sequence of Parallelograms.

the following conjectures: The closer the angles to 90, the closer to ½ perimeter the sum of the distances will be, and in any parallelogram that does not have 90, the sum cannot be greater than ½ of the perimeter (p. 173).

Formation of Samples

Supposer students themselves described the major difficulty they faced in creating a good bulk of information: "She never told us exactly what to look for." They struggled with decisions such as the type of examples they should include, the desirable quantity, and the availability of extreme and negative examples. Because there was no careful guidance, they had to develop their own methods to form the sample. A teacher of a low-ability Supposer class clearly expressed her frustration about the ability of her students to form a good sample: "My students did very little independent work using the Supposer. This came about because of some frustration in the lab setting. Students would gather data diligently, but with no sense of direction. They would ask, What do you want us to look for?" (Yerushalmy et al., 1987, p. 37). This teacher helped her students by encouraging them to make extensive use of the REPEAT option and to look for striking phenomena in their collection (such as congruency, similarity, etc.). Without getting into pedagogical and ability differences, I now discuss the various considerations students take into account when sampling with the Supposer.

Consideration of Nonstereotypic Instances.   People often fail to generalize appropriately when sampling stereotypic instances. Quattrone and Jones (1980) and Holland et al.(1986) found that people tend to learn more than they should from information about a group with which they are unfamiliar, then conclude that a whole sample could be replaced by a few stereotypic instances. Hershkovitz (1987) treated a similar situation in geometry and called it "the misconceptions which endure" or the tendency to use "super" examples. Wason (1974) and Nickerson et al. (1985) found that when people discover a rule or hypothesis that works for the given samples, they make no effort to test the invalidity of the hypothesis. To determine whether the Supposer has an effect on students' ability to overcome this obstacle I compared Supposer scores (see Yerushalmy, in press) and results obtained by non-Supposer classes (both groups are eighth graders of comparable ability, although the two tests were administered a few years apart). Students were asked to identify right angle triangles among nine diagrams of triangles. Three of the nine were right triangles and two of the three were in a nonstandard position (see Fig. 4.8). Among the Supposer students, 60% (compared with 17% in the comparison group) identified item b in Fig. 4.8 as a right triangle and 88.9% (compared with 61%) identified Item c in Fig. 4.8 as a right triangle.

In other comparisons, I found that Supposer students change more aspects of the given statement in making their generalizations, and their conjectures are more original. Originality of the conjectures on the posttest increased among Supposer students but decreased among students who took the traditional geometry course. I concluded that the ability to consider examples other than standard and stereotypic cases is a major cause of these results. I conjecture that students who are trained in observation and creation of various examples for any given situation are less likely to sample only stereotypic instances.

Consideration of the Size and the Source of the Sample.   Are amounts of information an advantage or a disadvantage? Nickerson et. al (1985) viewed the failure to sample enough information as a major bias in drawing a sample. They claimed that people are biased towards samples much smaller than optimal. Determining the most suitable number of geometric data to collect using the Supposer is one of the most complex dilemmas for

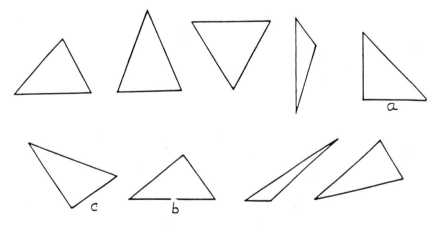

FIG. 4.8.   Identification of Right Triangles. From Hershkovitz, 1987.

students who are trained in deductive reasoning. I followed students' efforts to deal with it. As described previously, students were concerned about the size of their sample and often produced an irrelevant quantity of instances. At an advanced stage of the course, they tended to dramatically decrease the quantity of reported information. At that stage students chose to shift the emphasis from the number of data to the conjecture resulting from the data. They made their intention explicit when they dramatically reduced the number of data presented in their written reports and paid more attention to ideas and arguments. Aside from the quantity consideration, students attributed different weight to instances in the sample as a function of the source of the examples. As described, the Supposer makes it possible to produce a random member of a specific class and also enables the user to build his or her own specific shape. I hypothesized that at first students would use the random option (because it is the fastest way to get the shape) and that only after learning strategies, such as observing extreme cases, would they use the other option. My findings present a different picture. Students tried to explore their own specific triangles and did not trust the computer's random initial shapes. At this stage of the learning they lacked formal knowledge of methods of argumentation in geometry (such as the use of extreme cases), but they sought control over the information whenever the random members of the class did not meet their concept images. For example, a pair of 10th graders who conjectured that the concurrency point of any three altitudes is always inside the triangle rejected the construction made by REPEAT on obtuse and right triangles just because the concurrency point appeared on a vertex or outside the triangle. Instead, they chose to reconstruct the three altitudes one by one on a new triangle without using the REPEAT option. They were then finally convinced that the data provided by the uncontrolled REPEAT option were correct. Thus, Supposer students learned to appreciate data even when they did not support their original expectations.

It was also observed that students appreciated the increased chance of producing unexpected shapes that widened their range of examples. Such a tendency is rare according to the results of studies in inductive reasoning in nonmathematical domains that indicate that people prematurely limit the "hypothesis space" (Nickerson et al., 1985 p. 127), and oversimplify situations by presenting them as dichotomies. Certainly, the students did not limit their hypothesis space, but in some cases they were reluctant to consider randomly generated data. A study by Nisbett (cited in Holland et al., 1986) illuminates this behavior. Nisbett found that subjects accepted the creation of a sample by random choice as a superior technique but were hesitant to refer to it because of the introduction of information with too high variability.

Considerations Related to Special Examples   One of the criteria for a good sample is the existence of extreme examples and negative examples. As described by Anderson (1985), the lack of motivation to search for such examples is one of the serious difficulties of intelligent inductive reasoning. Different paths of reasoning lead to the inclusion of extreme cases. One path is to start with many regular cases, develop a conjecture, and then test it by introducing extreme examples. Another is to observe extreme cases that have a striking effect and then try to widen the base of the hypothesis by many common examples. The consideration of extreme cases sometimes took the students all the way to considering infinity as one of the cases that had to be observed. One such case occurred when students investigated the type of triangles formed by three consecutive numbers. One of the extreme examples was the consideration of the triangle with sides 1000, 1001, 1002 (which cannot be constructed with the Supposer) and the conclusion that the higher the numbers, the closer the triangle must be to an equilateral (for more cases, refer to Yerushalmy, 1986, pp. 197–202).

Hypothesis Formation: Methods of Sample Analysis

"The information is so easy to get. I know exactly what's going to happen. You can predict what's going to happen. . . . Then it does."

However:

"You have to get conjectures about all this stuff. That's really hard. That's not to do with a computer really. The computer is just supplying the information. That kind of spoils it with the conjectures" (Yerushalmy et al., 1987, p. 42).

The use of the Supposer to allow easy sampling does not automatically free students from the need to create samples confirming their previous or naive generalizations or to ignore the information that does not confirm their hypothesis. Findings from the psychological literature (Nisbett et al., 1983, cited in Holland et al., 1986) reveal that generalization strategies may be quite different across different content domains. Nisbett found that people use accurate statistical methods to evaluate variability and to form hypotheses when they believe or know that the problems or the samples are presented within a content domain that can be easily unitized and coded. The more objective the samples seem to the user, the better generalization should be expected. These findings led me to investigate possible effects of algebraic skills (for the generalization of numerical samples), of visual skills, and of the ability to explain and provide arguments on the types of generalizations students produce in geometry.

The Manipulation of Numerical Data.   Does the ability to maneuver with numbers, number operations, and algebraic sequences help students to generalize in geometry? Being able to compare numbers is essential in looking for patterns. Comparing numbers by observing differences and ratios is therefore intensively used while manipulating samples. Although the technique itself is well known to high school students, I collected evidence that misconceptions or insufficient knowledge about the structure of numbers causes false numerical manipulations that affect the quality of the inductions. For example, one student could not find an expected pattern because she unintentionally computed the ratios of two perimeters one way in some cases and another way in other cases. Recognizing her mistake, she decided to include two separate columns of results:

TABLE 4.1
Student's Data Table for Measured Parameters and Their Ratios

P:EFGH	P:ABC	ABCD/EFGH	EFGH/ABCD
30.3	42.9	1.4	.7
11.9	16.7	1.4	.7
26.7	37.4	1.4	.7
21.8	30.4	1.4	.7
12.4	20	1.6	.6
8.2	13	1.5	.6 etc.

In general, students confident in their algebraic ability used larger samples of numerical information than others. Here is an example of a student who tried intensively to code her numerical information into algebraic expressions: In answer to a problem asking her to conjecture about the ratio between the perimeter of a triangle and the sum of the distances of any point from the vertices of that triangle, this student collected 15 sets of data (there were two variables: the type of the triangle and the random position of an internal point), then used three computational strategies to reach generalization:

1. She looked for differences. They ranged from 3.64 to 8.44 and did not suggest any generality.
2. She looked at the ratio of perimeter/sum of segments. All numbers were in a smaller range, between 1.58 and 1.79.
3. She conjectured that the ratio was always close to 1:2, but not exactly 1:2, so she computed a table of differences: $x =$ (sum of segments) $* 2 -$ perimeter. This time the values ranged from 1.37 to 3.63. She then mentioned that all the results were positive numbers, tried to find an upper limit to the sequence, and in the end produced a deductive proof of one of two possible inequalities.

Not all students share this enthusiasm for algebraic manipulations. I identified cases in which students worked for a long time on the data trying to reach a conclusion but did not succeed. The inability to formulate a general algebraic formula for patterns caused difficulty in stating the generalizations. The conjectures were either false generalizations or applied to a very limited number of cases. Additional directions within the task formulation helped such students to reach a categorization of their samples.

Manipulations of Visual Information.   Working with large samples of diagrams, Supposer students had to develop methods to manipulate the visual information. While there are standard techniques to compare and order numbers, they are not attainable within the visual domain. The ability to overcome visual obstacles using the Supposer is described in detail in chapter 3 by Yerushalmy and Chazan. Here, I briefly present the main findings related to visual manipulations. Supposer users in my studies learned to reorganize the visual field of a given situation. By so doing they were able to see various data within the same picture. For example, students were asked to draw a triangle with its interior altitude and then to reflect the altitude over each of the two legs resulting in a shape like the one shown in Figure 4.9.

As the teacher hoped, the students were able to focus on different parts of the diagram, recognize the five triangles present and imagine lifting them off the diagram and rotating them in order to identify their correspondence. In addition, many students focused on aspects of the diagram that the teacher had not previously considered: they conjectured about the outside shape being a right trapezoid or about the sum of angles that create a straight line. They based their conjectures on selective attention to details of the diagram. Students were also able to communicate about their visual analysis because they developed ways to describe a visual process in well-defined parts. Some peeled a shape away whereas others built up a shape by parts. Quantitative evidence suggests that Supposer students are more likely to write conjectures based on a change in their view of the diagram. Thus, the developed visual skill improves the quality and the quantity of the generalizations.

Deductive Reasoning and Generalizations.   As concluded from results of an argument/proof test:

The performance of Supposer groups on the test indicates that the experience may have fostered an ability to make arguments. Supposer students made as many supporting arguments as the comparison class on two of the questions and more arguments than the comparison class on the third. The chances of a student in the experimental groups making a formal proof on problem two

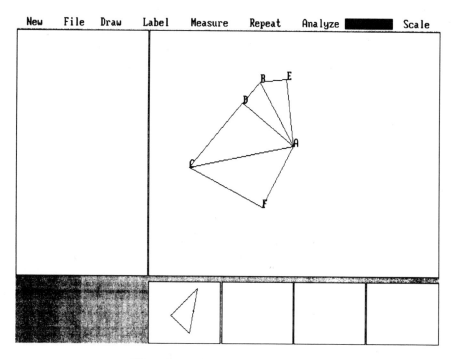

FIG. 4.9.   Reflections of an Altitude.

were 5 times greater than the chances of a student in one of the comparison classes. The students who worked with the Supposer were able to begin with the specific and work their way to a general proof; they were not trapped by the specific. (Yerushalmy et al., 1987, p. 62).

An earlier study presents similar results (Yerushalmy, 1986).

Here is one example in which the failure to confirm a hypothesis yielded a formulation of deductive proof: Toward the end of the course students worked on the following project:

> Draw a square ABCD. Subdivide AB into three parts: AE, EF, FB. Subdivide BA, CD, and DA in the same way. Draw the segments EG, GI, IK, and KE to form an inscribed quadrilateral. Investigate the properties of EGIK (see Fig. 4.10) and the ratios between perimeters and areas of the two quadrilaterals.

Most students conjectured (according to measurements of angles and sides) that EGIK is a square. They easily produced a proof for this conjecture (by proving congruency of triangles: EBK, GDI, ICK, and GAE). Then they measured the ratio between the two areas and found that

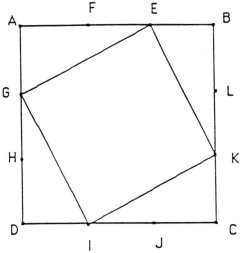

FIG. 4.10. Investigation of Inscribed Squares.

it was equal to 1.8. While trying to explore the same question, but with ABCD being any quadrilateral, they discovered that EGIK was not a square any more, and the four triangles were not congruent, although the ratio between the two areas remained 1.8. Because the teacher could not immediately provide proof (the result was totally unexpected), the students looked to various sources for confirmation: In the computer lab they decided to turn off the computer and look for an argument. The first step was to find another numerical representation for 1.8 (students had experienced before, especially in the similarity unit, that the decimal result of the computation should sometimes read as a fraction). A few students found that 1.8 = %. While constructing auxiliary lines to the original square, one student came out with a grid of nine squares. He then connected the construction and the fraction and provided the following argument:

> When you trisect the sides of ABCD you divide it into 9ths or 9 congruent squares. And, by connecting the points shown in my diagram, you get your congruent triangles as shown in the proof. And the four triangles are congruent to the four other triangles that they share sides with (by SSS). And those triangles divide rectangle AKPF into 2 9ths. That makes the square KJHF divided into %. The whole original square has 9 9ths so the ratio is % or 1.8 ratio.

The third part of this problem directed the student toward possible generalizations by subdividing the sides into more than three sections (see Fig. 4.11).

The student checked the results for $n = 4$ using the computer, and

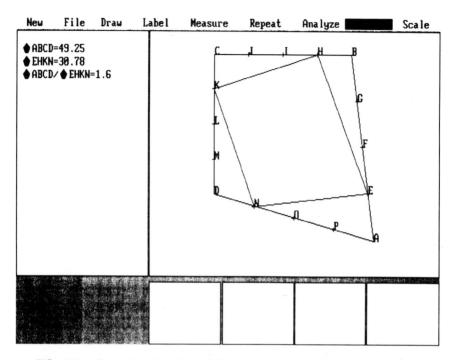

FIG. 4.11.   Generalization Derived From the "Inscribed Square" Problem.

obtained a ratio of 1.6. His previous proof led him to conjecture that the ratio (for $n = 4$) will always be $^{16}/_{10}$. He was enthusiastic to declare that he found a new generalization, and without even trying the construction with the Supposer, he decided that when subdividing each side into 5 the ratio between the areas should be $^{25}/_{20}$. He next checked the ratio for $n = 5$ and found it to be $^{17}/_{25}$ (which was computed as 1.4706). Because he could not reach an argument either way, he abandoned the problem at this point. Observations of this exceptional piece of work and the repeated results about the tendency of Supposer students to provide convincing arguments should help to show that there is a mutual effect between confrontation with false generalizations and the development of the need for proof.

SUMMARY AND CONCLUSIONS

In this chapter, I have described students' performance on two types of generalizations in geometry: generalizations of ideas and generalizations from instances (induction). Within generalization of any type, three major processes are involved (not necessarily within a constant order): formation of samples of examples to serve as a data base for conjectures, manipulations on the samples, and analysis of ideas in order to form more general ideas. Previous studies of generalization in the social sciences as well as a few works in mathematics education reveal that common biases to plausible generalizations include an insufficient quantity of samples and a tendency to choose examples that confirm an hypothesis. These studies also suggest that previous training in inductive reasoning, in the subject matter, and in statistics and probabilistic methods should affect the type and level of generalizations.

Following these studies, I created an evaluation scheme that included tests and other sources of data about the ability to generalize and to provide arguments in geometry. I have described students' overcoming obstacles and have tried to point out the reasons for the development of their reasoning skills; mainly I have described the influence of two factors: the Supposer and the inquiry learning environment.

I found that the use of the Supposer focuses students' attention on the nature of the sample: the quantity of needed information, the variability of the information, and the objectivity of the information. The learn to appreciate the ease of getting many examples but become aware of the need to form a strategy of collection in order not to get lost. They learn to use extreme cases, negative examples, and nonstereotypic evidence to back up their conjectures. Although the direct influence of the tool on the availability of information is clear, the processes by which students form an hypothesis from a sample or from an abstract formulation of ideas need to be more carefully observed.

Students' reflections on their own work show that they understand that conjecturing is the most difficult task they have; I tried to follow incidents as well as quantitative results to indicate the major factors involved in better generalizations. I reviewed four such skills: the ability to maneuver numbers using algebraic generalizations, the ability to generalize visual information by observing commonalities among examples, the ability to identify the major variables of a geometric situation (either verbally or visually described), and subject matter content knowledge (geometric deductive knowledge). Evidence shows that algebraic skills and visual skills each foster the making of generalizations. The ability to view a number or a figure in more than one representation yields unusual conjectures. Teacher modeling of inductive strategies while using the Supposer has an influence on students' work. First, they imitate the suggested strategy, such as the "what if not" strategy. Second, they absorb the legitimation from their teachers that there is no forbidden idea within geometry and that once there is enough evidence, any pattern is eligible. Through this work, it became clear that teaching inductive reasoning within the realm of deductive reasoning ruins no desirable mathematics skill. I am convinced that it is essential to create opportunities to generalize in any domain of mathematics using various software tools. Once the opportunity is provided, it is necessary to teach students various reasoning skills: variable analysis, numerical methods, and criteria to analyze the quality of the analysis. Students who are aware of the possible obstacles to generalization are less likely to fall into overgeneralization and stereotypic conclusions.

ACKNOWLEDGMENTS

The writing of this article was supported by the Spencer foundation through the National Academy of Education fellows' program.

REFERENCES

Anderson, J. R. (1985). *Implications of Cognitive Psychology*. New York: Freeman.

Brown, S. & Walter, M. (1983). *The Art of Problem Posing*. Philadelphia: The Franklin Institute Press.

Burton, R. R. (1982). Diagnosing bugs in a simple procedural skill. In Sleeman & Brown (Eds.), *Intelligent tutoring systems* (pp. 157–184). New York: Academic Press.(Sleeman and Brown, Eds.). Academic Press.

Chazan, D. (1988a). Similarity: Exploring the understanding of a geometric concept. (Tech. Rep. No. TR88-15). Cambridge, MA: Harvard Graduate School of Education, Educational Technology Center.

Chazan, D. (1988b). Proof and measurement: An unexpected misconception. In A. Barbas (Ed.), *Proceedings of the PME XII,* Hungary.

Cohen P. R. & Feigenbaum, E. A. (1982). *The Handbook of Artificial Intelligence,* (Vol. 3). Stanford, CA: HeurisTech Press.

Hershkovitz, R. (1987). The acquisition of concepts and misconceptions in basic geometry — or when "A little learning is a dangerous thing." In J. D. Novak (Ed.), *Proceedings of the Second International Seminar on Misconceptions and Educational Strategies in Science and Mathematics*. Ithica: Cornell University.

Hershkovitz, R., Bruckheimer, M. & Vinner, S. (1987). Activities with teachers based on cognitive research. In *Learning and teaching geometry K-12*. NCTM Year Book, pp. 222-235. Reston, VA.

Holland, J. H., Holyoak, K. J., Nisbett, R. E., & Thagard, P. R. (1986). *Induction: Processes of inference, learning and discovery*. Cambridge, MA: MIT Press.

Kitcher, P. (1983). *The nature of mathematical knowledge*. New York: Oxford University Press.

Kline, M. (1980). *Mathematics: The loss of certainty*. New York: Oxford University Press.

Matz, M. (1982). Towards a process model for high school algebra errors. In Sleeman & Brown (Eds.),*Intelligent Tutoring Systems* (pp. 25-50). New York: Academic Press.

Nickerson, R. S., Perkins, D. N. & Smith, E. E. (1985). *The teaching of thinking*. Hillsdale, NJ: Lawrence Erlbaum Associates.

Nisbett, R. E., Krantz, D. H., Jepson, D. & Kunda, Z. (1983). The use of statistical heuristics in everyday inductive reasoning. *Psychological Review, 90,* 339-363.

Polya, G. (1973). *How to solve it*. Princeton, NJ: Princeton University Press. (Original work published 1945)

Polya, G. (1962). *Mathematical discovery: On understanding, learning, and teaching problem solving.* New York: Wiley.

Quattrone, G., & Jones, E. (1980). The perception of variability within in-groups and out-groups: Implications for the law of large numbers. *Journal of Personality and Social Psychology, 38,* 141–152.

Rissland, E. (1977). *Epistemology, representation, understanding, and interactive exploration of mathematical theories.* Unpublished doctoral dissertation. Massachusetts Institute of Technology, Cambridge, MA.

Schwartz, J. L. & Yerushalmy, M. (1985–1988). *The Geometric Supposer* Pleasantville, NY: Sunburst.

Wason, P. C. (1974). The psychology of deceptive problems. *New Scientist, 63,* 382–385.

Yerushalmy, M. (1986). *Induction and generalization: An experiment in teaching and learning high school geometry.* Unpublished doctoral dissertation. Harvard Graduate School of Education, Cambridge, MA.

Yerushalmy, M. (1991). Enhancing acquisition of basic geometrical concepts with the use of the Geometric Supposer. *Journal of Educational Computing Research, 7*(4), 407–420.

Yerushalmy, M. & Chazan, D. (1990). Overcoming visual obstacles with the aid of the Supposer. *Educational Studies in Mathematics, 21,* 199–219.

Yerushalmy, M., Chazan, D. & Gordon, M. (1987). *Guided inquiry and technology: A year-long study of children and teachers using the Geometric Supposer.* Center for Learning Technology Reports and Papers in Progress, (Tech. Rep. No. 90-8. Newton, MA: Education Development Center.

Yerushalmy, M. & Maman, H. (1988). *The Geometric Supposer as the basis for class discussion in geometry.* (Tech. Rep. No. 9). Haifa, Israel: The University of Haifa, Laboratory of Computers for Learning.

5 Discovery Courses Are Great in Theory, But . . .

Christopher C. Healy
Los Angeles Public Schools

Almost everyone agrees that when students discover things on their own, the learning takes on a special significance. Students seem to have greater understanding and memory for what they have learned. Nevertheless, we teachers have a very difficult time allowing this kind of learning to happen in our classrooms.

There are a number of persuasive and seemingly logical reasons for not allowing much discovery to take place in our classes, and each has its merit. It takes too much time. I won't be able to cover the entire course. What if they discover the wrong things?

Due to a series of events, I fell into a course that pressed the word "discovery" to the maximum. I teach—well facilitate—the class originally known as No Book Geometry and now called Build-a-Book Geometry.

I began it in the fall of 1987 after teaching traditional geometry for 4 years. During that time our math department became involved in a program called Professional Links with Urban Schools (PLUS) in Los Angeles. College and industry contacts I made through PLUS stated unanimously that geometry was the most important class in high school, because "in geometry students learn how to think."

I didn't feel that even 50% of the students who passed my geometry classes learned how to think. I was frustrated with the failure rate, the textbook, and the incorrect impression given to colleges and industry, but I saw no solution until the summer of 1987.

During a 4-week institute that summer, I learned of the Geometric Supposer, reviewed the available geometry texts, and was introduced to word processing. Those were all I needed to convince me to try an all-discovery geometry class.

Most of this chapter is a mixture of comments and interactions from students in the first 3 years of the experiment. First, however, I want to describe what I mean by the discovery method as I have tried to use it.

The students who walked in the door in September that first year of the new course had no idea what they were getting themselves into (but then again, neither did I). As they entered, each was given a card randomly pulled from a deck. The card determined the seating arrangement for the first 2 weeks: all the aces sat together, as did all the 2s, 3s, and so on. I explained to them that each group would be given an "investigation sheet" with only a statement at the top. The rest of the sheet was to be filled in with the comments the students in the group made regarding the original statement.

These statements, which became known as the "given facts," were all the geometric knowledge I gave them for the entire year. Their job was to somehow discover the rest. These three statements were:

Parallel lines never meet.
A triangle contains 180 degrees.
A linear pair contains 180 degrees.

Students enroll in geometry for many different reasons. Some are looking for knowledge that is helpful on SAT tests and in college, while others just want to fulfill a graduation requirement. There are freshmen who have always done well in math, along with sophomores, juniors, and seniors who may have barely passed algebra. On the first day of Build-a-Book geometry, all inequities fade away, and the students realize they are dependent solely on each other. In a class with no rules, no one has an advantage over anyone else.

Responses to the given facts that first day were varied. Here is an assortment:

Parallel lines are sexy.
Nonparallel lines must meet.
A triangle is a dented circle.
A triangle has three sides.
A linear pair is two angles.
A pair of linear pairs is an upside and downside (of a line).

I read all the comments they had written and chose eight of them to be the topics for the next day. I copied the chosen statements off the papers of the first day onto the investigation sheets for the following day. This routine I repeated nightly, so that each day's investigation sheets were generated from the previous day's work. The class was thus responsible for the work the following day. I followed this format most of the first year with the following exceptions.

At times a group writes a concern about the actual meaning of a word on their investigation sheet (i.e., "What exactly is a line?"). Whenever I receive these inquiries or similar questions from class members, I note the word(s) in the back of my notebook, and when I have accumulated three or more of them, I write them on the board for homework. Each student is to define the words on the board and turn their definitions in the following day.

I have a student gather up the assignments as the students enter and give them to a random group. That group's assignment for the day is to read all the definitions and come up with a class definition of each word.

Each word and its proposed definition are put on the board on Monday, and a student leads the discussion to determine the final definition for the class geometry book. Frequently there are intense disagreements, and compromise is often the solution. Eventually most of the words end up in the book. Probably the most disliked day in class is Monday, because of the strain put on students.

While investigating, groups frequently come up with information they wish to share with the rest of the class. This is done through presentations. After each presentation and the ensuing questions, there is a vote on whether the material presented is true and worthy of entry into the book. This process produces some of the most difficult moments for me, because students have presented and voted down things that I feel are significant parts of geometry. Still, I believe it imperative that I not interfere.

The is no rule against getting information from other sources as long as the group or individual can present and support what they find. About the only things that aren't frequently questioned are those discovered using the Supposer. This software accurately measures geometric figures and shapes. It isn't perfect and isn't accepted as absolute truth, but it adds credibility to any presentation to be supported by the Supposer.

I am unable to ask questions or participate in class activities until students have developed a confidence that won't be automatically shaken because the question is coming from the teacher. It takes from 1 to 3 months for the mystique surrounding the teacher to be minimized by the discoveries students make.

The format has the general appearance I present here, but it is in constant flux. The students determine the direction and the format after the first few weeks. This flexibility is one of the major strengths and one of the most difficult things for teachers to accept. Nevertheless, when the teacher releases the creative nature of high school people and gives them the responsibility of learning and discovery, the teacher must also give up the authority to determine class structure and curriculum.

Testing is done biweekly (or so). I ask questions from their book and correct the test from their book. This causes some disagreements, because sometimes the students don't actually agree with all the definitions or "discovered truths" in the book. Students believe these tests to be the toughest tests they ever take, and the grades the first grading period are very low. By the end of first semester the average has improved. Using the discovery method leads to a marked decline in the failure rate, but the number of A's also declines.

This chapter is a taste of what opening the door to discovery can do. It increases the passing rate for geometry at my school. More students enjoy geometry and wish to pursue their study of geometry after leaving the course. Grades and SAT preparation are not sacrificed. Kids do learn how to think. But the most important changes can be described only by the students who have experienced the Build-a-Book class.

A STUDENT'S VIEW OF DISCOVERY

Christina (August 26)

When I registered for school today I took the classes my counselor wanted me to. I don't know if I can handle both biology and geometry. I feel better about biology because I have always done pretty well in science.

Geometry is another thing. Algebra wasn't easy for me, but I think everyone fails geometry. I don't think I have a chance to pass geometry, but it made my counselor happy to have me in "college prep" classes, and I can always drop geometry if I want to. I signed up to take it fifth period. I figure the later the better.

Larry (September 10 — the first day of school)

Hey man, who does this guy think he is? You can't run a class like that. How's he going to get away with this? Mr. Healy's a teacher. He can't just throw things out because he doesn't like them.

Today was the same old boring start of school. The only good thing about it is it's the last year I'll ever have to worry about.

Hey, I'll admit, I'm not college material, but I have to keep my options open. You never know when you might need something. So I took geometry, just in case I need it to get into college. It's not as if I'm expecting to go on to college, but like I said, you've got to keep your options open. I'm going to make a million dollars in real estate, and you don't need college for that. Actually I don't care what I do, but it has to include making a lot of money.

We're all sitting in fifth period, waiting for the teacher's patented first day speech about hard work, dedication and effort. The dude starts out, "I'm Mr. Healy, and this year in geometry . . . " and I break in saying, "We aren't going to have books."

It was great. I couldn't wait to see what he'd do. It's the first day of class. He doesn't even know my name, so what's he going to do? I figure it's my responsibility to test out each teacher in the first few days. Hey, it's a dirty job, but somebody's got to do it. I didn't know what to expect, but who cared? It was the end of the first day and if he couldn't handle it, so what?

Instead of getting on my case or sending me out of the room like a normal teacher this guy says, "Okay, we won't have any books." What's wrong with this dude? Who's going to run this class, him or me? He's got to be tricking us. We're not going to have a class like geometry without a book. This is serious stuff here. I couldn't care less what happens in the class, but there are other people who think that geometry is going to be important to them. They aren't going to be able to function without a book. Is this guy on drugs or something? He's playing with people's future here. The people in the class who are planning on going to college can't afford to have a teacher who messes around. I know they're hard up for math teachers right now, but this guy shouldn't be teaching.

Edmund (September 16)

As a freshman I had trouble just finding my classes. The high school is big and spread out. The first day was especially tough for me, because I don't have a lot of friends to help me out. I'm kind of a loner. When I finally got to my geometry class fifth period, I was just glad to get to the right classroom. The seats were in groups of four instead of rows, but other than that it was a normal math class. In junior high there were all these things on the wall to look at and learn about, but in this geometry class there wasn't anything on the walls — no theorems or axioms of geometry. But that wasn't the biggest surprise. The first day Larry, one of the students, interrupted Mr. Healy and told him we weren't going to use geometry books.

I was shocked that Larry had interrupted, and even more shocked when the teacher agreed not to use a book. Now I think Mr. Healy just planned not to use books all along. How could a real teacher let a class be determined by a student, unless the teacher was already thinking about working without a book?

After Larry came up with the idea of geometry without books, Mr. Healy gave each of the groups different facts and told us to write down anything we came up with. We could just use our brains to think about things any way we wanted to. I've never been able to do that in school — I thought students were supposed to learn things, not think. What we are doing seems very strange, but for me this is the most exciting thing I have ever done. I can think anything I want, and there are no wrong answers.

Like on the first day, our group was given the fact, "Parallel lines never meet." Our instructions were to write down any thoughts anyone had about it. Larry was in my group, and he said, "Parallel lines are sexy." I thought that was stupid and shouldn't be written down, but Mr. Healy's instructions were to write down anything, and Larry was so demanding that I didn't disagree.

The next day in class Mr. Healy even mentioned "Parallel lines are sexy." He said that any ideas need to be written down because you never know how the idea may make others think. That's when I was sure there would be no limits on me. I can think about anything — even something that has nothing to do with the thing we are given to talk about. I've never had freedom like this before, and I sure like it. It's perfect for me, but not everybody is into the idea of working this way.

I know Mr. Healy thinks we can do it, but I don't think he's thought of all the consequences. What would he do if someone decides not to work, or if we fail to come up with the right information? I'm worried that we won't learn "real" geometry. If we don't learn "real" geometry, we won't do well on the SAT. And if that happens, we won't be able to get into a good college.

I think this class is the best thing that ever happened to me, because I can learn the geometry information I'll need for the SAT and for college from books I read outside the class. I may never have another class where I have the freedom to think anytime I want to. Not only is there freedom to think, but the people in my group listen to everybody. I like to be listened to. They treat me as if what I say is important.

Anna (October 1)

My geometry teacher said that if Euclid could build geometry thousands of years ago, a bunch of high school students in the 1980s could do it too.

The idea of building geometry from the bottom up is fascinating, and I think it might be possible if the students in the class were all "A" students. But my class has all different kinds of students. The only things we have in common are the class we registered for and a passing grade in algebra. The people in the class are all in different grades, and they have such different personalities. It might have been an okay idea with an honors class, but I don't think we have very many modern-day Euclids in this class.

And Mr. Healy won't give us any hints about whether we are on the right track or whether our thoughts are totally fallacious. It's hard to see how we are going to learn "real" geometry, but I like the idea of a teacher having the confidence to let us experiment.

Mr. Healy is a nice guy and I guess he knows his geometry (how will I ever know?), but he's not very organized. In fact, if it weren't for my notes, whatever we've learned would have been lost. Our homework assignments are finding definitions for words that have come up in one of the groups during the day. Sometimes there's no homework, and other times there's a lot. The next day, when we turn the homework in, one of the groups reads all the assignments and develops a single group definition for each word.

Then the whole class gets to discuss the definition. The worst part of the whole process is that the definition the class agrees on becomes a fact in our book, even if Mr. Healy knows it isn't correct. How are we supposed to learn the geometry if no one ever tells us whether we are on the right track? I know Mr. Healy thinks this is a good idea, but how does he know it will really work? And why doesn't he give us some idea if we are right or wrong?

Whether we are right or wrong wouldn't make any difference if it weren't for me, because Mr. Healy is so disorganized that he never writes down our final definition. In fact he's been relying on my notebook ever since he found out about it. Organization isn't one of his strong points. In fact, I'm not sure what his strong points are. He doesn't teach us anything. He only provides us with materials like the computer and the Supposer, rulers, paper, building materials, etc. He's lucky I'm in our class—otherwise nothing would ever have been recorded.

The other thing is he doesn't know much about the computer. Sure, he knows how to turn it on and boot up a disk, but I don't know if he's ever even looked at the Geometric Supposer disk. Gerardo, one of the boys in the class, can operate the computer and figured out how the Supposer works, which is lucky or we'd be totally lost. The Supposer is really important for two reasons: (1) The Supposer is part of "real" geometry and it answers questions with real answers, and (2) It's got some real vocabulary words (too bad there aren't any definitions).

Patty (October 9)

Yesterday I thought I had showed everyone in the class that a line could cross one parallel line without necessarily having to cross the other. I don't know why it was important, but at the time it seemed like what I had to say was significant.

I was presenting the idea in front of the class. First, I drew two parallel lines on the board and had a third line cross one of the parallel lines and stop before it got to the other one.

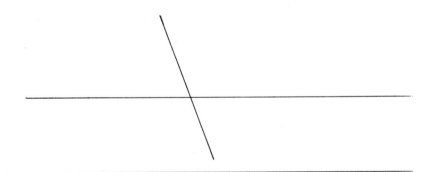

The class argued with me and voted that lines don't end, even if you can't see them continue. I didn't agree, but it didn't stop me. I drew the same picture, except this time after the third line crossed the first parallel line, I curved it so it stayed between the two parallel lines and never crossed the second line.

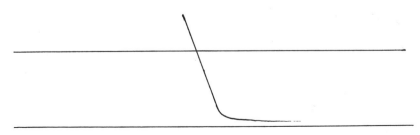

That was okay until Anna said lines had to be continuous and straight. It didn't take long until everyone agreed with her, but that didn't stop me either. I thought about it and drew a third picture, which began like the other two with a pair of parallel lines. In this picture the third line crossed one parallel, but avoided the other by "ducking" under it.

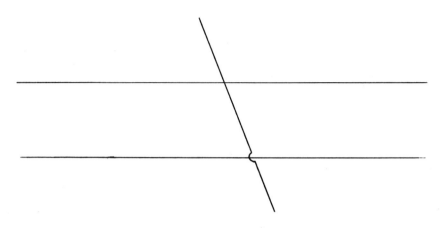

Actually not everyone was pleased with my picture, but they agreed to leave it in the book at least until some other group could investigate my "ducking" line.

Carlos (November 5)

In this class you make enemies out of friends arguing over things that you couldn't have cared less about six months ago.

Teacher (November 7)

Before Patty's demonstration the class had undergone some incredible turmoil with their definition of a line: the path of a moving point, like the exhaust from a moving car. According to their definition, a line doesn't have to be straight or have any other quality. The definition was a combination of ideas, and last Monday when we determined the class definition, there was quite a bit of discussion whether the path had to be straight. One girl who had failed geometry from a book last year couldn't see a line as not being straight because that's what the book said. And books are always right, aren't they?

Most people like to try to extend their skills. That's a portion of the reason for the success so far in the No Book class. They feel they are definitely in over their heads, but they are beginning to thrive in the land "beyond them."

Bernie (November 11)

My group was given an Investigation Sheet that had Patty's last picture on it and said, "The third line crosses the first parallel line and ducks under the second parallel line." At first, there was mostly disagreement about the "ducking" part.

Sandra said that a line can't duck, because it's on a plane, which she said is like a sheet of paper.

Then Tino made a lot of pictures of parallel lines and tried to figure out if the ducking thing could happen on a sheet of paper. He tried all sorts of parallel line shapes. I think he got carried away with things because before long he had a different geometric figure on each sheet.

After we talked we decided that there was no such thing as ducking on a plane. We were done, and we still had twenty minutes to go, so we sat and talked until Minerva crumpled one of Tino's drawings.

I thought she was going to toss it in the trash, but instead she asked us if the square that Tino drew was still a square inside the crumpled plane. I didn't know. I didn't even know if the plane was still a plane.

Tino was sure that the "squareness" was gone, but he wasn't go sure the "planeness" was gone.

According to Sandra a plane has to be flat, but Minerva said she'd heard of curved planes, so why couldn't there be crumpled planes.

That's when I thought about cellophane. I told them to draw a square on cellophane and then crumple it. Then hold the ball of cellophane over a flat surface and shine a flashlight through it. The square will reappear on the flat surface below. We never had the chance to check it out because the bell rang and the next day was a test, but I bet it works.

Arcy (November 16)

The thing I hate most about the Build-a-Book class is that I'm always tired. The reason is I stay up late trying to figure out how I can make the other people in class understand how I think and, especially, how I can change their minds to agree with me.

Chris (November 22)

Larry, this guy in my geometry class, is always talking about keeping his alternatives open. That class is a place full of alternatives, so I guess it's a good place for a lot of people. I don't know how much geometry we're learning, but it's more fun than I expected. We kind of make up the class as we go along. When I say "we" I mean the students. There are no rules in the class, no right or wrong, no ultimates. I took the class just to please my counselor, and now it's my favorite. What we say is important, and we talk everything over before we decide on anything. I think people should talk things over. One person shouldn't be a dictator. Maybe the whole world couldn't function that way, but I think it would be a better place if people talked over their choices before they made their decisions.

Last Monday we were going over our definition for the word "distance." Almost everyone thought that it sounded good to say, "Distance is the path between two points." But I knew that wasn't right, so I raised my hand to get Mr. Healy's attention.

When he called on me, I went up to the board and showed how distance could be between two or more points (like a triangle, or three points in a line).

It seems like Edmund and Larry always disagree, but after I showed the class on the board, both of them agreed with me. A few people asked me questions, and we voted on the final definition. What I said must have changed their minds because they voted to have "or more" in the definition. I know the definition's not that big a deal. But it was a really big deal that people listened to me and really cared what I said. When Edmund and Larry agreed with me it made me feel really good. When the rest of the class agreed on the definition, I knew that what I have to say is important and that other people are interested in listening to me.

Anna (November 29)

A few weeks ago Mr. Healy drew a triangle on the board and put an altitude in it.

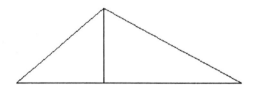

Then he asked us to come up with a word for the line inside the triangle. I figured he didn't mean "altitude" so I turned in the name "PLIT" (my acronym for Perpendicular Line Inside a Triangle). It was just one of those things you do on the spur of the moment, not something I really expected anyone to take seriously. The whole assignment was ridiculous.

The definition group liked my word "PLIT." So the next Monday (the day the class determines what will go into our book) the class discussed it. There wasn't much disagreement, and they chose PLIT for their word.

Okay, I admit, I felt really good about it. Even if no one else knew where it came from, I did. And I had "coined" something special for our book. It wasn't the word that everyone else knows, but it was my word.

Over the next couple of weeks some really interesting things took place with my word. Of course, Mr. Healy didn't say anything about us choosing a word that was different from the word the rest of the world uses. Because everyone knew what PLIT stood for, they thought it was easier to remember . . . at first.

The day after we decided on PLIT, someone in one of the groups discovered that a PLIT can be outside the triangle in certain kinds of triangles (obtuse triangles).

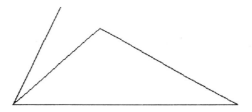

This wasn't a problem. We just added the term "PLOT" (Perpendicular Line Outside a Triangle) to our vocabulary the next Monday, and everyone was happy, until last week when one group found out that parallelograms have perpendicular lines like the ones inside triangles. Larry said it was okay and coined the word PLIP. Two days later we discovered PLOPs.

The next Monday when we were trying to add "PLIP" and "PLOP," Sergio raises his hand and asks Mr. Healy, "Why don't we forget all this PLIT and PLOP junk and just call an altitude an altitude?"

At first I was really hurt because the support he got from the rest of the class meant that my word (and all the generations that followed) would be gone forever. It never meant all that much to me anyway. At least I didn't think it did until I heard myself arguing in favor of keeping all the PL words.

I never thought I'd be arguing against anything that Sergio said, but it was kind of like a personal attack. Well, that's how I took it, I guess. So there I was, arguing against the one person in the class I didn't want to disagree with. And I was arguing against having "altitude" in our book, which is exactly the exact opposite of what I thought should have been done in the first place. This is crazy to get us to reevaluate everything we're doing or thinking. If you told me two months ago that I'd be arguing against Sergio or against "real" geometry I'd have said you were out of your mind. But you know, it didn't seem so crazy when I was explaining why "PLIT" was a better term for the concept of altitude.

At one point I said, "We are our own authors of geometry, and we don't have to be tied down by whatever the rest of the world believes to be true, because this is our class."

Laura (December 1)

I never cared what he said because I didn't get really involved in the class. I'm barely passing (if that) and nothing would have changed except for the group of people I'm working with in the class right now. This one guy, Larry, thinks he's God's gift to geometry, and it's "his destiny" to "open up the minds" of those hopeless creatures in the class endowed with less intelligence. He reminds me a little of Jo, my older sister, when she gets into that "I'm #1 and the rest of the world is dust" state of mind. I tried to act as the translator for Larry's ideas to the other two people in our group. I had to admit he had some good ideas, but the way he presented them wasn't clear and it was offensive to the other two in our group.

He wanted to create a circle with 100 degrees instead of the normal 360 degrees. Personally, I don't care how many degrees a circle has in it (I'm not even sure I understand what a degree is). But for our group to continue, a translator had to be found who could explain the Larryisms to the group before he lost his temper. Larry got so frustrated when he had an idea that the others refused to consider or couldn't comprehend, but I knew how they felt. Sometimes your brain just won't accept things unless they are rearranged. That's what I did, "rearrange" what Larry said.

We went through a week of Larry speaking to our group with me as the rearranger. I think the biggest problem was that the rest of the group could think in only one way (some people are more bound to tradition—like a circle has 360 degrees—than others), and Larry couldn't accept that. So it was anarchy or interpretation, and seeing as I get along with everyone in that group, I was the natural link between them.

Larry (December 3)

It's not my job to transport all these imbeciles to enlightenment. All right, I have an easier time than all the other people in the fifth period No Book geometry class. They still think they can't come up with "real" geometry. I don't care if we ever come up with "real" geometry—we're going to create a never-to-be-duplicated geometry. Just watch and see. The trouble is, while I'm out there on the edge of universal discovery, the rest of them are lost somewhere in the most basic ideas ever to cross a classroom. This Healy guy didn't know what he was getting into when he gave me a chance to challenge anything that anyone ever came up with. Just watch me work.

The only down side of this whole process is we don't get to create alone. We're in groups, so I have to be the raft on which most of my group depends for survival. It's not that I don't understand the position, but I'm not sure how to handle it all. I've been creating things ever since I can remember. I enjoy questioning what is an actual law of nature and what was merely the whim of some idiot in history, who didn't know which way was up. Some of those guys established laws for unknown reasons, and the rest of us have had to memorize it and accept it as gospel.

Take the idea of a circle having 360 degrees. What good does 360 do, anyway? Why did they choose that number instead of 300 or 400 or some other number? What's so sacred about 360? I started thinking about it a long time ago, but I never said anything. I mean I know how to get through school. Teachers don't want you to think about the world. They want you to memorize what they think is important about the world. If you can swallow the facts they want you to know and regurgitate it on one of their tests, you pass. If not, you fail.

I've known how to play the game since I was in elementary school. It's not one of the things I revere about education, but if you're going to play the game you've got to know how to win. You have to agree to play the game according to their rules, because without an education you aren't worth anything in this world. I'm not saying I agree, but I know the facts. Until I'm in charge. I've learned to operate in their world. When I run the world, it'll be the way I want it, according to my rules.

We're making our own world in that geometry class. That's one of the things that makes it so special. I never thought that class would be worth anything unless I wanted to go to college. I'm thinking about college more now than I ever did before. This class encourages us to challenge old facts. I'm not sure Healy would agree with all the changes we're working on, but he said it was our class, and so far he hasn't interfered. I bet it's killing him.

Getting back to the 360 degree circle. When I brought how ridiculous 360 degrees was to my group, they just sat there and couldn't see what difference it made. So I told my mom who works at the Star News newspaper to look up where they got the idea of 360 degrees. Using her computer checking system she found a book in some library, and I went and checked it out.

According to this book, sometime in the 12th century a bunch of scientists and mathematicians gathered together in Germany. One night the mathematicians noticed that the horizon appeared to be a circle from where they were standing. Meanwhile an astronomer mentioned that 360 stars were visible. So somehow the idea got into the mathematicians that that was how many degrees there were in a circle. Is that wild or what?

I don't know if it's true or not, but it didn't matter. When I took that information to my group and told them about it, you should have seen them. They couldn't believe the number of degrees in a circle was determined in such a useless way. Like I said, I don't know if I believe it, but that doesn't matter. With that information their closed minds momentarily opened a crack, and I took advantage of it. As soon as they noticed the possibility of some ancient law being fallible, I introduced the Metric Circle, which is based on 100 degrees. I helped them discover the wonder of my Metric Circle and the ease with which it could be used. They were ripe for indoctrination.

Laura (December 7)

By the end of the week Larry was convinced that we could discover and develop major improvements. Everyone in the group was involved in the whole idea and offering their suggestions. This must be the way decisions are made in big business.

Mr. Healy gave us the opportunity to convince the remainder of the class to let us stick together for more than two weeks to investigate the Metric Circle. Larry spoke first and convinced the whole class that he thought they were incapable of understanding, which made them determined not to let us stay together.

I'm not the type who gets up in front of a group of people easily. In fact I hate it. But I had been making a real contribution to our group, and I knew there was no way we were going to stay together if Larry was the last person the class heard before voting.

Larry walked back to his seat with the statement, "See if I care how you vote!" The podium was empty.

I got up to "translate" again, only this time it was in front of the whole class. I was so scared that when I started to talk, you could barely hear me. Then the strangest thing happened. I saw that the whole class was listening to what I said. I told them that we were working well together and that we had made some discoveries that we wanted to share with them, but we weren't ready to do so.

I said, "We aren't keeping secrets, we just need time to verify our discoveries. If you vote to give us another week together, we will continue to work on the circle idea. And a week from today we will be ready to present the entire plan to you. Then you can decide if we will be given the second week together."

It sounded so good I couldn't believe it was me talking. Everyone listened. Better than that, they completely reversed their opinion and voted unanimously to let us have the week's extension. What a feeling!

After I finished and sat back down, do you know what Larry said to me?

"In the two weeks we've spent together this is the first time I've heard you talk."

Where had he been all the time I was translating for him? Listening isn't his thing I guess. He's more into using people to accomplish things. Funny though, I don't feel used. It just feels good to know that I can help people learn in this class.

I may not find out about geometry in this class, but I found out that I have the ability to influence people.

Edmund (January 11)

I still don't see what the big deal is. A couple of weeks ago I figured out a way to get the same results as the Pythagorean Theorem using an Isosceles Right Triangle. I did it by folding the paper and it worked out fine, but no one cares if you have a proof of something for only one isolated case. When I showed it to Mr. Healy, he said the same thing. He seemed impressed and told me to keep working on it, so I did.

I found out it works for some other right triangle. When I showed it to him this time, he was really excited. He asked me to present it to the rest of the class, using the board to demonstrate it. I'm not exactly a public speaker, but I wanted the rest of the class to see it. And I knew Mr. Healy wouldn't show it to them — that's just the way he is.

Today was the day for my presentation. I had it all planned on graph paper, but I was pretty sure that the rest of the class wouldn't care what I'd done. I just didn't want them to make fun of me. I still don't speak English very well. I know how to read and write it well, but presenting this to a class of people like Larry and the others could have been very embarrassing. So I had it as organized as I could. I thought if things were well planned, people would give me more of a chance before telling me to sit down or be quiet. When I went up to do the presentation, I was organized and ready for the class to hassle me.

But I froze. I didn't completely stop, but I got so nervous that I lost my notes—or they got disassembled. The presentation was a disaster. I got the picture up on the board, and I even showed them why it works, but they didn't understand. When I finally got to the end of my notes, the class was lost, and I knew it. All through the presentation they just sat there. It's not that they aren't smart. I just couldn't present it right. I was up there for nearly half the period, until Mr. Healy finally interrupted. I was so grateful he rescued me from my disastrous presentation. Mr. Healy thanked me and then asked the class if they would like to have me explain it again!

Everyone voted for me to do it again. I didn't use my notes, and it seemed to go better. I still had trouble explaining it, but this time a couple of the people in the class asked questions, and I guess that helped everybody. It seemed like I had been up there the whole period when Mr. Healy finally rescued me for real.

He thanked me as if I'd done a good job. Then he asked how many students really understood what I'd presented and only seven people raised their hands. He didn't stop there, though. Next, he asked how many felt that they kind of understood. There were nine of those. The ultimate embarrassment, he asked how many didn't understand at all. Eight people raised their hands. I'm glad I got through to at least some of them. But I know when a good teacher really understands what he is talking about, he gets through to everyone.

I know what I am talking about because this is my proof. I didn't get it from anywhere else, so I have no excuses for not communicating with everyone. I know a third of the class understanding is better than nobody, but that means I missed getting the idea across to two thirds of the people. At least the presentation wasn't as bad an experience as I thought it would be.

Larry (January 23)

The semester test was a disaster. What is Healy going to do with the class now? I'm getting out of this class, but what'll happen to the ones who need to learn "real" geometry for their SATs and stuff?

The Metric Circle may not have caught on while I was in this class, but wait till I've made big bucks in real estate. I'll use my money and my influence to help the world find an easier solution to the 360 degree circle. I think the world would operate a lot more efficiently if the complicated stuff were simplified—like using the Edmund Park's Proof to explain the Pythagorean Theorem. Edmund's proof is the first explanation I ever understood of why the Pythagorean Theorem works. I know it would take a lot of influence and money, but I'll do that for future suckers like Sergio.

I think I'll get the Park Proof published at one of my book-making places. I'll get Anna and Diane to be in charge of that end of things. They're good at organizing, and you need that to make a good book. I'll need a few people who know how to work with the public. Laura, Sergio, and Carlos know how to handle people. I can use them to build my empire. I'll put Edmund in a think tank to come up with ideas, which I'll convert from the fifth dimension into language everyone can understand. We'll make a fortune.

I can see it all now. Geometry Camp in the summer instead of band camp. There'd be no rules, you could think about anything. If anyone came up with any great ideas we could market them right then and there. And why stop there? We could have Algebra Camp, Trigonometry Camp, Calculus Camp, and who knows what else.

Laura (January 31)

I like this class because we use our imagination not just our brains.

DISCOVERY CLASS SECOND SEMESTER

Anna (February 14)

It was great. A few weeks ago our group was investigating the possible existence of bigons. We assumed a bigon was a two-sided figure. I have my opinion about bigons, and I was really into the argument we were having about their existence. I still can't believe we get into such incredible disagreements. Enoch and I agreed, but Arcy and Patty really disagreed. Cynthia was somewhere in between. So I called Mr. Healy over and asked him to draw a bigon.

You know I used to think he was this person with all this knowledge (I thought math teachers were probably smarter than anyone else), but that he was keeping it from us, like it was some sort of game. When I found out how unorganized he is, I realized he's fallible just like the rest of the world. Now I don't know how smart he is, but it doesn't matter anymore.

Mr. Healy didn't know what he was getting into when I asked him to draw a bigon. I didn't know what he'd draw, but I was sure he wasn't going to agree with what Arcy and Patty said. Well, his picture didn't look like either of ours. We all got on his case when he drew his picture of a bigon.

It's funny. Our class used to believe Mr. Healy was the basis of knowledge for geometry, and we used to bug him for answers. No matter what he says now, we don't feel any obligation to agree with him.

Here we were discussing "bigons," something I'd never heard of before and getting on a teacher's case for having an opinion. Boy, this sure isn't what I expected to be doing in geometry. I thought the existence of bigons or anygons was supposed to be things we were told about, but not in this class.

Even though the topic of bigons was a big thing, like so many other things my groups have been involved in, nothing ever became of the idea. After four days of investigation, discussion, Supposer demonstrations and debate, our group decided to let bigons be bygones.

Chris (March 5)

I'm going to college.

Teacher (March 10)

The No Book class is special in the eyes of people from all over. People have been visiting the classroom almost every day — high school teachers, college professors, authors, etc. No matter who is visiting, the kids in the class are not impressed. It doesn't even affect them. They have their own task to accomplish and no matter what the interruption, they aren't distracted.

I've told the class repeatedly how unique they are, but it has no effect. Why is that? I'd think that after all the publicity, and all the visitors the students would begin to get an idea that they were accomplishing something at least a little unusual. It's probably all for the best anyway, because they still have a long way to go in this class.

Bernie (March 18)

We need to come in during spring vacation and work on geometry. We wouldn't have any limit on how long we could work together. I think it would make everything better.

Teacher (April 7)

I wasn't about to give up my vacation for geometry, but I did sit down with my Apple IIe and the Supposer to verify the Park Proof. The Supposer isn't perfect. It is remarkably useful for a traditional geometry class that studies traditional things, but it doesn't always do what the students in the No Book class want. I've been aware of that shortcoming, but it was just another obstacle, and those kids have become experts in overcoming obstacles. The class profited by the opportunity to use this unique software.

I'm no expert with the Supposer, and I kept thinking about my lack of expertise as I manipulated the information to try to duplicate on a random right triangle the picture Edmund had presented. It wasn't easy to duplicate, because the Supposer was definitely not made with the Park Proof in mind. However, the Supposer does all the measuring. I knew if I could get the construction right, it would verify the proof. It took quite a while, and I made a number of mistakes before I finally arrived at the picture I thought represented what Edmund had demonstrated.

One of the things I like best about the Supposer is that after doing the construction with the computer you just press a button and the results appear on the screen before you to verify your conjecture. Only this time it didn't confirm his proof.

I repeated the construction, making sure no error existed, and again it didn't verify Edmund's Proof. In fact, it proved he was incorrect. The Park Proof had been sent out to high school teachers, college professors, and mathematicians across the country, and evidently no one ever checked its credibility.

The day after vacation during fifth period I stationed myself on the opposite side of the class from the group that Edmund was in, and I announced that the Park Proof was flawed. The class reacted in disbelief, but Edmund seemed to take it well.

Later in the class, after the groups began to function smoothly, I went over to Edmund to explain.

"Edmund, maybe I shouldn't have told everyone at the same time, but I couldn't think of a good way to announce it. I'm really sorry, but your proof just doesn't work."

He just looked up at me and said very matter-of-factly, "I know. It only works if the ratio of the legs is two to one, but that's the kind of right triangle nearly everyone draws."

I was dumbfounded. This high school freshman had taken us all in, and no one had discovered his secret. How could it be?

Thinking he must have discovered this inequity at some point and not been able to share it due to the publicity his proof had received, I asked, "How long have you known about this?"

"Since the day before I presented it to the class, but I didn't want to confuse anyone at that point."

He thinks on another level from the rest of us. [Note: The summer following the class Edmund completed his proof algebraically. It was determined to be a new proof of the Pythagorean Theorem and was subsequently published in the *Journal of Mathematical Behavior.*]

Chris (April 22)

I used those big index cards to build it. First, I cut out three congruent isosceles right triangles. Next I put all the right angles together and glued the matching sides together. Then I measured the hypotenuse and cut out an equilateral triangle whose sides were the same length as the hypotenuse. Lastly, I glued the sides of the equilateral triangle to the hypotenuses.

I know the Chris Shape construction isn't as exciting as the Park Proof, but it's mine. I still think the Park Proof is valid no matter what anyone says because it's the first time I ever understood the Pythagorean Theorem.

It took me a long time to figure out how to build the Chris Shape, and I made a lot of mistakes before I got it right. I eventually built a total of four congruent (I think that word works in three-dimensional shapes) Chris Shapes using the big index cards. I brought them to Mr. Healy, and we had a long discussion after class.

Since then there've been investigations into the Chris Shape, especially the volume. One group went to the science department to get sand, beakers, and scales to measure volume. Our group thought we could build a cube out of Chris Shapes, if we could only find out how many Chris Shapes there are in a cube. It took some doing because four of them make a shell of the cube and there was a big empty section in the middle. We found out you could fill that space with a triangular pyramid made out of equilateral triangles. Finally we discovered that the volume of a Chris shape is one sixth the volume of the cube. Discovering new information is fun, especially if it is named after you.

Diane (May 2)

We've all changed with this class, but I consider myself one of the people that changed the most. I think I look at questions deeper, more seriously than I did before, even if it isn't a geometry question. I have learned that taking into consideration every possible answer/clue and not skipping anything gets you the answer. This class has helped me think, express my ideas, and know how to get them across. It's true this is probably the hardest class we'll ever take. We were all lucky to take this class. Whether it was by accident like me or knowing about the class, we all learned.

Carlos (May 14)

You actually have to use a part of your brain you don't use very often in school. The thinking part. The class questions and situations force you to think. No one is better than others. We're all given a chance to speak our thoughts and opinions. I love it. I loved being forced to think.

Cynthia (May 28)

Honestly, when I found out what this class was like, I FREAKED OUT! I was ready to drop out, but I survived and I love this class. I learned a lot more in this class than geometry, like thinking and respecting others' opinions. I have learned a lot from the others in this class. Especially how they think and feel towards certain topics.

Teacher (June 5)

One question that all skeptical people must ask of a class where discovery is the curriculum is how do the students fare on tests that are given to both traditional classes and the experimental class? Over a two-year period the Build-a-Book class average on the standardized tests given in June has been similar to that of the traditional classes. The first year the Build-a-Book class finished with an average 5 percent below that of the traditionally taught course, but the second year the Build-a-Book average was 6 percent above the traditional course's. The highest scores on those tests came from the Build-a-Book classes, but so did some of the lowest.

A comparison of grades the following year in Algebra II reveals no trends. The Build-a-Book class seems to have no measurable effect on the mathematical progress after students leave the class.

STUDENT COMMENTS FROM JUNE 1989

1. Our book is basic. It doesn't give you the unnecessary information a regular book gives.

2. We have a chance to learn what we want to learn, not just memorize what we are supposed to learn.

3. I think our book will be better (than other books) because ours was made by normal humans.

4. Our book is the way we have wanted to make it. It contains things we understand and believe are correct, for some reason. I approve of the book because most of what is in it makes sense. Proven facts, for example, are proven by ourselves by hard thinking and logic.

5. Our book is pretty good, especially the part about the parallelogram scandal we had a while back. I think we have learned to debate against others, keeping our personal feelings to ourselves.

6. I'd say the thing that most affected me is the fact that we were independent in the class. Now I know never to underestimate anything.

7. I really liked the way the class had so much responsibility. I liked it when you left the classroom sometimes and let us go over the book with no adult in the room.

8. I loved the idea of speaking out and expressing my ideas. Though I'm not always right, it's still fun. I believe this class has been good for my character. In no other class can we speak up and express our feelings, though sometimes the discussions turn into fights.

9. I am a very shy person, and this class has given me the opportunity to open up and speak my mind. This class is valuable for the students because I believe that through this class you learn how to deal with all the different types of people and yourself. Also you learn you are capable of expressing your opinions and evaluating different situations, not only things that have to do with geometry but with events that occur in our daily lives.

AN AFTERWORD FROM THE TEACHER

Teaching in the way that I have been for several years has reinforced several important ideas in my mind.

1. Students need to have ways of assuming authority and responsibility for their own learning.

2. If one permits students to exercise authority and responsibility, many of them learn to do so.

3. The specific content that students learn in this method of teaching and learning is often less important than the implicit lessons they learn about their own abilities to formulate problems and plan solutions.

4. The standard methods of assessment that are used to gauge achievement are largely insensitive to those things that are really special for students and teachers.

III PROBLEMS OF TEACHING

6

Instructional Implications of Students' Understandings of the Differences Between Empirical Verification and Mathematical Proof

Daniel Chazan
Michigan State University

Schwartz (1989) suggested that students using the Geometric Supposer[1] computer microworld should investigate geometry in both scientific (empirical) and mathematical (deductive) ways and should use what Polya (1954) called plausible and demonstrative reasoning.[2] In classrooms, teachers typically ask students to make a construction with the Supposer, create hypotheses and test them with the Supposer's measurement capabilities, write conjectures, and then provide supporting arguments (formal or informal proofs) for their conjectures (Yerushalmy & Houde, 1986). High school teachers using the Geometric Supposer to teach Euclidean geometry noticed that some students did not seem to appreciate the teachers' insistence on mathematical proofs when they had measurement evidence to support their conjectures. They did not distinguish between evidence and a deductive proof as ways of knowing that a geometrical statement is true.

The teachers' observation spawned a research study. A researcher and three teachers constructed a unit to teach students about the differences between measurement of examples and deductive proof, and to address distinctions made by philosophers of science and mathematics but typically not included in high school courses. The researcher also constructed a questionnaire (based in part on the work of Martin & Harel, 1989) to

---

[1]The Geometric Supposer, a software system developed by Judah L. Schwartz, Michal Yerushalmy, and the Education Development Center (Newton, MA) is published by Sunburst Communications, Inc.

[2]Gleick (1987) described the way mathematicians working on chaos integrated inductive and deductive work, sometimes eschewing formal proofs. This way of working is similar to the one being described.

ascertain students' beliefs about measurement of examples and deductive proof. The questionnaire was distributed before and after the unit. Based on responses to the questionnaire, students who held misconceptions or alternative conceptions were interviewed (Chazan, 1989). Students' conceptions were grouped under two headings (Chazan, 1988): evidence is proof and proof is simply evidence.

Some students, based in part on common linguistic usage, believed that measuring examples proves that a statement is true for all members of a set with an infinite number of elements. When discussing a statement about all triangles, one student said:

> If I did it on a bunch of triangles, like different kinds of triangles, and then if I would find it to be all true then I'd just accept it, you know, any triangle — if the two mid points connected, then their opposite sides they'd be parallel, I'd just accept that. . . . If you keep on doing this like maybe ten more times and it just keeps on doing that, I'd just say it would just have to be that way.

Students who held this view frequently mentioned the idea of kinds or types of triangles.

> We're given an acute and an obtuse, and it appears to be right . . . right, obtuse, acute, and like isosceles or something like that, that's pretty much all the triangles that you can have. So it's almost the same effect as having every.

> You'd have to do each — like do one an isosceles, one an equilateral. Like you have to use the different triangles. And then, if you show that it's true for each triangle, one case of each triangle, then you're saying well he's showed the illustrations of all the different triangles — that's good. Whereas if you just do — if you do like four isosceles triangles, they'll say that's true for isosceles.

Other students did not understand that the proof referred to by their teachers was different from measurement evidence. Specifically, they believed that a deductive proof is about one example and can prove only for that one example.

> Basically, it's [the deductive proof] a proof for that particular diagram or that particular shape. I'd like to try it [the deductive proof] again [on a new particular shape].

> On this proof, it's given statement and reasons and you only have that on that one . . . I think it [an argument based on measurement of four examples] kind of does [prove for all cases]. . . . The [deductive] proof — I don't think the [deductive] proof says that. I think if there were some thing after or before the [deductive] proof, or after the [deductive] proof that said, for any two lines that are equal and parallel, the opposite side is equal then. . . .

The interviewees' conceptions were not as different from canonical notions as it might seem. Even interviewees for whom the two methods of argumentation were on equal epistemological footing—that is, interviewees who believed that both (or neither) measuring examples and a deductive proof could prove a statement about all members of a set with an infinite number of elements—still preferred a deductive argument to an argument based on the measurement of examples. One might attribute their preference to their teachers' oft-repeated insistence that "a statement isn't true unless we have a proof" or to a desire to please the interviewer, but their rationale indicates otherwise. These students suggested that deductive proofs provide illumination or explanation in a way that measurement of examples does not. In the words of one student, "This one [the deductive proof] is more clear on why—why it's true."

Analysis of data from the initial and final questionnaires and from the interviews indicates that at the end of the unit, fewer students considered evidence to be proof (the activities which combatted against this conception were successful), whereas more students were skeptical about the limits of applicability of deductive proofs (Chazan, 1989, p. 210). Some students seemed to become more skeptical about deductive proofs as a result of becoming more skeptical about measurement of examples. In addition, all three teachers felt they did not spend enough time addressing students' skepticism about deductive proofs.

ANALYSIS

In describing numeracy, the recent report of the National Research Council (1989) suggests that "The study of mathematics can help develop critical habits of mind—to distinguish evidence from anecdote, to recognize nonsense, to understand chance, and to value proof" (p. 8). The new National Council of Teachers of Mathematics, in *Curriculum and Evaluation Standards for School Mathematics* (1989), suggest that "*All* students, especially the college intending, should learn that deductive reasoning is the method by which the validity of a mathematical assertion is finally established" (p. 143).

Though the results of the study described here are not as bleak as they might initially seem, they suggest that these goals are difficult to reach. The unit used in the study argued that measurement of examples has limitations as a method for verifying the truth of geometrical statements and presented activities to suggest that the method of deductive proof both lacks these limitations and has strengths of its own. Nevertheless, these activities, particularly the activities in favor of deductive proof, were not successful with a sizable portion of the students in the study. Although teachers emphasized that a deductive proof guarantees that a statement is true, some students thought there might be counterexamples to proven results.

One possible explanation for this limited success distinguishes between the method of deductive proof and a particular deductive proof. Scheffler (1965) argued that the students' skepticism is justified for individual deductive proofs, whereas the teachers' position is reasonable when describing the method of deductive proof. Thus, although teachers were discussing the method of deductive proof, students were thinking of individual deductive proofs.

Scheffler criticized "the traditional notion that knowing implies not only truth but also certainty" (p. 29) and suggested that knowing implies only truth and not certainty. According to this view, one has good reason to claim that a particular theorem is true, but is never certain that one has proven it, because the deductive proof of the theorem may be flawed in some way. Students, as novices in the art of proving, may be especially justified in doubting their ability to judge whether a particular proof has been carried out correctly.

Offering another explanation, Gila Hanna (1983) emphasized that because we are never certain about the validity of a particular argument, social groups play an important role in determining whether an argument is an acceptable proof. With this lens, students' skepticism about deductive proofs is not a cognitive misunderstanding but an indication of their limited initiation into the social group of mathematicians.

In contrast, recent developments in the philosophy of mathematics suggest that students' skepticism about mathematical arguments is important and valuable. Philosophers, such as Lakatos (1986)[3] rejected rationalistic, a priori views of mathematics as the domain of certainty and suggest that mathematics, like the sciences, is a quasi-empirical domain. For example, Lakatos argued that non-Euclidean geometries demonstrate that Euclidean geometry is not a theory with " . . . an indubitable truth-injection at the top (a finite conjunction of axioms) — so that truth, flowing down from the top through the safe truth-preserving channels of valid inferences, inundates the whole system" (p. 33). Instead, in his view, mathematical theories, like scientific ones, have their "crucial truth value injection" at the bottom.

> The important logical flow in such quasi-empirical theories is not the transmission of truth but rather the retransmission of falsity — from special theorems at the bottom ('basic statements') up towards the set of axioms . . . a quasi-empirical theory — at best — [can claim] to be well-corroborated, but always conjectural. (pp. 33–34)

---

[3]Although I highlight the views of Lakatos and Putnam, Quine, Wittgenstein, Lehman, Kitcher, Peirce, and others share this view.

Putnam (1986) suggested that in mathematics the "basic statements" used to tests theories "are themselves the product of deductive proof or calculation rather than being 'observation reports' in the usual sense" (p. 51). In his view, acceptable grounds for considering a conjecture as "verified" include

> [that] extensive searches with electronic computers have failed to find a counterexample — many 'theorems' have been proved with its aid, and none of these has been disproved, the consequences of the hypothesis are plausible and of far-reaching significance, etc. . . . (pp. 51–52).

Nevertheless, in his view, in mathematics, the method of deductive proof and the method of quasi-empirical verification live side-by-side.

> [The method of deductive] proof has the great advantage of not increasing the risk of contradiction, where the introduction of new axioms or new objects does increase the risk of contradiction, at least until a relative interpretation of the new theory in some already accepted theory is found. (p. 63)

Thus, either of these philosophers considers students' skepticism warranted.

Cumulatively, these three views suggest that the distinctions between deductive arguments and arguments based on measurement of examples are complex and fine. In striving to have students value proof and understand its role in validating mathematical assertions, teachers should not gloss over the fine points and nuances.

SUGGESTIONS FOR PRACTICE

The remainder of this paper presents four suggestions for improvements in the teaching of deductive proof in high school Euclidean geometry courses where the Geometric Supposer is in use and where students are asked throughout the year to use both plausible and demonstrative reasoning while exploring geometric constructions.

First, teachers should treat proof as a social activity. According to Fawcett (1938), proofs presented by teachers in class should not confer the status of theorem upon a statement unless the class unanimously[4] agrees that the proof is a good one. Students should be encouraged to question the steps of a theorem as well as the validity of its conclusion. Similarly, when students begin to write their own proofs, preferably for conjectures they have developed from their own exploration with the Supposer, the role of the social group in validating a proof should be emphasized. The idea is to

---

[4]Except for disciplinary problems.

avoid having teachers assume the role of validator of proofs. When using this strategy, teachers must be willing to admit an invalid proof or a proof of an incorrect statement if they are unable to convince students by criticizing the proof or providing a counterexample.

Students should also be encouraged to suggest postulates to the group. If a student convinces the class to accept a postulate, the statement should remain as a postulate until proven from other postulates or unless students question its truth or its usefulness in proving other statements.[5]

Second, throughout the course, teachers should emphasize proof as a *part* of a mathematical process and not its end point. In addition to asking, "What have we just proved?" teachers should ask, "For what geometrical objects does it hold?" Teachers should have students examine and critique finished proofs. Thus, at first, there should be a diminished emphasis on having students write proofs. Students should be encouraged to try to find counterexamples to textbook proofs and to expose assumptions not presented in the proof.[6] Students may become more convinced by deductive proof as a method of argumentation if they complete missing assumptions, look for counterexamples, and cannot find any.

Third, when deductive proofs are introduced, teachers should emphasize their explanatory role, that is, the insight they provide about why a statement is true.[7] At the same time, much greater emphasis should be placed on the intent of a proof to prove for all objects described by the givens and on understanding what set of geometrical objects are designated by the geometrical description provided by the givens. One way to do this is to present the proofs in an order that helps students understand which geometrical objects are being discussed. The first proofs should be for statements, such as, "Any point on the angle bisector is equidistant from the two rays which make up the angle" or "Any point on the perpendicular bisector of a segment is equidistant from the end points of the segment," which involve a locus, because many of the objects in the set being discussed can be illustrated in a single diagram.

The next proofs should be about sets of objects whose names make them

---

[5]It may turn out that different students want to take different statements as postulates. Such alternatives could be explored to emphasize that the choice of which statements to take as postulates (and definitions as well) is to some extent a matter of choice.

[6]High school geometry textbook proofs frequently have shortcomings. For example, the textbook proof used by Chazan (1989, p. 89; Chakerian, Crabill, & Stein, 1987), which is the first proof presented in this textbook, assumes that the figures are in a plane and that the segments are connected A to D and B to C with B and C on the same side of AD. The conclusion would not hold if the given were true and the points connected in a different order.

[7]Hanna (1989) distinguished between proofs that prove and proofs that explain. Most proofs in a high school geometry course are of the latter type. This does not mean that all students understand these proofs, but that in contrast to existence proofs, these proofs provide some illumination.

easy to describe—for example, all triangles or all parallelograms—and should use few auxiliary lines. An example of an elementary proof of this kind is the proof that the sum of the interior angles of a triangle is 180 degrees.

Next, students should see proofs that require a larger number of auxiliary lines for sets of objects that are easily named. With these proofs, teachers should emphasize that the auxiliary lines could be drawn for any member of the set. At first, the diagrams accompanying the proof might not include the auxiliary lines, and the first steps of the proof might describe the rationale for being able to construct such lines. Gradually, the mention of auxiliary lines should be moved to the givens. After introducing a proof, teachers should show students many diagrams and ask them to indicate the geometrical objects for which the conclusion of the proof holds true. Such tasks should include members of the set without the auxiliary lines needed for the proof.

Finally, students should see proofs for sets of objects that do not commonly have names. They should practice drawing different members of the set of objects described by the givens and listing characteristics of these objects that are not constrained by the givens.[8] These activities should be used to introduce the vocabulary "quantifier" and "set of objects" and their relevance to geometrical statements.

Fourth, teachers should create activities to challenge students' conceptions. After students have had experience both measuring examples and writing deductive proofs, teachers should investigate students' conceptions of these methods of argumentation in order to use a style of teaching that Alan Bell (1986) called *diagnostic teaching*. The key aspects of diagnostic teaching are "the identification and exposure of pupils' misconceptions and their resolution through 'conflict discussion'" (p. 331) in which teachers present evidence that conflicts with students' notions and where students holding different views talk to each other. The questionnaire used in the study described in this chapter could be employed to identify students with misconceptions and determine their number.

If a large number of students think that evidence is proof, then activities from the study's proof unit could be used (Chazan, 1989, pp. 76–81). These activities suggest two points at which uncertainty enters into the measurement of empirical examples that distinguish it from the method of deductive proof, though both a particular empirical verification and a particular attempt at a deductive proof are open to the charge that they were carried

---

[8]There are many such characteristics for a particular proof.For example, in the textbook proof used by Chazan (1989, p. 89), the lines L and M may be any distance apart, the size of the segments AB and CD must be the same, but it can be any particular measure, and AB and CD may be anywhere on their respective lines.

out poorly—an incorrect measurement or a faulty step in a deductive proof. With measurement of examples, one can check only a finite number of cases with limited precision. If a statement has a universal quantifier and is about a set of objects with an infinite number of members (e.g., all isosceles triangles), then one can never be certain by using measurement that all examples will support the statement. One may have overgeneralized; there may exist a set of objects satisfying the givens for which the conclusion is not true.

Using these activities gives teachers opportunities to point out that within the mathematical community a deductive proof for a statement that has a universal quantifier and is about a set of objects with an infinite number of members claims to prove that the conclusion is true for all members of the set. This can be emphasized by examining an hypothetical situation. Imagine that the same deductive proof, the exact same steps, are presented as proof for the same conclusion but for only one member of the original infinite set of objects. Contemplation of this hypothetical example suggests that the argument in its singular intent and in its universal intent are equally uncertain and that the uncertainty of a deductive proof does not stem from the infinite number of objects within the set.

These activities can also be used to point out that measurement of examples involves tools that by definition have a margin of error. Measurement tools lead to both false positives and false negatives. All statements based on measurement must be qualified (implicitly or explicitly) by the limitations of the tool. Thus, even a statement about the equality of two measurements in a single drawing cannot be argued, in the mathematical sense of equality, by measurement. Within the mathematical community, it is understood that if the results of an accepted deductive argument indicate that two quantities are equal, they are equal in a mathematical sense. That is, the quantities are exactly equal no matter what scale is used; measurement discrepancies do not call such a conclusion into question.[9] Such activities might prompt students to become more skeptical about deductive proofs and might to take their opportunities to critique textbook proofs more seriously.

---

[9]All of this is not to argue that measurement of examples can never be used to make a mathematical argument. Although measurement of examples cannot provide extremely convincing grounds to believe an assertion about all members of a set of objects with an infinite number of members, it can provide much stronger grounds for disbelieving such an assertion. For example, a statement that begins "For all triangles, . . . " and asserts the equality of two measurements is effectively called into question by a measurement counterexample, by measurements that show an inequality that is much larger in magnitude than the precision and accuracy limitations of the measurement tool. Thus, there is a lack of symmetry between the power of measurement to argue against statements about all members of sets with an infinite number of members and its power to argue for such statements.

Teachers who want to convince their students of the value of deductive proofs might argue along the lines indicated by Lakatos (1976) and Putnam (1986). Although all proofs are not equally illuminating, Lakatos argued that deductive proofs provide insight by connecting a conjecture to a previously accepted body of knowledge. Furthermore, as Putnam argued, the great advantage of the method of deductive proof is that, if a particular proof is to be believed, it shows that a new result does not conflict with previous theory and does not add to the risk of contradiction within this theory. In contrast, empirical verification can show only that a particular statement is or is not supported; it cannot forge logical connections to previously accepted knowledge or indicate whether there is a conflict with previous ideas.

CONCLUSIONS

While suggesting that students should understand the role of deductive proof in validating mathematical assertions, the National Council of Teachers of Mathematics Standards suggests reduced emphasis on two-column proofs and increased emphasis on the interplay between inductive and deductive reasoning.[10]

When used thoughtfully by teachers, new software environments, such as the Geometric Supposer can be an aid in carrying out these changes in classroom emphasis. For example, the Geometric Supposer allows students to explore mathematical concepts empirically and to develop their own ideas about geometric shapes. Teachers can then introduce students to deductive reasoning and have students compare and contrast the two modes of reasoning.

One might hope that from this process of comparison and contrast, students would come to value proof more highly and understand the role of proof in validating mathematical assertions. Yet, as the results of this study suggest, reality is not so simple. Even after comparing and contrasting deductive proof and measurement of examples, many students still hold conceptions that are different from some aspects of standard conceptions.

These results should not be discouraging. The role of proof in mathematics is a complex and challenging subject; even philosophers of mathematics characterize this role in different ways. This study demonstrates the feasibility of exploring this subject with students. The suggestions for practice outline ways in which such teaching can be improved. The

---

[10]"The Standards suggest 'local axiomatics' as a replacement for emphasis on 'geometry as a complete axiomatic system.' The organization of geometric facts from a deductive perspective should receive less emphasis" (p. 159).

suggested activities can lead to provocative philosophical discussions in which students present their understandings and come to understand some aspects that differentiate mathematics from other pursuits.

REFERENCES

Bell, A. W. (1986). Outcomes of the Diagnostic Teaching Project. In L. Burton and C. Hoyles (Eds.), *Proceedings of the Tenth Meeting of the International Group for the Psychology of Mathematics Education* (pp. 331–336). London: University of London.

Chakerian, G. D., Crabill, C. D., & Stein, S.K. (1987). *Geometry: A guided inquiry.* Pleasantville, NY: Sunburst.

Chazan, D. (1988). Proof and Measurement: An Unexpected Misconception. In A. Borbas (Ed.), *Proceedings of the Twelfth Annual Conference of the International Group for the Psychology of Mathematics Education* (pp. 207–214). Veszprem, Hungary.

Chazan, D. (1989). *Ways of knowing: High school students' conceptions of mathematical proof.* Unpublished doctoral dissertation, Harvard Graduate School of Education, Cambridge, MA.

Fawcett, H. P. (1938). *The nature of proof.* New York: Bureau of Publications, Teachers College, Columbia University. (National Council of Teachers of Mathematics Thirteenth Yearbook)

Gleick, J. (1987). *Chaos: Making a new science.* New York:Penguin.

Hanna, G. (1983). *Rigorous Proof in Mathematics Education.* Toronto: Ontario Institute for Studies in Education.

Hanna, G. (1989). Proofs that prove and proofs that explain. In G. Vergnaud, J. Rogalski, & M. Artigue (Eds.), *Proceedings of the Thirteenth Meeting of the International Group for the Psychology of Mathematics Education* (Vol. II, pp. 45–51). Paris.

Lakatos, I. (1986). A renaissance of empiricism in the recent philosophy of mathematics? In T. Tymoczko (Ed.), *New directions in the philosophy of mathematics* (pp. 29–48). Boston: Birkhauser.

Lakatos, I. (1976). *Proofs and refutations.* Cambridge: Cambridge University Press.

Martin, W. G. & Harel, G.. (1989). Proof frames of preservice elementary teachers. *Journal for Research in Mathematics Education, 20*(1), 41–51.

National Council of Teachers of Mathematics. (1988). *Curriculum and evaluation standards for school mathematics.* Reston, VA: Author.

National Research Council. (1989). *Everybody counts: A report to the nation on the future of mathematics education.* Washington: National Academy Press.

Polya, G. (1954). *Mathematics and plausible reasoning* (Vols. 1 & 2). Princeton: Princeton University Press.

Putnam, H. (1986). What is mathematical truth? In T. Tymoczko (Ed.), *New directions in the philosophy of mathematics* (pp. 49–66). Boston: Birkhauser.

Scheffler, I. (1965). *Conditions of knowledge: An introduction to epistemology and education.* Chicago. Scott Foresman.

Schwartz, J. (1989). Intellectual mirrors: A step in the direction of making schools knowledge making places. *Harvard Educational Review, 59*(1), 51–60.

Yerushalmy, M. & Houde, R. (1986). The Geometric Supposer: Promoting thinking and learning. *Mathematics Teacher, 79*(6), 418–428.

7 Posing Problems: One Aspect of Bringing Inquiry into Classrooms

Michal Yerushalmly
The University of Haifa

Myles Gordon
Education Development Center, Inc.

Daniel Chazan
Michigan State University

INTRODUCTION

Our image of how students should learn mathematics is tied to the word *inquiry,* a word with a long history in educational contexts and with many connotations. By using inquiry, we bring to the reader's mind the process of learning employed by creative people at the forefront of their fields — people interested in a particular area and continuously motivated to learn more about it, who set themselves problems, design methods to explore them, and then try to create solutions. (This characterization is based on Schwab's (1962) description of *pure inquiry.*)

In this vein, inquiry teaching in mathematics means that students learn mathematics by choosing a topic, posing problems, creating approaches to the problems, and recreating historical discoveries. We believe such an approach is neither realistic nor practical; students are not expert mathematicians. In our image of inquiry teaching, teachers organize inquiry experiences for their students by posing inquiry problems to explore. A central activity of our approach is inquiry by individual students or small groups. Typically in our work, student inquiry occurs in a computer lab interspersed with sessions in a regular classroom. Tools such as the Geometric Supposer act as intellectual amplifiers and inquiry facilitators, helping students explore in the manner of experts.

As the designers of the Geometric Supposer note, inquiry teaching is uncommon in high school mathematics classrooms:

> There is something odd about the way we teach mathematics in our schools.
> We teach it as if we expect that our students will never have occasion to make

new mathematics. We do not teach language that way. If we did, students would never be required to write an original piece of prose or poetry. We would simply require them to recognize and appreciate the great pieces of language of the past, the literary equivalents of the Pythagorean Theorem and the Law of Cosines. (Schwartz & Yerushalmy, 1985–1988, p. 293)

Inquiry teaching is at odds with common school practice for several reasons. First, an inquiry approach is potentially replete with doubt, confusion, dead ends, frustrations, and wild goose chases. Common conceptions of teaching suggest that teachers should not willingly lead students into such uncertain terrain but, rather, should eradicate or smooth over confusion. If teachers do lead their students into difficult terrain, they should at least help them figure out how to resolve confusions. Experts faced with confusion rethink and recategorize; they stand back and reexamine. Second, in contrast, teachers are taught to reduce confusion by atomizing material into smaller chunks as they typically do when they teach students to factor quadratics or do long division. Third, current evaluation procedures do not test students on inquiry tasks; they do not measure inquiry skills such as testing conjectures, finding counterexamples, or posing new problems. Fourth, inquiry is time consuming, and time is precious in schools where teachers must cope with a host of conflicting demands on their time and energy.

In implementing our approach to teaching geometry, we encountered these conflicts between an inquiry approach and current school practice, between our image of how we would like students to learn mathematics and the constraints of school settings. This chapter presents observations about strategies for designing inquiry teaching materials, indicating which ones help to preserve an inquiry spirit and defuse the conflicts between traditional school practice and our approach, and which ones do not. We hope that such strategies help others planning to implement inquiry approaches in schools.[1]

This chapter is primarily intended for researchers interested in inquiry learning and in the use of computers to promote inquiry and for mathematics educators interested in implementing inquiry approaches in schools (see footnote 1). Although not explicitly about the evolution of an innovation during implementation or about collaboration between teachers and researchers, it can be read as the result of such a collaborative evolution.

INQUIRY PROBLEMS IN GENERAL

Our first major compromise with the pure inquiry model was to include as a central tenet of our approach that teachers, as students' guides, take

---

[1]Footnotes throughout provide information for those interested in posing inquiry problems for use in high school Euclidean geometry courses using the Geometric Supposer.

responsibility for providing questions or problems for students to explore.[2] Thus, a problem assumes a different meaning from that commonly used in mathematics classrooms. Inquiry problems are not tidy textbook problems, easily solved and with only one answer; they are real problems — though not necessarily real-world problems — resembling those an expert would explore. They are related to the teacher's agenda, are open-ended, can be approached in many ways, and have many solutions; in short, they are worth exploring. Students and teachers must understand the differences between inquiry problems and textbook problems and the differences in appropriate student performance in solving each kind of problem.

Creating or finding problems worth exploring is not easy. Once one exists, good open-ended ways to pose or communicate it must be created. The challenge for the problem poser is to communicate the problem in a way that provides enough guidance so the task of the problem is clear but not so much that all inquiry converges to a single point. Communication of inquiry problems becomes a locus of tension between open-ended inquiry and structured school work. The challenge is compounded because each person (teacher or student) views the balance between too much and too little instruction differently.

In this chapter we examine materials we used to communicate to students both the particular problems used as the basis for inquiry and our expectations for appropriate inquiry. We focus on strategies for designing printed materials, because comparing and contrasting such written materials is relatively easy. At the same time, we acknowledge many other less tangible ways to communicate expectations to students. (Perhaps the most important and effective way to communicate new expectations is to model the process of working on inquiry problems, a complex endeavor which is hard to evaluate. This paper reports on one facet of a larger ongoing project to understand how to integrate inquiry into the teaching of high school geometry. Future research will focus on modeling inquiry skills.)

INQUIRY PROBLEMS IN GEOMETRY: AN ANALYTIC FRAMEWORK

From 1984 through 1988, we worked closely with high school students and teachers in the Boston area in 23 classes where Euclidean geometry was taught using the Geometric Supposer in an inquiry approach. We observed classrooms and met with teachers monthly. Many conversations with

---

[2]We have observed schools outside this study, where teachers rely on students to pose problems before going into the lab. This approach places a heavy burden on teachers and students and may not be realistic for wide application.

teachers centered on actual inquiry problems. Reactions to the problems varied from teacher to teacher and from class to class: different kinds of students and different kinds of teachers needed different problems. We encouraged the teachers to modify the problems to fit their perception of their classes' needs.

From the experience of creating and posing inquiry problems, we learned strategies to preserve the spirit of inquiry in activities practical for classrooms, and we created an analytic framework of what we call considerations for designing inquiry problems in geometry. The reader looking at the list of six considerations should imagine a teacher creating and posing an inquiry problem for a geometry class. Initially, the teacher chooses the geometric content of the problem, and before drafting a written statement of the problem might considers:

Kind of problem
Size or scope of the problem
Students' ability or background

Then, while drafting a written statement of the problem, the teacher considers how to word:

A statement of the goal of the problem
A description of any constructions in the problem
Process instructions

Below, we offer observations based on empirical evidence about the success or failure of pedagogical strategies used by teachers in three geometry classes during 1985–1986[3] (Yerushalmy, Chazan, & Gordon, 1987) to address these considerations. The evidence was collected by examining students' work, observing classrooms once every 2 weeks throughout the year, and meeting with teachers once every 3 weeks. (For a detailed description of our methods of data collection, see Yerushalmy et al., 1987.) To be considered successful, problems had to meet all of the following criteria:

Preserve the spirit of inquiry
Be enjoyed by students
Be the catalyst for significant student work by almost all students
Be considered successful by teachers in reaching their goals

---

[3]Although, as explained in Recommendations and Conclusions at the end of this chapter, our observations presented here stem from that year's work, they have been confirmed by our ensuing experience.

The evidence suggests that the success or failure of inquiry problems is determined by the strategies teachers used to address the six considerations listed previously and that these strategies determine both the clarity of the problem and the extent of student inquiry.

The remainder of this chapter outlines observations about strategies for designing problems that are clear and also leave room for student inquiry. Because these observations concern strategies used to address the six considerations, the considerations are used to organize the discussion.

CLASSROOM OBSERVATIONS

Before Drafting a Written Statement of the Problem

Kind of Problem. Our first two observations relate the success of a problem to two aspects of its nature:

Its category:

A construction problem (see Problem 7.1)
A conjecture problem (see Problem 7.2)

Task: To develop a procedure for reproducing this figure.

Procedure:
- Make a drawing similar to this figure.
- Collect data.
- Describe below the procedures for reproducing this figure
- State your conjectures.

Drawings & Data

Conjectures

Procedure for reproducing figure:

For quadrilateral ACBE above, under what conditions will ∠CAE be a 90° angle?

Problem 7.1. (From Yerushalmy and Houde, 1987)

Task: To explore figures formed by drawing one midsegment in a triangle.

Procedure:

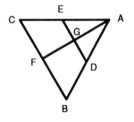

- Construct any △ABC.
- Draw midsegment $\overline{DE}$ connecting $\overline{AB}$ and $\overline{AC}$.
- Label the midpoint of $\overline{BC}$ with point F.
- Draw $\overline{AF}$ and label the intersection of $\overline{DE}$ and $\overline{AF}$ with point G.
- Measure the elements of the figure.
- Record your data.
- State your conjectures.

■■ Drawings & Data ■■■■■■■■■■■■■■■■■■■■■■■■■■■■■■■■■■■■■

■■ Conjectures ■■■

Problem 7.2.   (From Yerushalmy and Houde, 1987)

Its instructional role:

To help students discover theorems
To familiarize students with relationships in a construction
To encourage students to apply concepts already learned

The first observation concerns the relative success of construction and conjecture problems at different points in the year (see Problems 7.1, 7.2, & 7.3):

Observation: Mechanisms for checking results (to know when they are correct) are an important element in the structure of successful inquiry problems.

Construction problems were especially successful early in the year for several reasons. First, the Geometric Supposer makes trial and error strategies easy to carry out. Students are motivated to try a variety of constructions. They have a tool to test their strategies. Second, in most construction problems there is a level of solution that does not require generalization. Most students interpret the construction problems as "Construct a figure that looks like this (or that has these properties). . . . "[4] In

---

[4]In another paper (Yerushalmy & Chazan, 1990), we examine how these students viewed diagrams. At the beginning of the year, they treated diagrams as specific instances, not as

Task: To explore the relationship among the interior angles in different types of triangles.

Procedure:
- Construct a triangle.
- Measure each angle.
- Draw the triangles and record the angle measurements on the chart below.
- Repeat this procedure on five other triangles.
- On the following page, state conjectures about your findings.

Triangle Drawings	∠ABC	∠BCA	∠CAB
1.			
2.			
3.			
4.			
5.			
6.			

Problem 7.3. (From Yerushalmy and Houde, 1987)

such problems, the characteristics of the solution are known from the start; students are given criteria to judge their solutions and know when they have a correct answer. They can check their methods of construction by making measurements on the resulting diagram to determine whether their method works. The problem does not dictate a particular construction method. If the construction is not too elementary and is adequately described, then the underlying task is not vague yet allows room for open-ended inquiry.

In contrast to a problem whose solution does not require generalization, a problem that does require a general answer does not provide all the characteristics of its solutions. Students can be sure of their answers only when they have a proof for their conjecture. Before students learn how to devise proofs, they find problems that require general solutions and conjecturing more difficult than those that allow for specific solutions.

The success of problems also depends on their pedagogical role, in that:

Observation: The pedagogical roles of problems had implications for the amount of structure required.

models of a class of figures; later, they treated them as general models and were able to argue that specific characteristics of a given diagram were not representative of the whole class.

Teachers assigned problems with at least three different roles (discovering theorems, familiarizing students with relationships in a construction, or applying concepts already learned).

In some cases, when teachers wanted students to discover the theorems, postulates, and definitions of geometry, they gave inquiry problems before the concepts were introduced. The teachers had specific agendas—they wanted certain conjectures to appear—and these problems typically relied on charts to organize students' data collection and focus their attention (see Problem 7.3).

A second pedagogical role for problems was to familiarize students with a set of relationships in a particular construction before the teacher taught a theorem based on that construction. When problems were used in this way, the teachers were less concerned about the production of the particular theorem; in some cases, they preferred that, rather than discover the theorem, students should understand and become familiar with the relationships in the construction. The theorem to be taught was extracted from their understanding of those relationships. For example, when teaching about the sum of the interior angles in a triangle, instead of using Problem 7.3, a discovery problem, a teacher might ask students to explore the construction in Problem 7.4:

Task: To explore angle relationships in the following construction

Procedure: Draw any triangle ABC. Through C, draw a segment parallel to AB. Record a diagram and measurements. Repeat this process on other triangles. State your conjectures below.

Task: To explore angle relationships in the following construction.

Procedure: Draw any ∆ABC. Through C, draw a segment parallel to AB. Record a diagram and measurements. Repeat the process on other triangles. State your conjectures below.

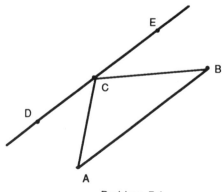

Problem 7.4.

Task: To explore the figure formed by reflecting the intersection point of the *altitudes* in each side of a triangle and connecting the three image points.

Procedure:
- Construct an acute △ABC.
- Draw the three altitudes.
- Label G as their point of intersection.
- Reflect point G in each of the three sides of △ABC producing points H, I, J.
- Draw △DEF and △HIJ.
- State your conjectures about the relationships among the points, elements, and triangles.
- Repeat the procedure for other types of triangles.

▬ Drawings & Data ▬▬▬▬▬▬▬▬▬▬▬▬▬▬▬▬▬▬▬▬▬▬▬▬▬▬▬▬▬▬▬

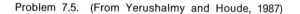

▬ Conjectures ▬▬▬▬▬▬▬▬▬▬▬▬▬▬▬▬▬▬▬▬▬▬▬▬▬▬▬▬▬▬▬▬▬

Problem 7.5. (From Yerushalmy and Houde, 1987)

Once students recognize the angle relationships present in this construction, even if none of them conjectures that the sum of the interior angles of a triangle is 180° or can prove this conjecture, the teacher can use the relationships they do find to prove it.[5]

The third pedagogical role of problems was to help students apply the concepts they had already learned. In this situation, because they were not asked to discover basic concepts, their individual conjectures were less important than in discovery problems, and teachers were less concerned with every possible conjecture. Following a discussion of similarity, for example, Problem 7.5 can serves as a concept application problem.

Using these three pedagogical roles of problems, teachers' levels of need for particular student results dictate different levels of teacher guidance and directions. For problems intended to fulfill the discovery role, the instructions are directive and leading, to enable students to discover the results most important to the teacher. In problems intended to fulfill the roles of familiarizing students with relationships in a construction and applying

---

[5]The construction in Problem 7.4 was created from the construction in Problem 7.3 by adding the auxiliary line necessary for the proof of the sum of the interior angles theorem. Note that Problem 7.4 differs from Problem 7.3 in several ways. The construction in Problem 7.4 is more complicated, allowing for more conjectures, and the presence of the auxiliary line makes the proof more accessible to students, providing greater flexibility for their exploration.

concepts, the instructions are less directive and leading. Not surprisingly, these types of problems are more successful in preserving the inquiry spirit. The different roles for problems are more or less successful according to our criteria discussed previously. For example, much to the teachers' consternation, students had trouble both finding patterns in their data in Problem 7.3 and in developing conjectures for problems like Problem 7.6, where the task is to chart exterior angles. Students may find it difficult to discover the one central relationship the teacher is seeking. They may discover and be distracted by other relationships less central to the course and of less interest to the teacher. The process instructions may also contribute to the relative ineffectiveness of such problems, an idea examined later in the discussion of process instructions.

Size or Scope of the Problem.   Theoretically, the size of an inquiry problem cannot be gauged apart from the learner because it depends on the learner's effort and creativity in exploring the problem. This assertion is illustrated by examining a problem that one student selected as the most trivial and uninteresting of all: "Investigate the sum of the interior angles of a triangle." Yet even this problem is the starting point for a long and interesting exploration if students do not equate it with the written

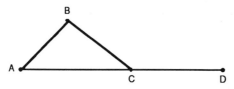

∠BCD is called an exterior angle for △ABC. Conjecture how the measure of exterior ∠BCD is related to the measures of the interior angles of the triangle.

Drawings of △ABC	m ∠BCD	m ∠BAC	m ∠ACB	m ∠CBA
Acute △ABC				
Obtuse △ABC				
Right △ABC				
Isoceles △ABC				
Others				
Conjectures				

Problem 7.6.

Try to split a triangle into triangular sections that have the same area. First, try to get four sections with equal area. When you have a solution, make sure it works in all kinds of triangles. Record a drawing of your solution and explain what kind of lines you added to the triangle to get the drawing.

Problem 7.7.

statement just given. A creative inquirer might explore polygons with more than three sides and find a pattern relating the number of sides and the sum of the measures of the interior angles; might look at the sum of two angles in any triangle and explore how the sum varies by the type of triangle; might examine exterior angles; or might even generalize to three dimensional objects. These explorations of the initial problem were created using Brown and Walter's (1983) "What if not" strategy.

We did not, however, observe this kind of expansion of problems by students:

Observation: Students explore problems as they are written. Because they do no more than the instructions suggest, we are able to define the size of problems by examining the instructions on the page.

In the classroom, the size of an inquiry problem is a function of the expectations of members of the class. In our experience, students do not go beyond the instructions given in the problem and are unwilling to expand or change a problem without specific instructions to do so. For example, in Problem 7.7, students did not generalize the number of triangular sections, that is, they did not attempt to divide the triangle into 2, 3, 4, 5, . . . n equal triangular areas.

The observation noted above is clearly disappointing, although not surprising (for a similar finding in a different setting, see Jensen, 1986). In our view, an important part of exploring a problem is changing the formulation, asking the question, "What if not?" (Brown & Walter, 1983) about some aspect of it. No matter how a problem is posed, this question opens new avenues of inquiry, yet in many schools, such changes are considered inappropriate by both teachers and students.[6]

---

[6]Though this finding is discouraging, there are ways, besides building wider exploration into the statement of the problems, to make generalization part of students' repertoire for solving problems. One way is to model such behavior in the classroom and make clear that changing and manipulating the elements of a problem are part of the task of doing a problem. In teaching with the Geometric Supposer, the teachers had already taken on a large and difficult task, and for that reason, we did not spend a lot of time on modeling the students' behavior; other issues had greater priority.

> One segment can cut or divide any triangle into triangular sections. For example, an angle bisector divides any triangle into two sections, and three medians divide any triangle into six sections. Give the type(s) and number of line segments that divide any triangle into 2, 3, 4, 5, ... n sections all having the same area.

Problem 7.8.

For the most part, teachers felt that the Supposer problems were too large and vague. They rewrote them and relied on process instructions (for a definition, see Process instructions, p. 14) to clarify problems and break them into manageable parts. As a side effect, parts of problems were jettisoned and problems became smaller (Lampert, 1988; Yerushalmy et al., 1987). For example, Problem 7.8, which teachers revised and simplified into Problem 7.7, is in our view larger because it explicitly asks students to generalize their findings to any number of triangular sections of equal area.

Finally, we have one more observation related to the size and scope of problems:

> **Observation:** Students do not like working on one problem for an extended period of time. In general, problems with few solutions are less successful than those with many avenues of exploration and possible solutions.

This observation and the previous one both support and contradict the teachers' intuitive decision to make problems smaller. If size is viewed purely as the amount of time and work students need to complete a problem, then the larger problems are unsuccessful. After 3 or 4 consecutive days' work, students tired of working in the computer lab.[7] When they were interviewed after a year of using the Supposer, some, though not all, said they prefer to learn in ways that require less work. Such students prefer a traditional classroom, where the teacher does a few examples of one kind of problem in class and the homework consists of a set of similar problems (Yerushalmy et al., 1987).[8]

If size is instead defined by the number of avenues of exploration or solutions available, then larger problems are more successful than smaller

---

[7]Splitting one large construction problem about reflection into a series of connected subproblems (all construction problems) proved a successful strategy. The students' work on the subproblems was similar, in a positive way, to their work on the "smaller" construction problems.

[8]This attitude coincides with Schoenfeld's (1988) observations about students' 5-minute theory of problems. The students he observed gave up on any problem that they could not solve in 5 minutes. They seemed to think a problem, by definition, should be solved quickly.

ones. Because one of our criteria for the success of an inquiry problem is that it has many solutions, this reasoning may seem tautological. Yet, problems with many solutions are successful also according to our other criteria, that is, significant work from most students, student enjoyment, and teacher satisfaction.[9] For example, one reason both teachers and students enjoy construction problems is the range of different solutions. (Students also enjoy conjecture problems with different solutions.) At the same time, small problems created early in the year to lead students to basic concepts, which had one preferred solution and suggested the measurements students should make, are not successful (for examples, see Problem 7.3 or Problem 7.6). As noted, in the discussion of Problems 7.3 and 7.4, adding an auxiliary line produces a problem that generates a larger number of conjectures and brings the proof of the desired theorem into students' range. We used this strategy more generally to change unsuccessful small problems into larger problems with a large number of possible conjectures with easier proofs.

Students' Ability or Background.   There are at least three interrelated aspects to the consideration of students' ability: their general mathematical ability and achievement, their knowledge of geometry, and their inquiry skills (cf. Krutetskii, 1969a, 1969b). Although the effect of students' general mathematical ability could not be carefully examined, our experience suggests that the amount of structure and direction students need from written materials varies according to their general mathematical ability and according to the school's expectations for self-directed activity. Concerning the other two aspects of ability, we observed the following:

> **Observation:** As students' knowledge of geometry and their repertoire of inquiry skills grows, inquiry problems become more successful.

For example, students' ability to produce conjectures improved with increasing geometric knowledge. In the beginning of the year, when students had little knowledge of geometry, their conjectures were a hit-or-miss business. As they learned more geometry, they derived their first conjectures from deductive geometric knowledge and used the Supposer to elaborate and verify them. Thus, as students gained geometric knowledge, they made more conjectures. Further, as their inquiry skills developed and they learned, for example, to appreciate generalization and to identify

---

[9]DiSessa's (1985) claims about small problems in physics complement this indication of the success of problems with many possible solutions and avenues for exploration. He argued that small problems "can hardly establish the context for inventing a technique for solving a class of problems" (p. 113). In mathematics, he pointed out, small problems can never motivate students to invent definitions in the way a mathematician does.

fruitful situations for exploration, they used numerical manipulations and found interesting conjectures even in "dull" problems (for a detailed description of this development with a different sample of students, see Yerushalmy, 1986).

When Drafting a Written Statement of the Problem

The preceding discussion of three considerations a teacher might take into account before drafting a written statement of an inquiry problem indicates the bind in which we found ourselves. Although students responded poorly to small problems that were created to lead them to basic concepts, had a single preferred answer, and suggested the measurements students should make, their teachers were uncomfortable with large open-ended problems, which they felt were too vague for the students. The need to find out how to pose large but specific problems led us to develop another set of considerations when drafting a written statement of an inquiry problem: a

STATEMENT OF THE GOAL

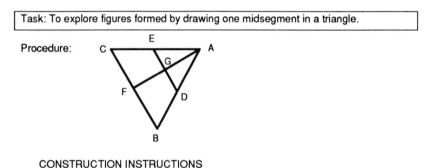

> Task: To explore figures formed by drawing one midsegment in a triangle.

CONSTRUCTION INSTRUCTIONS

> - Construct any △ABC.
> - Draw midsegment DE connecting AB and AC.
> - Label the midpoint of BC with point F.
> - Draw AF and label the intersection of DE and AF with point G.

PROCESS INSTRUCTIONS

> - Measure the elements of the figure.
> - Record your data.
> - State your conjectures.

Problem 7.9. Statement of goals, constuction instructions, and process instructions for Problem 7.2.

Task: Split a triangle into different numbers of triangular sections of equal area.

Procedure: First try to get four sections of equal area. When you have a solution, make sure it works in all kinds of triangles. Record a drawing of your solution and explain what kind of lines you added to the triangle to get the drawing.

Problem 7.10.   Adding a statement of goal to Problem 7.7.

statement of the goal, a description of the construction, and process instructions. These considerations are indicted individually in Problem 7.9.

A Statement of the Goal of the Problem.   Greeno suggested that "when a problem has an indefinite goal, the problem solver cannot know what the solution state will be like until it is achieved" (1976, p. 480). As the construction problems described previously illustrate, however, it is possible to pose a problem with a definite goal (e.g., "Draw a rectangle") that provides students with information about the solution without specifying the exact solution.

Conjecture:[10] A statement of the goal of an inquiry problem helps students work productively.

Originally, when we wrote inquiry problems, we did not include a statement of the goal of the problem for students (see, as examples, Problems 7.7 and 7.8). We learned, however, that such statements help students. Now it is our common practice to use them. The format used in Problem 7.10 from the Geometric Supposer Problems and Projects books published by Sunburst Communications, Inc. shows how the addition of a goal statement to Problem 7.7 helps students make a more thorough investigation of the problem by providing some indication of the desired direction of inquiry. The task is specified, and the phrase "different numbers of" has been added to provide further direction.

As this problem illustrates, a sentence that directs students to the goal of the task makes the problem less vague by answering the question, "What are we trying to do?" (Although such a statement seems valuable, sometimes it is difficult to write one without specifying more of the solution than is

---

[10]We use the term conjecture, as opposed to observation, because we have no direct data to support this statement.

actually desirable or being too vague; see Problem 7.4 for a vague task statement.) In Problem 7.10, the question of whether triangles of equal area must be congruent provides a connection to the curriculum; the statement of the goal of the task includes a mathematical property or relationship that links the lab problem to class lessons. The statement of the goal of a task, therefore, not only explains to the students what they should be doing, but by linking lab activities to class, it also clarifies why a particular lab problem was assigned.

A Description of the Construction in the Problem.   In all the Supposer problems we used, a construction was described. In construction problems, the construction itself is the goal; in conjecture problems, the construction is what students explored. This section evaluates methods of describing constructions, specifically the effectiveness of diagrams as vehicles for stating the specifications of a desired construction.

Observation: An unaccompanied diagram is not a sufficient description of the construction to be made. A diagram accompanied by a written description proves to be a more successful method of describing the construction to be made.

Problem 7.11 asks students to describe methods for drawing a construction and provides a diagram as an example of the construction desired. (The students had learned about similarity and properties of quadrilaterals and triangles before this problem was assigned.) In this case, the use of only a diagram to specify the desired construction was unsuccessful: students did not produce solutions to this problem and, according to teachers' reports, had difficulty understanding the assignment.

In contrast, Problem 7.12, which was assigned somewhat earlier in the year and included written specifications as well as a diagram, was

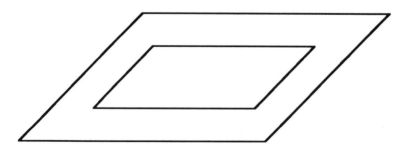

Problem 7.11.

A) This problem asks you to describe the different methods for drawing a triangle similar to but inside ∆ABC such that the two triangles share no points in common. Provide data to verify that your methods work.

_____

_____

B) Draw the sides of the new triangle inside ∆ABC such that they are equidistant from the corresponding sides of ∆ABC.

Example:

C) The new triangle is located anywhere inside ∆ABC.

Example.

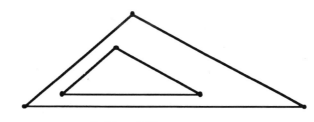

Problem 7.12.

successful.[11] The problem asks students to construct a triangle within a triangle and defines the relationship between the two triangles (similarity). Next, the problem is broken down into parts. Students are asked to construct particular types of similar triangles to be drawn, and diagrams serve as models for the written descriptions.

Students produced many solutions to Problem 7.12, and they described their solutions in clear geometric terms, not in step-by-step lists of the keys to press in order to make the construction. The contrast between their difficulty with Problem 7.11 that presented only a diagram to specify the construction desired and their productive response to Problem 7.12 suggests

_____

[11]In some problems, particularly conjecture problems, diagrams can be dispensed with altogether, and the description of the construction presented as procedure, or list of steps, for the student to carry out. We do not suggest that all descriptions of a construction must include diagrams. Indeed, because initially students treat diagrams as specific instances, not as models, avoiding diagrams early in the year may be preferable.

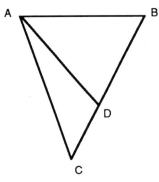

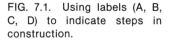

FIG. 7.1. Using labels (A, B, C, D) to indicate steps in construction.

that they need written descriptions to help them identify and isolate key attributes of a diagram. This interpretation makes sense, because a diagram is a specific member of a class and has a large number of attributes. It is hard to know simply by examining a diagram which of its attributes must be reproduced.[12] For example, in Problem 7.11, the diagram does not specify clearly enough which configurations are considered correct solutions. The diagram appears to be a parallelogram, but the student is not told whether the desired construction also must be a parallelogram. In order to evaluate thoroughly the use of diagrams as specifications of a construction, one needs to understand how students view diagrams, an issue explored earlier in chapter 3 (see Yerushalmy and Chazan on Visual Obstacles in Learning Geometry). Early in the school year, students in this study made construction tasks into "Draw this specific figure. . . . " They treated diagrams as specific instances, not general models. Had Problem 7.11 been presented to them early in the year, they might have assumed that the final product must include two parallelograms, maybe even parallelograms with the same rotational orientation as those in the diagram. As the year went on, they learned that the diagrams accompanying their instructions were models for a class of figures. Thus, although diagrams are helpful models for specific instances of a construction, they are inappropriate for communicating the characteristics of a desired construction especially for beginning students.

In many problems where the construction is specified by a written description (with or without an accompanying diagram), the steps of the construction are described by labels that refer to the points in the resulting diagram. For example, in the diagram in Fig. 7.1, A, B, C, and D are the labels.[13]

---

[12]A sequence of diagrams can be used to aid students in determining which attributes should be reproduced, but the diagrams must be carefully chosen; students may find common features the problem poser did not intend.

[13]It might seem that "talking in labels" would become easier with the Supposer, for the following reasons: every new triangle is labeled ABC; right angles in right triangles and obtuse angles in obtuse triangles are always at vertex A; and when the construction is repeated, the

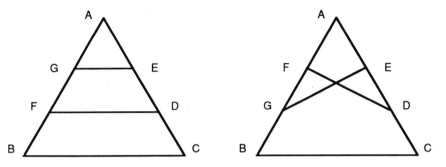

FIG. 7.2. Two different interpretations of consturction instructions. It might seem that "talking in labels" would become easier with the SUPPOSERS, for the following reasons: every new triangle is labeled ABC; right angles in right triangles and obtuse angles in obtuse triangles are always at vertex A; and, when the construction is repeated, the labels remain the same—only the picture changes. Even with the SUPPOSERS, however, labels do not always produce an unambiguous description of a construction; e.g., two different kinds of diagrams can result from the following instructions: Draw triangle ABC. Subdivide segment AC into three segments. Subdivide segment AB into three segments. Draw segments EG and DF.

Observation: When labels are included in the problems, students write their conjectures using labels, not geometric language.

When a diagram is accompanied by written instructions that use labels, the labels may distract students from the geometric relationships in the construction. For example, for a problem about exterior angles where the columns of data were identified by labels (see Problem 7.6), students conjectured that the number in one column added to the number in the next column was always the number in the third column. They did not mention that the relationship they described indicates that the sum of two remote interior angles in a triangle is equal to the exterior angle at the third vertex.

Process Instructions. Process instructions tell students what they need to do beyond the construction that must be made. They suggest the measurements to make or the types of figures to explore, or they remind students to test conjectures on other triangles and to write their conjectures. More general instructions or metacognitive hints are also considered as process instructions. For example, one teacher wrote the instructions for a

---

labels remain the same—only the picture changes. Even with the Supposer, however, labels do not always produce an unambiguous description of a construction. For example, two different kinds of diagrams can result from the following instructions: Draw triangle ABC. Subdivide segment AC into three segments. Subdivide segment AB into three segments. Draw segments EG and DF. (See Fig. 7.2.)

large assignment shown in Fig 7.3. The instructions are sufficiently general to be used with many problems, and they help students step through a model of the kind of inquiry desired by the teacher.

Observation: Explicit written process instructions help students.

In a problem posed earlier in two different ways—Problems 7.7 and 7.8—the key difference between the two ways of writing the problem lies in the process instructions. Regardless of which way the problem is written, students do not need to analyze a diagram to discover the construction to be completed. The process instructions in Problem 7.7 state the general goal and then detail the steps to be taken in exploring it, which helps students to organize their inductive work. The process instructions in Problem 7.8 provide examples and ask for a generalization focused on the number of triangular sections, without describing the work to be done or separating different cases.

Even though students using Problem 7.7 did not generalize the number of triangular sections, clear and detailed process instructions did not prevent them from making disparate generalizations about other aspects of the problem, for example, that the vertex of origin can be changed or that the medians can be used from different vertices in the subtriangles (see Figure 7.4 for generalizations of different kinds for Problem 7.7). Problem 7.8, which focused on generalization, kept students from carrying out a systematic analysis of the cases. Those who restricted their investigation to

1   You will select one of the problems to work on.
2   You may work with a partner or alone. If you choose a partner, indicate his/her name under your name. Each must turn in his/her own work.
3   You will make a brief _restatement_ of what the problem asks for.
4   You will make an _outline_ of the steps you think necessary to explore and solve your problem.
5   You will collect, examine and study the data you think will help you to make conjectures about the relationships in the problem. This data collection is for you. (Use log sheets for this purpose.) Although you may enclose these sheets, I will not grade them. You will have 4 days in the lab to collect data. If you need more time, you will have to go to the math lab on your own to complete your collection of data.
6   A conjecture sheet will be due _____. This conjecture sheet must include a diagram and a list of your conjectures, clearly numbered. This summary sheet will be graded and returned in order that you will be able to complete the last and most important part of the project.
7   The last segment of your project is to prove "formally" as many of your conjectures as possible, but no fewer than 3. More credit will be given for more proofs.

FIG. 7.3.   An example of explicit written process instructions.

Try to split a triangle into triangular sections that have the
same area. First try to get four sections with equal area.

When you have a solution, make sure that it works in all kinds
of triangles.

Record a drawing of your solution and explain what kind of lines
you added to the triangle to get the drawing.

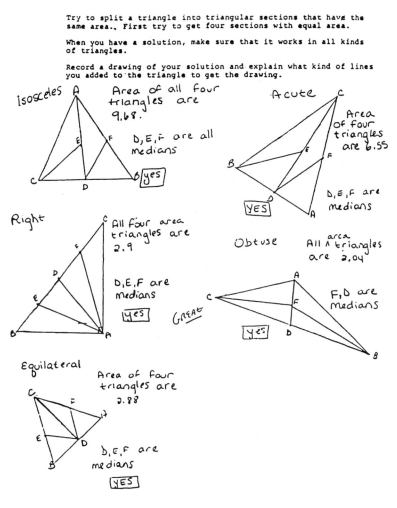

FIG. 7.4.   Generalizations of different kinds for Problem 7.7.

one type of triangle (e.g., isosceles) were more successful in making
generalizations. The explicit process instructions given in Problem 7.7 were,
therefore, helpful to students doing this problem.

Our next observation concerns the nature of process instructions:

Observation: When students are given charts that dictate which data should be
collected, the problems are not successful. When students are asked to record
data in charts they create and label, charts prove to be a useful way to help
them inquire systematically.

Using charts and tables that dictate which measurements should be made
proved to be an unproductive strategy for giving process instructions.

Despite the attractiveness of charting as a technique for organizing data, overemphasis on it paralyzes students' ability to direct their own inquiry. For example, in a class where tables and charts were used frequently, students ignored written instructions and turned directly to the tables and charts, limiting their inquiry to the headings specified in them. When interviewed about their work with the Supposer, they reacted negatively to this form of process instructions. As one said:

> On the worksheets the problem is all mapped out for you. The problem that they just gave us, you have to find the solution and find the work. They give you step by step, number one, number two, number three. (Yerushalmy et al., 1987)

Guiding student inquiry by providing a chart that dictates the measurements to be made reduces student inquiry to an unthreatening rote collection of data. It is easy to specify clearly in the problem exactly what needs to be done to create a successful solution, but as the student's comment shows, it is uninteresting. We are not, however, arguing that charts are never appropriate tools in the inquiry process. They are useful when students determine which measurements and drawings are to be collected and organize them in their own charts (see Appendix I). In a critical sense, the act of organizing a table or chart is an important part of the inquiry process itself.

Our third observation concerns changes during the school year:

> **Observation:** As the year progresses, students are able to work on their own with less direction (that is, less explicit process instructions). This phenomenon is observed both with work on the Supposer and with other classroom activities.

For example, at the end of the year, an observer visited a class working with one type of geometry construction device known as Mira, a clear plastic drawing tool for investigating reflections (thus, "Mira"), as well as compass and straightedge. That students could do this work with little direction from the teacher indicates how comfortable they were with construction tools and their willingness, absent at the beginning of the year, to try their own constructions. The following excerpt is taken from the notes of the classroom observer:

> I was impressed by the students' ability to make constructions and follow directions without asking millions of questions. . . . Students were recording the constructions neatly on their papers. . . . There was a lot of commotion in

the room. Students were talking most of the time, although a high percentage of the talk was on geometry. . . . The kids seemed comfortable working with tools, even one (Mira) that they had never worked with before.

RECOMMENDATIONS AND CONCLUSIONS

Our goal is to create materials that describe problems clearly and unambiguously so students know what needs to be done, yet still leave room for student inquiry. The observations presented here are based on our experience. To summarize, we present the following recommendations for posing inquiry problems with the Supposer.

First, we recommend three strategies for writing clear materials for the Supposer: state the goal of the problem at the top of the page; provide explicit process instructions to remind students of what they should do as inquirers; and once students understand that diagrams can be models, use diagrams to exemplify written construction instructions.

Second, avoid small-scale problems that use charts to tell students which measurements to make in order to discover a single conjecture desired by the teacher. Students told which data to collect have difficulty seeing numerical patterns in the data and do not necessarily discover the particular relationship that interests the teacher. They also find this process of collecting data and doing the problem uninteresting because it precludes individual creativity. We recommend enlarging such problems and using them in a different manner. For example, one might ask students to add the auxiliary lines necessary to write a proof, which allows a more complex initial construction to be created. If the students cannot find the particular conjecture desired, they can at least find conjectures the teacher can use to derive the one desired. At the same time, each student is able to explore more freely and theoretically, at least, has an opportunity to develop a proof of the desired conjecture. Keep in mind, however, that conditions for effective inquiry go well beyond problems and how they are written.

The level and evolution of students' knowledge and abilities are critical factors. When students do not have the necessary background in geometry to make deductive arguments, they do not have mechanisms for checking general answers. With such students, it is best to start with construction problems and other problems with specific solutions. Because early in the course students may not be able to distinguish between diagrams used as specific instances and those used as models, avoiding diagrams as models early in the year may be helpful.

The written word is not sufficient for transmitting expectations. Modeling inquiry strategies and parts of the inquiry process is important. For example, the "What if not" strategy should be modeled explicitly to help students become adept at changing aspects of the written statement of the problem.

LOOKING AHEAD: INQUIRY, PROBLEMS, SOFTWARE, AND DEVELOPERS

Beyond the Supposer geometry contexts, our work suggests more general recommendations for introducing inquiry teaching into schools. At the opening of this chapter, we suggested that the utility and power of a software tool environment (i.e., a program designed around a set of capabilities rather than an explicit curricular content or instructional framework) becomes apparent only in the context of a problem. The observations included here indicate that well-crafted problems clarify the instructional approach, define the relationship between the use of the software and the curricular content, and provide students with direction. Furthermore, our observations make clear the relationship between the formulation of the materials and the success of the problems.

We believe that the formulation of inquiry problems is important to the successful development of guided inquiry approaches using other tool-based software environments in other domains. Our scheme of considerations is an initial framework for such formulation. With the exception of the description of the construction, the considerations are general enough to apply to other environments; clearly, the development of other software like the Geometric Supposer and further research on the use of this sort of tool in the curriculum are essential for their evaluation and refinement. Already we have some indication that our concern about the formulation of problems is warranted and fruitful. In working with a piece of software of a similar, "toolish" nature in algebra, we have found that teachers' foremost concern and difficulty is the creation of problems that exploit the power of the program. Our experience analyzing the formulation of inquiry problems for the Supposer helped us in this endeavor.

Our experience also highlights the challenges and difficulties of bringing inquiry approaches into classrooms. The students and the teachers we worked with had some difficulties with both the new expectations and the roles they had to adopt in an inquiry approach, difficulties that we believe are not unique to our approach and are found with most inquiry approaches (Kaput, 1986). Hardware, software, and sources of inquiry problems are not yet sufficiently available. In addition, students need modeling and support from teachers to take on new expectations and to leave behind the security of learning without the exercise of inquiry, and teachers need modeling and support as they explore innovations that require new teaching skills, especially the delicate skill of saying enough without saying too much.

ACKNOWLEDGMENTS

A version of this paper appears in *Instructional Science,* 1990 Vol. 19.
The work discussed in this paper was conducted at the Center for Learning Technology, Education Development Center, Inc., under a subcontract from the Educational Technology Center at the Harvard Graduate School of Education. Preparation of this report was supported in part by the U.S. Office of Educational Research and Improvement (contract # OERI 400-83-0041). Opinions expressed herein are not necessarily shared by OERI and do not represent Office policy.

REFERENCES

Brown, S. & Walter, M. (1983). The art of problem posing. Philadelphia: The Philadelphia (Pa.) Franklin Institute Press.

DiSessa, A.A. (1985). Learning about knowing. In E. L. Klein (Ed.), *Children and computers.* San Francisco: Jossey-Bass.

Greeno, J. G. (1976). Indefinite goals in well-structured problems. *Psychological Review, 83*(6), 479–491.

Jensen, R. J. (1986). Microcomputer-based conjecturing environments. In G. Lappan & R. Even (Eds.), *Proceedings of the Eighth Annual Meeting PME-NA*. East Lansing, MI: International Group for the Psychology of Mathematics Education – North American Branch.

Kaput, J. J. (1986). *Information technology and mathematics: Opening new representational windows.* (Topical Paper 86–3). Cambridge, MA: Harvard Graduate School of Education, Education Technology Center.

Krutetskii, V. A. (1969a). An investigation of mathematics abilities in school children. In J. Kilpatrick & I. Wirzup (Eds.), *Soviet Studies in the psychology of learning and teaching mathematics* (Vol. 2). Chicago: University of Chicago Press.

Krutetskii, V. A. (1969b). An analysis of the individual structure of mathematics abilities in school children. In J. Kilpatrick & I. Wirzup (Eds). *Soviet Studies in the Psychology of Learning and Teaching Mathematics* (Vol. 2). Chicago: University of Chicago Press.

Lampert, M. (1988). *Teachers' thinking about students' thinking about geometry: The effects of new teaching tools.* (Tech. Rep. No. TR88-1. Cambridge, MA: Harvard Graduate School of Education, Educational Technology Center.

Schoenfeld, A. H. (1986). On having and using geometric knowledge In J. Hiebert (Ed.), *Conceptual and procedural knowledge: The case of mathematics.* Hillsdale NJ: Lawrence Erlbaum Associates.

Schoenfeld, A. H. (1988). When good teaching leads to bad results: The disaster of "well taught" mathematics courses [Special issue]. Educational Psychologist, *23*(2), 145–166.

Schwab, J. (1962). The teaching of science as enquiry. In J. J. Schwab & P. F. Brandwein (Eds.), *The teaching of science* (pp. 1-103). Cambridge, MA: Harvard University Press.

Schwartz, J. L., & Yerushalmy, M. (1985-1988). *The Geometric Supposer.* Pleasantville, NY: Sunburst.

Yerushalmy, M. (1986). *Induction and generalization: An experiment in teaching and learning high school geometry.* Unpublished doctoral dissertation, Harvard Graduate School of Education, Cambridge, MA.

Yerushalmy, M., & Chazan, D. (1990). Overcoming visual obstacles with the aid of the Supposer. *Educational Studies in Mathematics, 21,* 119-219.

Yerushalmy, M., Chazan, D., & Gordon, M. (1987). *Guided inquiry and technology: A year-long study of children and teachers using the Geometric Supposer.* (Tech. Rep. No. TR88-6). Cambridge, MA: Harvard Graduate School of Education, Educational Technology Center.

Yerushalmy, M., & Houde, R. (1987). *Geometry problems and projects: Triangles.* Pleasantville, NY: Sunburst.

8 Teachers' Thinking About Students' Thinking About Geometry: The Effects of New Teaching Tools

Magdalene Lampert
Michigan State University

This chapter draws on the thinking of a group of secondary school geometry teachers who were participants in the Laboratory Sites Study of the Educational Technology Center (ETC) at Harvard University. The purpose of the Laboratory Sites Study was to understand the process of implementing technology-enhanced guided exploration in school classrooms. A diverse group of school sites were chosen for the study, including an inner city magnet school, a large urban comprehensive school, a suburban school, and a small rural school.

The data analyzed here were collected as a substudy of the Laboratory Sites project, which looked at comprehensive questions of implementation in relation to materials produced at ETC for teaching science, mathematics, and programming. The substudy reported here is concerned with teachers' points of view about using one piece of educational technology—The Geometric Supposer—to substantially change the way they teach geometry. The Supposer[1] is designed to change fundamentally the way instruction is delivered in classrooms by enabling students to engage directly in the exploration of subject matter. This chapter reports on the teacher-users' thinking about how their teaching changed as they incorporated the Supposer into their work, as well as their thoughts about the technology.

The teachers who participated were interviewed during the fall and spring of the 1986-1987 school year, observed as they taught with the Supposer,

---

[1]The Geometric Supposer was developed at Education Development Center (Newton, MA) by Judah Schwartz and Michal Yerushalmy. The software is published and distributed by Sunburst Communications.

and observed as they participated in monthly Users' Group meetings with ETC researchers. Common themes in their thinking were identified during the fall, and in the spring, observations and interviews were used to further probe issues of concern to the teachers.

GEOMETRY TEACHING AND LEARNING

The content of high school geometry is conventionally organized around students' learning to prove the theorems of Euclidean geometry. Before they get to the 10th grade, these students have been taught the definitions of various kinds of plane figures, and they should know how to draw and label them according to mathematical conventions. They may also have been introduced to the idea of proof in a course in introductory algebra, but in most secondary school curricula, that topic is reserved for the geometry course. This pattern of instruction has changed little in the last 50 years, in spite of "the new math," technological developments, and changes in the field of geometry itself (Usiskin, 1987). Comparing this conventional pedagogy with the sort of reasoning that is involved in actually doing mathematics helps to understand what using the Supposer means to geometry teachers.

Doing a Proof in Mathematics and in High School Geometry

Within the world of mathematical discourse, establishing a geometrical truth such as intersecting lines form opposite angles that are equal begins with the definitions for intersecting lines and opposite angles. In conventional deductive form, these definitions and some algebraic manipulations using supplementary angles[2] are logically related to produce the conclusion that whenever two lines intersect, the opposite angles formed are equal. This must be true simply because opposite angles are supplementary to the

---

[2]Supplementary angles are two angles that, when placed next to one another, form a straight line—180° angle—with two of their sides, as in the case of these two intersecting lines (see Fig. 8.1).

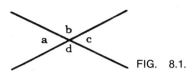
FIG. 8.1.

(Angles a and b, b and c, c and d, and d and a are supplementary; b and d are opposite angles, as are a and c.)

same angle. The conclusion is reached by deduction and generalized thereby to all pairs of intersecting lines; it does not depend on actually drawing any lines or even looking at two lines that intersect.

But much more than this simple deductive argument is required to prove this assertion in the form that is typically taught, and sometimes learned, in high school geometry courses. A student who wants to demonstrate that he or she has learned how to prove that intersecting lines form opposite angles that are equal needs to produce something like Fig. 8.2.

Theorem: If two lines intersect, then the opposite angles formed are equal.

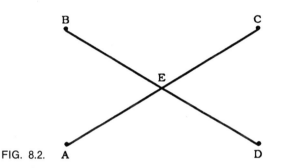

FIG. 8.2.

Given: Line BD intersects line AC at point E.
To prove: Angle AEB = Angle CED

Statements	*Reasons*
1. Line BD intersects line AC at point E	1. Given
2. Angle AEB + Angle BEC = 180°	2. Supplementary angles
3. Angle BEC + Angle CED = 180°	3. Supplementary angles
4. Angle AEB + Angle BEC = Angle BEC + Angle CED	4. Quantities equal to the same quantity are equal to each other
5. Angle AEB = Angle CED	5. Subtracting the same quantity from both sides of the equation

Q.E.D.

Among the basics of constructing such a proof are definitions and labeling conventions. Students have to learn these first before they go on to the reasoning process that is involved in proofs.[3] Another basic is the

---

[3]In less academic geometry courses, it is not unusual for students never to get beyond definitions, drawing diagrams, and labeling.

two-column form for proof. To generate a geometrical argument in this form, the theorem is written in what teachers call the *if-then* form, and then the *if* part of the hypothesis is translated into a statement of what is *given* and the *then* part into a statement of what is *to prove*. This is done simultaneously with creating the diagram to illustrate the conditions that are given. This illustration turns the general condition being stated into a claim about somewhat more particular entities: in the illustration, the intersecting lines become lines BD and AC that intersect at E. They form angles BEC, CED, DEA, and BEA,[4] so the opposite angles that must be shown to be equal are either BEC and DEA or CED and BEA.

Of course, a pair of intersecting lines could also look like Fig. 8.3.

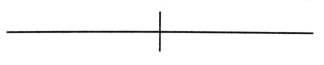

FIG. 8.3.

or like Fig. 8.4.

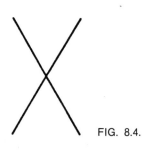

FIG. 8.4.

or like any other configuration of two lines meeting. Any letters, in fact any symbols, could be used for labeling them. But in any illustration of the general condition, the lines and their point of intersection must be *specified* in a way that is a concrete exemplar of the given condition. In the activity of creating the diagram, general terms of the hypothesis, such as *intersecting lines,* become specific: two actual lines are drawn on paper and labeled.

In a secondary school geometry lesson, some attention is given to the meaning of this mathematically significant translation from the conditions

---

[4]Some teachers and textbooks require that one always distinguishes between lines and line segments by highlighting the points that are labeled on a line and putting arrows at either end, but in most situations, this formalism falls away consciously or unconsciously early on in the course. Here it is assumed that BD is a segment of line BD and AC is a segment of line AC.

of universal logical to a particular empirical illustration, but whether the proof is about the particular elements of the diagram or the more general elements of the theorem becomes somewhat ambiguous. Whether students come to know that the proof is universal whereas the drawing is particular, probably depends on the authority asserted by the teacher rather than on their appreciation of the subtleties of logic.[5]

The list of statements and reasons make up the body of the proof. They are always written in parallel columns, and they must always begin with what is given and proceed through a series of steps so that the last is a statement of what one set out to prove. The proof then ends with the triumphant Q.E.D. — a claim in authoritative Latin that one has demonstrated what was to be demonstrated. There is never any question that what needs to be proved will be proved; typically students write the first and last steps before going on to fill in the middle ones.

What goes between the first and last statements is more of a problem, because that is where logical thinking comes in, or doesn't. In the case of the proof that the opposite angles formed by intersecting lines are equal, one begins with definitions and manipulates them with a bit of algebra to get from the given lines to the conclusion. In other proofs, one might also need to use previously proven theorems as reasons for the statements in the argument.[6] As with arithmetic word problems, it is useful to know the topic of the chapter in which a proof problem is given in order to narrow down the possible choices for reasons. Many students admit to memorizing the steps in proofs that are given in their books or demonstrated by their teachers. Teachers rarely ask students to write a proof that they have not seen before, except in honors or advanced placement sections.

A typical scenario for a geometry class of average ability is to have the teacher go over the proof in class and then give a homework assignment that has students write the proof to show that Angle BEC = Angle AED. To do this correctly, students reproduce the steps described in class, but change the angle names to match the new set. They are not expected to do much in the way of reasoning.

---

[5]This ambiguity becomes significant if one wants students to be able to distinguish between deduction and induction as sources of mathematical certainty. For those initiated into mathematical conventions, there is no question but that proof is about deduction. But what is being taught — and presumably learned — in high school geometry is not just how to do a proof. Students are also learning how to learn mathematics: "don't do what seems to solve the problem (i.e., measure to see if two angles are equal), but do what the teacher tells you is the right thing to do."

[6]One teacher reported to me that she had a problem with students who wanted to put everything they could remember somewhere in the proof they were working on. This is a wonderful case where the culture of the classroom, in which the idea is to let the teacher know what you remember, and the culture of mathematics, in which the idea is to bring relevant definition and theorems to bear on a logical argument, come into an unproductive conflict!

What is Learned in Learning a Proof?

Presumably, after seeing a proof like the one described previously, students should be convinced that whenever two lines cross, the angles across from each other are equal—even if the students themselves did not invent the reasoning that leads to that conclusion. That is the way acquiring geometric knowledge happens if one believes that acquiring such knowledge follows the form of using deductive reasoning to arrive at mathematical truth. Starting with definitions and using algebraic principles, geometric elements are combined to generate new relationships that are known to be true by virtue of being logically inevitable. The conclusion is known, because it follows logically from what is given.

But is that what happens in high school geometry classes? It might be. But there are at least two other possibilities. One is that students know that intersecting lines form opposite angles that are equal, because the teacher or the textbook say so. They demonstrate that they have this knowledge on a test and perhaps even call it forth when it is useful in another proof. But they acquired it through acceding to authority and memorization, not because it was logically demonstrated to be true. A second possibility is that students know that opposite angles are equal, because whenever they have drawn two lines that cross, the angles across from each other looked equal. They might even have drawn some intersecting lines and measured the angles with a protractor to find that every time they do it, the angle measures are the same. They need to draw only a few pairs of intersecting lines to be sure that the next time they do it, the results will be the same.

Both of these scenarios lead students to wonder why they should bother to prove what they already know is true. But students soon stop raising this question, if they ever bother to raise it in the first place, because they have learned to go along with what the teacher says. Geometry is a required course in the college preparatory track, and especially for the ambitious, the need for a passing grade is enough incentive to do whatever is required to learn about proofs.

Teaching Proof and Teaching Mathematics

Many geometry teachers and high school curriculum developers continue to assert, however, that learning to prove geometrical theorems helps students to think logically in math and in general. Some teachers teach proof, because they want students to appreciate the particular mathematical beauty of Euclidean geometry, which generates a great deal of mathematics from a few axioms and definitions using deduction. Others simply recognize that their students will not pass the final exam and be able to go on to the next math course unless they write proofs in the conventional form. So teachers of geometry cajole and convince, they require and explain, they do whatever it takes to get their students to be able to do proofs. And they divert students away from measuring actual geometric figures—that is not the way Euclid did it, and it will not help on exams. By participating in this kind of learning, students acquire a very limited perspective on mathematical thinking, however. Common methods of teaching geometry and the assumptions they express about student learning mix a formalist philosophy of mathematics with a reliance on teacherly authority as the source of mathematical knowledge and truth. Formalism defines mathematics as a set of logical procedures by which conclusions are deduced from abstract propositions. In this view, everything that is known is derived by rules of logic, which is thought to give mathematics its special claims to certainty. Formalism came upon a significant challenge early in this century, however, when some mathematicians established that they could produce contradictory sets of results by applying legitimate logical procedures to the same set of axioms (Brouwer, 1913; Kline, 1980). This bit of logical acrobatics inspired all sorts of arguments and generated several alternative theories about the nature of mathematical knowledge, and it shifted attention in the field from theorems to the axioms from which they were deduced. Several non-Euclidean geometries developed from different sets of axioms, and it seemed as if the certainty of mathematical knowledge might be lost forever in a sea of relativism (Kline, 1980; Polanyi, 1960).

The identification of mathematical creativity with the deductive process has been more recently challenged by philosophers taking a careful look at how mathematical knowledge has developed over the centuries. Mathematicians' accounts of their work do not give the impression that everything flowed logically from a small set of axioms (Davis & Hersh, 1981; Hadamard, 1945; Lakatos, 1976; Polya, 1954). Instead, mathematicians make leaps into "truth" using induction or—even worse from the formalist point of view—intuition, resorting to proof only when they suspect that something they have asserted is not true.

These developments in thinking about the nature of mathematical knowledge do not seem to have much effect on the practice of secondary school mathematics teachers. Before they began working with the Supposer, all of the teachers described in this chapter taught geometry as the logical development of theorems from the Euclidean axioms. They followed textbooks that assumed this perspective on the subject and expected their students to learn definitions, labeling conventions, and the two-column form for proof. They felt strongly that theorems needed to be taught in a particular order so that each new proof could be built on previously established truths. They controlled the agenda according to which knowledge was acquired, with the help of their textbooks, and they told students what they needed to know and when it made sense to know it. Sometimes, they did activities designed to let students discover mathematical theorems empirically, such as having them draw intersecting lines and measure the angles that are formed to find that in every case, the opposite angles are equal. These activities supplemented "teaching as telling" and were done primarily to motivate students and vary the routine.

In these classrooms, as in most, the relationship between what teachers do and what students learn is defined not only by the course content but also by the particular kind of social interaction that is a routine part of the culture of schooling (Doyle, 1985; Florio-Ruane, 1987; Green, 1971; Jackson, 1970; Powell, Farrar, & Cohen, 1985). This culture interacts in complex ways with the kind of mathematics that is and can be taught. Teachers tell things to students. Sometimes they even explain them, although most teachers I have asked are hard pressed to tell me what that entails. Teachers give students assignments, students do them, and they are checked. If students don't do their assignments correctly, teachers do more telling or explaining, and then they give a test. If students know what they have been taught, they do well on the test. That is how the culture of the classroom defines knowing, and students and teachers participate together in that culture. Teachers are party to a social contract with students and their parents that binds them to current representations of what is to be taught and learned and current procedures for measuring those accomplishments. It makes sense in this culture to memorize what the teacher says you need to know, even if it does not make logical sense to you. Using the Geometric Supposer to support guided inquiry over the course of a year in the midst of this culture was disconcerting to both teachers and students; it caused the renegotiation of common understandings about what was to be taught and learned, and how students' knowledge was to be measured.

THE SUPPOSER INTERVENTION

The lab problems that accompany the Geometric Supposer software are designed to have students consider geometrical relationships inductively before being exposed to deductive proof (Yerushalmy & Houde, 1986). Students use the technology to construct and measure many specific figures before the classroom discourse turns to a discussion of what the patterns of these measurements imply for relationships in what one teacher calls *the universal triangle*. The lab problems are designed to lead students to the same abstract geometrical theorems as the more conventional curriculum, but the activities they entail can lead in many other interesting directions as well.

For example, students might be given this sort of problem on the Supposer: "On different kinds of triangles (acute, obtuse, equilateral, scalene), construct a line that is parallel to one side and bisects one of the other two sides. What can you conjecture about this line in relation to the sides and angles of the original triangle?" The software enables the production and measurement of multiple instantiations of each kind of triangle, the instant construction of the parallel bisector in each, the speedy measurement of all lines and angles, and the automatic computation of ratios between pairs of measures. Students work on problems at the computer in pairs, and they are provided with charts on which to record whatever measurement data they choose to collect. One pair of student might be looking at a figure and data like that in Fig. 8.5,

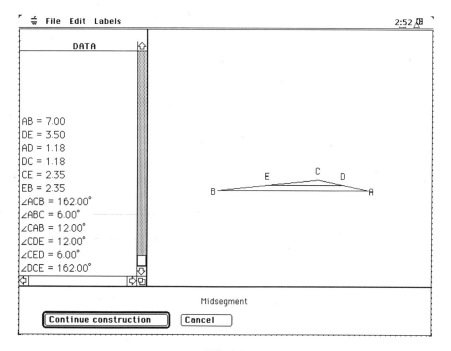

FIG. 8.5.

whereas another pair might be looking at something like Fig. 8.6.

Several more variations might be produced by each pair in a lab session. The software is designed so that students do not need to remember the definitions of terms in order to produce these figures. In the class following a lab session, students report and discuss their conjectures. Some of their conjectures are chosen by the teacher for the development of deductive proofs, first in paragraph form, then in the traditional two-column form. Initially this development is led by the teacher, and later it is primarily the independent work of students.

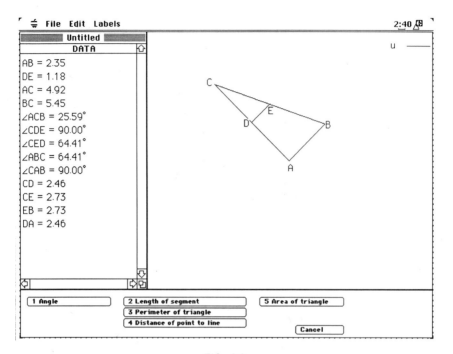

FIG. 8.6.

In the classrooms I studied, the software, the computers, and the commitment to spend regular class sessions doing lab problems functioned together to redefine both the nature of geometric knowledge and the teachers' and students' assumptions about their respective roles in the acquisition of that knowledge. The Supposer became a new authority on what it meant to do geometry and thus on what teachers needed to teach and what students needed to know and know how to do. The technology was in no sense a replacement for either the teacher or the textbook, however. It was an additional resource in the classroom that put both of those more familiar elements in a different perspective.

In the early weeks of their attempts to use the Supposer technology, the phenomenon of most concern to the teachers was sharing their control of the intellectual agenda with students – they wanted students to engage in the kind of independent exploration that led to the invention of conjectures but worried about the consequences of this kind of activity for covering the curriculum. As students were taught to collect data about geometrical relationships, look for patterns, and make conjectures about what sorts of relationships might be always true of figures in a certain class, they engaged in problems that are posed neither by the teacher nor the textbook. As they proceeded to make and test conjectures, they were able to take off in different directions through the subject matter. In contrast to theorems in the textbook, which are chosen by the teacher for the teaching of proof, Supposer-related conjectures are experienced by students as geometric relationships that need to be proven before they are accepted as true. Thus, the work of proof is owned by students in a way that it is not in the traditional curriculum. They construct their own intellectual roadmaps through geometry as they assert geometrical relationships and test their reasonability. This student ownership of the agenda is in radical contrast to what occurred in these classrooms before the Supposer became a tool for teaching and learning, when the content of the geometry course and order in which it was presented was determined by how the teachers decided to proceed through the textbook.

The teachers who experimented with the Supposer were faced with a serious conflict. The culture of the schools in which they were working had not prepared either the teachers or their students to feel secure that students following their own intellectual roadmaps would learn what they were supposed to know. Yet the new technology was seductive – to both students and teachers – and drew them along mathematically interesting paths that did not coincide with the routes defined by the textbook. Students went off on mathematically productive tangents that no one was able to keep track of. As they made conjectures that they wanted to prove, teachers were barraged with questions. Even teachers went off on tangents, as the Supposer captured them in some interesting mathematical puzzle. This is both exhilarating and frustrating; the participants enjoy what is happening, but they are not sure what connection it has with what they know as learning high school geometry. They are faced, at a very practical level, with figuring out how to guide the inquiry process once students are engaged in it. The situation the teachers experienced is like that of a tour operator whose bus has been replaced with a collection of glitzy motor scooters in the middle of the Place de la Concorde. Many of the "tourists" see places they want to explore, but do not know how to get to them. Others did not even know where to go or how to begin to make choices. Everyone is complaining because their expectations for the tour are not being met, while at the same time they are anxious to jump on a scooter and take off down the road. To make matters worse, the cameras that were to record where everyone had been are left on the bus. The theme that dominates the teachers' thinking over the course of the year is how to make a situation like this one fit into the culture of schooling without losing the excitement and engagement the Supposer engenders.

The Supposer innovation brought about a situation in the classrooms of the teachers I interviewed that is analogous to a cultural transition. During the year of the study, the authority to define what is to be learned and how it is to be taught is negotiated on a daily basis, over the course of the school year, putting previously unquestioned practices into a new perspective.

Although it is reasonable to imagine that changes in teaching practice follow changes in teachers' beliefs and attitudes, the Supposer innovation did not work that way. Teachers' beliefs and attitudes changed over the course of the year, as they were affected by what they observed their students doing with the Supposer. This sequence has been proposed as a model for teacher development, based on the notion that teachers embrace a change in their practice if they perceive it as practical, that is, if it produces student learning (Guskey, 1986). This cause–effect explanation does not take full account, however, of the complexity of how teachers define student learning. Changes in their ideas about what should be learned in a geometry course left the teachers with several questions at the end of the experimental year about whether the Supposer could be considered practical.

Teacher Thinking About Subject Matter: Finding a New Way to Map the Terrain

Because the textbook generally plays such an important role in the organization of mathematics curriculum and instruction, and because there is little to challenge its authority in defining high school geometry, it is not surprising that when teachers begin using the Geometric Supposer, they merge their definitions of the subject of geometry with the contents of the book they had been using to teach it. For all of them, the book is the measure of what students are supposed to know at any point in the course. They rely on textbooks for guidance about the order in which to introduce topics, because they assume that the books present material in the order in that geometrical knowledge logically develops.

The mathematical elegance of Euclidean geometry makes it difficult for teachers to accept a diversion from the order given in the book: they worry that students will get confused or that what they are learning is not really geometry if it comes out of the proper sequence. The order of topics, arranged around axioms and theorems, is meant to teach students something about what geometry is.

One teacher in the group put this quite plainly:

> The textbook is a logical progression, it absolutely is. As a matter of fact, the nature of geometry is sequential; that's how Euclid did it. You accept some statements as true because they make logical sense and then you deduce things from them. That's how geometry progresses. (G.S., Int. 1[7])

---

[7]Teacher talk is designated by the speaker's initials. "Int. 1" means that the quote is taken from interviews done in Fall 1986; "Int. 2" quotes are from Spring 1987.

Another teacher, who agreed with this description of geometry, said that the Supposer had thrown off her sense of how the material should be sequenced and that she did not yet have a sense of how to construct a new sequence to replace the one that was familiar:

> In terms of specifics, I'm very confused, because it's so nitty gritty in the book [what students need to know to do the problems, that is], and then when you go to use the Geometric Supposer, it's kind of "Well, they'll get that idea when they do problem #18, so do I really even have to discuss it?" I mean in terms of the postulates you need for doing that proof or whatever. (A.D., Int. 1)

For all of the teachers in this study, the development of geometry in the classroom had proceeded according to what they thought to be the internal post hoc logic of the discipline. They had all taught geometry several times, and they had a realistic sense of where they should be in the progression of axioms, definitions, and theorems at any given point in the school year. When they began using the Supposer at the beginning of the year, they combined lab work on the computer with textbook exercises, so that they could maintain the familiar schedule, rather than give up any of what they had done before:

> I did very traditional stuff the first couple of weeks, so they have learned their vocabulary fairly traditionally and we also did several things [with the Supposer] in small groups in my class. I still feel comfortable they've gotten everything we'd normally give a class up to this point. And then it's been enriched by the Supposer. I'm concerned and wondering if the stuff we're doing with the Supposer can be transferred to a more traditional testing and textbook oriented curriculum, if you could teach the subject purely from the Supposer. (G.S., Int. 1)

This teacher is reflecting not only on how to teach or when to use the new technology but also on a more fundamental question about how order defines the content of a high school geometry course.

Although each of the teachers found ways to maintain this order throughout the school year, using the Supposer radically altered their views of geometry itself, of the aims of teaching it, and of the way it should be taught. One of the teachers felt personally threatened by what she saw students doing with the Supposer, because one of the reasons she liked teaching geometry was her appreciation of the "beautiful logical development of the whole corpus of Euclidean geometry." She wanted her students to like geometry for its "self-contained completeness." But her goal was at risk as she watched her students conjecture about what might be true of the shapes they had generated on the Supposer. Her students were "making generalizations all over the place that they did not have the background to prove":

> We did some of these projects, just to get a sense of the Supposer and collecting data. We made conjectures and then just threw them in there [without proving them] to explore what similarity was. . . . *They've got a lot of neat conjectures, and they can't do anything with them because they don't have the theory yet,* that is, they can't do anything in the sense of proof. This bothers me because one of the things that is neat about geometry for me is that you can really do a deductive process with it. My teaching the deductive process has gone out the window. . . . It's like I'm in a totally new ballgame and I don't know what the rules are. (J.H., Int. 1, italics added)

To this teacher, "not having the theory yet" means that students do not have a corpus of already proven theorems they can use to prove the conjectures that result from their work on the Supposer. This contradicts what it has meant to her to do geometry, because the ideas that students are encountering are not coming in logical deductive order. In her view, doing geometry means:

> You have to be clear about what you know is true at the start and where you want to end up; you have to have that set out in your mind and you have to have available some place up here [in your head] for what relationships exist that you know about and then be able to put them in the right places to apply them to this situation. *And that comes from where you are in the course of the year.* You can begin with something as simple as proving triangles congruent and wind up with proofs about the internal and external triangles on a circle. The progression is really remarkable. (J.H., Int. 1, italics added)

Again, there is a merging of the track one takes through the course syllabus with how the subject is defined.

Near the end of the school year, I asked this teacher how she was thinking about the relationship between students going off on Supposer explorations and the elegant logical corpus of Euclidean geometry. Her first response was to talk about the difficulties she was having trying both to give time for exploration *and* to complete the syllabus. She was still associating the syllabus with the logical progress of postulates and theorems and still feeling something of a tension between that progression and the process of inductive inquiry intended by the Supposer. She said that another teacher in her school had done better at integrating the two, but she was still going back and forth in a "linear" way, feeling that although she wanted to integrate, it would be "much more of an effort for me to think that through." She hoped to do a better job the following year. Then she spoke about her "sabotage" of the deductive process she enjoys so much:

I've sabotaged it all, I give the kids all kinds of axioms, but—it's because I so value the problem-solving experience and I don't think I have lost a lot in the deductive process. I provide them with more axioms than before, and that is not a small thing. But it isn't the same kind of issue as I thought it was earlier because now I am able to enjoy the course in a little different way. There is no question but that the deductive process is still extremely important.

The thing is that we have in no way lessened that. And in some ways, maybe we've strengthened it. [With the Supposer now] you've got to be able to say *why* something is true. (J.H., Int. 2)

The meaning of deduction had broadened for this teacher, and it seemed as if her students were also having a more personal experience of the deductive process because they had to state their own conjectures and were expected to be able to say, from a logical standpoint, why those conjectures are true or not.

Another significant change in this teacher's thinking was the way she found her way through the subject matter as she attempted to guide students from their conjectures to the knowledge she believed it was important for them to acquire. After Supposer labs, she spent class time discussing conjectures that were not related to the topic on her agenda, because "some of the things they come up with are just remarkable, and we need to get all that up there." Discoveries were written on the blackboard; in recognition that they deserved a place in the public discourse whether or not they were part of her agenda. But she also made sure "that the things that are important to me get stated." She attempted to draw many connections between students' discoveries and the curriculum in any given lesson, so that "kids can begin to appreciate that everything matters." The theorems she believed important were ones to be used at some other point during the year to prove other theorems. Because of the Supposer, however, she moved toward these important ideas along a path that followed her students' thinking, rather than following the classic agenda from axioms to theorems that is often believed to represent Euclid's thinking.

Where do teachers get this idea that doing geometry is a logical progression from a few axioms and definitions to theorems and more theorems, all of which follow one another in a neat deductive sequence? One explanation is that they have never done geometry as it is done by geometers or even seen it done. There is no required college course in geometry for math majors, so their model for doing geometry probably comes from their own high school course, heavily supported by the textbooks they are using. As one of the teachers commented:

The way you were taught geometry is not always the way it's taught now, but I don't know which is best. With the Supposer, there is terrific pressure on you to just jump ahead and show them things or let them discover things in the Supposer that actually you shouldn't because the theorems are supposed to follow a certain rigid order. (B.L., Int. 1)

Another said, "I know what they're supposed to know in terms of the curriculum I'm supposed to cover." (A.D., Int.) Both of these comments intertwine the process and sequence in which one learns geometry with the presumed "rigid order" of the subject matter.

After several weeks of experiencing a tension between the ideas students were coming up with in Supposer Lab and the ideas that were contained in successive chapters of the book she was using, one of the teachers decided to abandon the book for what she considered the "more natural" order of students' thinking as generated by the Supposer problems. In the process, she gained some insight about how the order of the theorems and axioms in Euclidean geometry could be rearranged and still follow a logical sequence:

> I've really gotten away from the book in terms of the specific topics in the chapter. I found it to be better if I did the order which went with the Supposer. But I still use the textbook if there are appropriate homework problems. . . . I could see from the problems I asked them to prove at night (based on work in the Supposer Lab) that it was very easy, for example, to use the first three postulates and then just go right into CPCTC [Corresponding Parts of Congruent Triangles are Congruent], whereas the book waits for CPCTC....it logically followed; it was a real nice step to do just then, and the kids would understand it really easily. (A.D., Int. 2)

This teacher's decision about the agenda is a negotiation between what she saw that "the kids would understand really easily" and what she knew they needed to learn at some point in the year.

Other teachers made less radical adjustments in their use of textbooks, but they all commented on the amount of extra organizational, intellectual work involved in diverging from the order of postulates and theorems presented in the book.

> It's an awful lot of work for the teacher . . . just sitting down and trying to organize the unit. In a geometry book, the order does make a difference, let's face it. And if you're going to go away from that order, it takes a lot of thinking and a lot of work to organize the unit, a lot of thinking ahead. (A.D., Int. 2)

Reorganization of the subject matter was mentioned by all of the teachers as one of the most difficult tasks that resulted from their experiments with the Supposer. Each of them talked of plans to spend time over the summer reviewing the lab problems to figure out where they fit into the corpus of material that was supposed to be taught in a geometry course. They all seemed disposed to reorder the material in response to students' thinking, but they felt constrained both by time and by their familiarity with the conventional curriculum. One teacher said:

> My mind is so straight and all I see is just what I know, and my mind doesn't seem to go off on all the tangents like the kids do. . . . You've got to take the time to study a lot, and you have to think a lot before you give the projects out, and that's what I have to do more of. . . . I never realized the kids will come up with so many more ideas,or so many different things than what I thought of. (P.O., Int. 2)

This was the kind of work J.L. felt she did not have time for, and this kept her from integrating her Supposer classes with the syllabus she was expected to cover. When she did have time to read the papers on which students recorded their data and made their conjectures, she felt as if she could produce a lesson that was both responsive to the syllabus and attentive to their discoveries. Whereas she had previously been able to rely on the textbook for logical order, she now had to figure out the order of theorems and axioms on her own.

As teachers reflect on the tension between celebrating what students discover inductively while they are using the Supposer, and being responsible for students' knowing the postulates, definitions, and theorems that are presented in order in the textbook, they raise fundamental questions about what it means to know something in mathematics, about how much of that knowledge is internally generated by the knower (discovered), and how much comes down from the authority of the discipline in the sense that it has been proven according to acceptable methods of logical deduction. What is the relationship between the process of individual inquiry and existing bodies of knowledge? To what extent can we trust that students' exploration in a subject will result in their learning what it is important for them to know? (Petrie, 1981; Kitcher, 1984.)

These questions arise because of the potential of the Supposer technology to tap students' capacity to acquire geometric knowledge on their own, that is, without getting it from a teacher. The teachers who use the Supposer are thus challenged to expand their sense of their role to include directing student inquiry and legitimizing the knowledge that is acquired in that process.[8] They are also faced with the need to construct a new kind of social interaction in the classroom so that they can pay close attention to students' thinking and follow their leads through the subject without wholly relinquishing the authority to determine what will be learned.

---

[8]Comparing this teaching task to the more typical kind of teacher work that Putnam (1987) described as "constructing curriculum scripts" gives one a sense of the magnitude of the problem they face.

The Role of Induction in Changing Teachers' Ideas About Their Role in Geometry Teaching and Learning

Before they used the Supposer, this group of teachers believed that geometry is done without data collection and conjecturing on the part of learners; they saw doing geometry as a process of moving from teaching definitions and axioms and postulates to proving theorems, then using those theorems to prove more theorems. But they also felt that this process does not work for many of their students. Even students who acquiesce to it are alienated by it. The thinking belongs to teachers and texts. In the Supposer, teachers see a tool that counters this intellectual alienation. As one teacher said, it provides "the opportunity for students to do their own thinking and not just a lot of responding to what the teacher is asking for." (J.H., Int. 2)

The Supposer is seen by these teachers as a motivator both because the technology has some appeal and because students can do lots of things without teachers always telling them what their next move should be. The teachers are realistic about how much work they still need to do, especially to convince students of the need for proof,

> but at least now it is about something they [i.e., students] have shown some interest in exploring, whereas before it was all coming from me and it seemed totally contrived. The motivation for proof—that still, most of the time, comes from me. If I never threw out the idea of "Let's prove this now," I doubt very much if many of them would try it. But at least they're tuned in.

> It motivates them to be interested in the problem for the problem's sake more than teaching it traditionally would. And that is a motivation that is absolutely critical in education, particularly in math education. This stuff just doesn't seem relevant to the overwhelming majority. But [with the Supposer], they've invested the time in exploring, and they enjoy working with the computer. I think there's that empowerment there. (G.S., Int. 2)

Watching what their students came up with on their own, once they were educated to collect data, look for patterns, and make conjectures, was a surprising experience for the teachers in this experiment. They saw that their students were able to construct new knowledge from what they had been taught before and that they could actually generate new knowledge by induction. The more they saw their students do on their own, the more willing the teachers were to let students go. The result was an interactive process of empowerment: students taking charge and teachers trusting them to do so, because they recognized capacities they did not know were there.

But how much mathematical knowledge can students acquire without being taught? How much of it comes from observing patterns in physical phenomena and inventing concepts to describe them? These deep philo-sophical questions became matters for everyday consideration as the Supposer teachers tried to figure out how to incorporate students inductive discoveries into lessons. One of them commented on her reaction to what she had observed in a lab session in which her students were experimenting with the Supposer.

> I see that they know an amazing amount. Not only do they know stuff I haven't taught them, but they know stuff it never occurred to me to teach them, and they've got it *in their gut*. (J.H., Int. 1, italics added)

Allowing the Supposer into her classroom revealed to this teacher that students can come to know a lot of geometry "in their gut." Students make discoveries with the Supposer that are not related to what they are being taught. These discoveries may derive in part from geometry that was learned in earlier courses, but they are also attributable to the students' intuitive appreciation of mathematical relationships. At the end of her year of experimenting with the materials, J.H. said:

> The amazing thing about [the Supposer problems] is that they are open-ended. The kids can go in so many directions and so they're coming up with stuff that *I* never thought about before. . . . It gives them the opportunity to create their own mathematics, to go where other people haven't necessarily forged before you.

> For many folks, this is the very first time they have a chance to create their own mathematics, to do the kind of thinking required to justify their conclusions, to do a logical connecting. (J.H., Int. 2)

Where do these intuitions fit into the school learning and teaching of geometry? And where do they fit in the process of doing formal mathemat-ics?

Geometry has always been thought to be about "teaching thinking," but the users of this phrase had in mind deduction, not induction. The teachers using the Supposer were not clear about how to relate inductive inquiry to traditional content. But they observed that when students discovered a geometrical relationship the patterns they observed in numerical data, they got excited about it and maybe were more likely to remember it.

This kind of thinking both excited and troubled the teachers. For one thing, it made the job of keeping track of who had learned what, and where they should go next, quite difficult. But also, the teachers saw the process of inductive discovery as threatening their capacity to teach students the conventions of logic that require that a conjecture be proven before it is true. The teachers said they teach students that "it's not true until you prove it," because they believe that is how mathematics is supposed to work. But they also acknowledged that discovering a relationship for oneself (or "constructing it" as cognitive scientists say), makes it true in a way that may be more powerful than truth that is accepted because a teacher says it is true or because of the way truth is defined in an academic discipline.

One teacher commented:

> I don't find any problem with [the Supposer using numbers and measurement]. I think its good, at least for this level. Giving them specific problems and allowing them to work out problems, that's the only way they're going to get *their own conclusions*. I think the universal triangle works with very intelligent kids, but not with average kids. (A.D., Int. 1, italics added)

She thought her students might be more likely to learn geometry from trying to find patterns in visual and numerical data than from trying to deduce relationships among abstract figures.

But another teacher worried that she was not spending enough time teaching proof because she was doing Supposer labs. She did, however, think the Supposer was giving a deeper understanding of the relationships among figures.

> Maybe proof isn't everything. Maybe that isn't all there is to geometry. Maybe knowing that equilateral always means all sides and all angles equal, and what an isosceles triangle is, is more important than doing proofs. They are coming up with the terminology. . . . They are talking more geometry. . . . They are knowing the difference between a rhombus and a square now because we did that [Supposer] project on quadrilaterals. And they realize that a square and a rhombus have some of the same properties, but they are not the same. They were able to come up with conjectures like that. They were able to come up with a lot of things on their own before they were taught the difference between them. . . . They learned it better because they did it on their own. (P.O., Int. 2)

Induction and Deduction: Complementary or Contradictory?

At the same time that they celebrated its results, the teachers saw the inductive discovery process as something they had to monitor very closely so that students did not get the wrong idea about the nature of their knowledge:

> We had constructed a figure [on the Supposer] so that these two base angles here were made by perpendicular lines. They both measure 90 degrees. The students did that with a lot of similar triangles and analyzed all the ways that

it will be true. Well that's kind of a danger, and you have to keep cautioning them that it's not always going to be true. They have to prove it by using a proof of it. It is beginning to dawn on them that "just because I observe it doesn't mean that it's true *because we're harping on that quite a bit.* . . . We have to keep telling the kids that just because you discover something doesn't mean it's true unless you can prove it and that proof has to be without measurement, without reference to any kind of measurement. (P.O., Int. 1, italics added)

The teacher believed that she must regularly exert her authority to remind students that the relationships they observed to be true were not true until they were formally proven. It was not clear what this teacher meant when she said they "analyzed all the ways it will be true," but this process was not a substitute in her view for doing a proof.

Doing a proof has both a mathematical and an organizational function in the high school geometry classroom. It demonstrates to students that inductively derived conjectures are not enough to establish geometric proof. But it also serves as a public synthesis of the diversity of discoveries that students come up with as they work at lab problems on their own. Proof is the teacher's opportunity to take charge again of what is being learned and to feel secure that students do not miss an important point.

The Supposer lab problems are designed with this kind of balance between students' discoveries and covering the curriculum in mind. Working backward from the theorems students are expected to know, the problems are devised so that students inductively see the reasonability of a relationship before they are faced with constructing a logical argument for its applicability to all figures of a given type. Although it is not always accomplished in practice, this balance is appreciated by the teachers and often enabled them to integrate Supposer work with the rest of their agenda:

What we're doing is we're picking our [Supposer] project by what we're teaching next. We had just come through teaching side-angle-side, angle-side-angle, and side-side-side, and the next lesson was going to be isosceles triangles, so we picked a project that would tie together formal proof with introducing some of the isosceles theorems.

It worked beautifully, because *they were already assuming the theorems from their work on the Supposer.* They had already said, "Wait a minute, the bisector of the vertex angle is always going to be the perpendicular bisector of the base," and I said, "Not always. You can't do that, you can't assume that until you can prove it." And we did. So now they can use it. But they had already discovered it. So it's really neat because you can have them discover and then say, "Okay you have to prove it before you can use it." And then you come to the point where you can use it all the time, because you can prove it. (B.L., Int. 1, italics added)

Working on the Supposer gives students some investment of their own in the material teachers want them to learn. At this level, however, they still need to be indoctrinated to the need for deductive proof.

THE SUPPOSER IN THE SCHOOL CULTURE

Given all the tensions they feel between the sort of learning that the Supposer intends and the curriculum they are supposed to teach, why are teachers willing to experiment with a new approach? Besides the external incentives (being associated with a prestigious research project, wanting to please outside observers, and so on), the teachers in this project regularly mentioned how working with the Supposer enhanced their capacity to engage students in the process of doing mathematics, and that seemed to turn the intellectual chaos into a worthwhile activity. But the culture of the school does not naturally lend itself to supporting this kind of divergent mathematical discovery. So the teachers had to figure out ways to negotiate between the sorts of independent student activities they wanted to encourage and the familiar social and intellectual expectations everyone has about what should go on in school.

One of those expectations is that there is a common curriculum for all and that everyone follows it in the same order. Another is that math problems have right and wrong answers, and the more right answers you get, the more you know. And, of course, everyone assumes that teachers already know everything that students will learn and that information passes from teachers to students. These expectations are not always met in Supposer classrooms, and both teachers and students need to invent new schemes for making sense of what is happening instead.

The Sequences of Teaching and the Sequence of Learning

Although the teachers in this group saw geometry as a logical sequence of deduced theorems, the Supposer challenged them to think about whether students actually learn it that way. One teacher described an experience of communicating with a student about a Supposer project that put her sense of the learning sequence in a new perspective:

There is a Supposer project where there is a triangle that has parallel lines drawn on it this way, and your job is to duplicate the figure without using the parallel option. My God! They were just coming up with all sorts of ideas about how to do it; they were doing it, and one kid subdivided the sides and connected them and he got parallel lines this way, but when he connected them this way, they weren't parallel, and it was just driving him crazy.

Why did it work this way, and why didn't it work this way? All I could say was "In 2 weeks, I'll be able to tell you." But it really bothered him. He came up to me the next day and said, "I really need to know why." So poor old Jackie had to do a fade while we wait for the theory. (J.H., Int.)

What Jackie wanted to learn at that point was not what his teacher had in mind to teach. Because of his engagement with a Supposer problem, he wanted to go off in a different direction from the one that follows the Euclidean-geometry-oriented curriculum.

One important aspect of this experience is that the Supposer takes the ordering of the learning agenda away from the teacher. Another is that the Supposer has the capacity to engage students directly in wondering about the generalizability of an observed geometrical relationship. When this teacher said she needed to "wait for the theory" in order to answer the student's question, she meant that the theorems he could use to prove his conjecture about parallel lines had not been proven yet in this class, and so they were not to be considered part of the public store of reasons that students could call upon in developing proofs for conjectures. There was no deductive basis for arguing the truth or falsity of the conjecture he had discovered inductively, and so the teacher was stymied how to answer the student's question. On another occasion, this same teacher found herself "just giving them a lot of axioms so they could proceed." That is, she taught provable theorems as though they did not need to be proved (i.e., as axioms), so that students could use them as reasons in their arguments without knowing the proofs. This was a serious diversion from the classic course in Euclidean geometry, which is special because it relies on only a few axioms. By adding more axioms to this classic list, the teacher supported the process of discovering geometry, but she also redefined what geometry can mean. She diverged from the expectation that the teacher and the book determine the agenda, and she adjusted her lessons to students' maps for exploring the territory of geometry.

Another teacher talked about "all the tangents kids can go off on" when they are working on a Supposer lab problem. These tangents diverge from the planned substance of a lesson, and he tried to figure out how to mediate between this kind of learning and his curriculum:

What tangents do you take off on? That's where the curriculum can bog you down. Or you can eliminate parts of the curriculum and still be able to proceed, it just means you take a slightly different path. There are all of those considerations, and then there are the considerations of whether they'll need it in some other mathematical area down the line. In fact you do, you need a big chunk of geometry. (G.S., Int.)

This teacher was concerned that if the corpus of geometry did not get communicated to his students in a particular sequence, and to all of the students at the same time, they would miss something in the curriculum or something they would need to know in a more advanced math course. He saw it as the teacher's (i.e., his) responsibility to make sure no one missed anything. Yet he also seemed to be putting the curriculum in some larger perspective by recognizing it as only one path through the subject matter.

The textbook offers teachers a way to keep in mind a clear path through the subject matter, and the Supposer challenges that security. In addition, books function in a classroom as a treaty between teachers and students about what they are supposed to be doing together in school (Powell, Farrar, & Cohen, 1985). Another teacher in the group reflected on the difficulties she had disrupting this long-standing agreement:

> I have always tried to set up problems so that kids can draw their own conclusions. The problem is that the Geometry textbook is so structured, and that's where I get all the problems... Richard (the advisor from the Lab Sites Project to the Supposer Group) said you have to pick and choose as far as what you want to discuss from the book. I'm not sure the kids are going to be happy about that.

> At this level, the students really like to have things spelled out and if you don't go over all fifteen problems in the book, they're very anxious about whether they did them correctly, whether they got the right answers. . . . What I hope to do is to take a day every couple of weeks and go over anything we haven't talked about that they're uncomfortable with, just putting the pieces together, and we'll see how that goes. It's going to be tough. It's going to be very different. (A.D., Int.)

Another teacher also said she "went over the problems in the book so students would feel secure." (J.H., Int. 2) They would have to take an exam at the end of the year, and both she and they felt more trust in the book than in the Supposer to prepare for that exam.

The question of what students learn about geometry from their own independent exploration on the Supposer, apart from how the teacher manages to incorporate those explorations into the whole class agenda was salient to the teachers as they tried to decide how much time should be spent on divergent inquiry as opposed to whole-class study. Most of the teachers were willing to experiment, however, and to see what would happen later in the course. But they did not yet know how their students' self-directed explorations fit in with what they were supposed to teach and students were supposed to learn. As one teacher said:

> I don't think they're going to get much out of [doing their own explorations after they finish the assignment] now. I think once they get to learn more geometry and we do the other projects they'll say "Oh, we did that before," and I think they'll remember them, but they're not saying too much because they don't know what is ahead of them. (B.L., Int.)

What this teacher says about students' explorations raises questions about how she defines learning geometry. She suggests that although independent exploration contributes something to learning, the explorations become knowledge only after the students learn more geometry according to her planned agenda. Like G.S., quoted previously, she is trying to figure out where the diversions from her agenda fit into the learning process.

When I asked the advisor to the teachers in the Supposer group what he thought about the problem of students' divergent learning paths, he said:

> You have to come in and teach from the philosophical view that not all learning happens when it is supposed to happen. Some people teach kids how to solve linear equations and they'll show them how to do it and they'll give them review sheet after review sheet and at the end of those two days, dammit, those kids are supposed to know it. But maybe in two months, after they've had to do a more advanced topic, usually with equations, they say, "Oh yeah," and they learn how to solve linear equations. The same kind of thing, I think, happens with all kinds of learning. (R.D. Int.)

Both R.H. and B.L. see an interaction between the path a student takes through a subject and the path that is chosen by the teacher, but they seem to value them differently. The difference may be attributable simply to experience, however, in that the teacher advisor had been through an entire year with students using the Supposer, whereas the other teacher was just beginning to see how it might fit into her way of teaching.

When is a Conjecture a Right Answer?

It is not only in the area of following the order of the problems in the book that the Supposer teachers need to renegotiate their treaties with students. The routines for using the Supposer to come up with conjectures before proving them deductively means that another essential aspect of classroom culture needs to be redefined. When students are given the assignment to produce conjectures from the data they have collected, the idea is that they should come up with as many conjectures as their data can reasonably support without concern for whether they are provable. Many of these are later discussed in class, and the ones that can be proven are retained as theorems. Others are refined or rejected because counterexamples are produced that demonstrate that they do not apply as generally as the student initially assumed.

In mathematics, the process of creating plausible conjectures and then finding the limits of their applicability is the heart of the matter, and the Supposer is designed to give this experience to teachers and students. But in school, a rejected or corrected conjecture becomes equated with a wrong answer — and students are reluctant to produce those for fear of negative teacher evaluations. This fear is disabling when lessons are based on deciding the limits of a particular conjecture and when students are to be rewarded for coming up with lots of conjectures for discussion.

One teacher said of her students, toward the end of their year of working with the Supposer:

> As far as coming up with conjectures, they still have a sense that there's a correct answer there. They still search, you know, with the idea that there are correct answers and incorrect answers to those. I don't think you could ever get away from that. [But] I think it's a real negative kind of, um, emphasis, if they always think "well just because they say something, it's wrong." And it's not. . . . I think it's something, as an adult we understand, and I'm not sure kids can. Because in every other subject they're, you know, most of the time you're either right or wrong. That's the kind of tests we give, objective tests. Um, so I'm not sure, I think it would be kind of losing battle to ever try at this age. (P.O., Int. 2)

Learning from Teachers and Learning from Peers

When students come to school, they usually behave as if their teachers possess a body of knowledge that they are to acquire. They expect to learn from their teachers, and their knowledge is legitimized by the teacher knowing they have it. Students do not come to school expecting to learn from their peers or to have what they know confirmed in conversation with their peers, but that often occurred as students worked together on Supposer lab problems.

The Supposer lab is a classroom that has microcomputers all around the walls, one for every two students. During a lab session, students generally work with a partner on a project that they have been assigned by the teacher. Because each computer is separately booted, each pair of students may have a different figure in front of them, even though they are working on the same project. After they take the measures of one figure, they call up another figure of the same type and measure its parts as well. The software is carefully designed so that not all of the figures have a base that is parallel to the bottom of the screen, and so the work students are doing actually looks quite different from one pair to another. Usually, after some initial structured activities, students decide for themselves what parts of a figure they want to measure, pursuing patterns in the data they are collecting and deciding to test conjectures by getting the sum, difference, product, or ratio of measures. This further diversifies the potential paths they take through the given problem.

This is an unusual structure for academic tasks, and it means there is a greater potential for peer communication than there would be if everyone were facing the teacher and/or the blackboard. (Doyle & Carter, 1984; Morine-Dershimer, 1983). All of these structural innovations in the way geometry is communicated to learners results in a substantial increase in students' capacities to learn mathematics independently from their teachers.

Most teachers tell you that they would like to see students "work more independently," and the teachers in this group were no exception. But with the Supposer in their classroom, they saw one version of such student independence and were surprised at what students were curious about and what they were able to do. One teacher said of her first lab session:

> I'm blown away! I didn't give my kids a menu or anything and they took off!
> (J.H. meeting, 10/9/86)

She was pleased, of course, but she was also a bit shocked by how quickly things were out of her hands. Her students had already had half a year of geometry without the Supposer (because of the way the curriculum is structured at her school), so she felt her class might be more bold than others. But in another school with the traditional sequence, pairs of students also reportedly dove into geometry with the same enthusiasm "even though they were strangers to the Supposer and to each other." In this school, the teacher observed that:

> There was a great deal of interaction between pairs of students seated at the same machine, and the discussions the kids were having were actually about geometry. . . . Word travels fast in the lab as kids make discoveries – like that you can add angles or that you need to put the vertex letter in the middle when you label angles. (B.L. meeting, 10/9/86)

Another teacher said that students "who don't talk to one another in the halls" were talking about geometry and that a lot of teaching was going on in that talking. In her school, they decided to have students share a computer terminal because they did not have enough for every student to have one. Later they decided this was a good arrangement because of all the peer teaching that occurred.

Several other teachers commented that definitions and the conventions of notation were learned as students worked together on their Supposer problems. One said:

> Studying notation and labeling on the Supposer is more interesting than on paper; it's a pick and shovel job by hand, but with the Supposer they could just see that ABC and CBA were the same. (L.H. meeting, 10/9/86)

Another said that one effect of the Supposer lessons was:

> . . . to immerse kids in geometry situations which as they explored them, caused kids to want the language and definitions in order to describe what they were discovering. They would ask, "Isn't there a word for these angles?" (M.S. meeting, 11/3/86)

At one of the Supposer Users' Group meetings, another of the teachers described a lesson she did with her class when the same sort of need arose:

> I asked them, after they had been working with the Supposer for a while, "What do you think a right triangle is?" and wrote their definitions on the board. I was excited that the kids had worked out for themselves how to label angles and that they realized which letter had to be in the middle. (B.L. meeting, 9/17/86)

Another teacher commented that it was hard at first for her students to figure out how to read an angle on the Supposer, but that they were able to figure it out by trial and error (A.D. meeting, 9/17/87). This information about terminology and labeling was formerly the property of the teacher, to be doled out to students according to a careful agenda. With the Supposer, students no longer needed their teachers to gain access to these basics.

As students learn from one another the mechanical conventions that the software uses to do things like label angles and add angles, they are also confronting the idea that you can add angles and that the way angles are labeled is functional as you move from one part of a figure to another. And they are learning these things because *they* need to know them to pursue the questions *they* were working on.

What Role Does Technology Play?

The idea that students are actually doing geometry independently as they work with the Supposer was appreciated without reservation by all of the teachers interviewed. They seemed surprised at this development and even more surprised by the fact that students were working together with their peers *on mathematics.* As one teacher described a lab session:

The thing that is most amazing to me is that mathematics is going on all the time, all the time. I assigned kids very arbitrarily to partners, and rather boy–girl, and with some eye to balancing personalities, but in most cases, these kids don't know each other. But the very first day, they were in there working together! It was just wonderful

They were really caught up in whatever was happening in the problem itself. It was a good open-ended one and it caught their imaginations. (J.H., Int. 1)

Asked whether she thought it was the technology that was responsible for their immediate engagement in the problem, she replied:

Well, it's the technology that makes it possible for them to check it out themselves. But . . . the technology also grabs them in a way that they wouldn't be, even if I gave them a really good problem at their desks. (J.H., Int.)

From this teacher's perspective, then, the technology makes it possible for students to carry on their own mathematical inquiries, "to check it out themselves," and this potential draws them directly into the process of discovering geometrical relationships. The mathematical appeal is complemented by the general appeal of having a novel technological tool available for their use in the classroom.

Another teacher commented on the appeal of the software, suggesting that the appeal for students stemmed more from what the technology enabled them to do with mathematics than from its bells and whistles:

It's not animated, it doesn't make any sound, it's not appealing in any other way other than that it is just another way of looking at the subject. To someone who likes it, this is a fantastically interesting subject, but to someone who doesn't get into this cut and dried stuff, it's dull and boring. This is a better way of enticing the students to stick with it. (B.L., Int. 1)

The teachers saw that their students were "enticed" by the software, that they didn't "fool around with it," but used it to do mathematics, even with the potential distraction of working with a partner on an independent project. But the mathematics they were doing was different from what it would have been if they had not been using the Supposer, and that difference was not fully apprehended by the teachers. The teachers' appreciation of what *students* were doing with the software mathematically was related to their own use of the Supposer to do mathematics. They talked about this as an unusual opportunity and a renewing experience. And some believed that actually doing mathematics in the classroom made them communicate with their students in a different way. The technology is a tool that enables this to happen. It frees up both teachers and students to engage in a new kind of relationship with their subject.

A department head who was one of the teachers in the Users' Group wrote to me before the school year began:

> I chose to use the *Geometric Supposer* for much the same reasons I have varied classes, textbooks, approaches, manipulative aids for the past twenty years—a need to keep vital as a teacher.
>
> My hunch is that this software will empower my students early on and they will likely come up with several hypotheses that I have never entertained. They will thus *see me playing with their hypotheses* in an attempt to convince myself of their truth or falsity. They will also work very hard (more so than usual) *to convince me* of the truth of their arguments. (M.S. letter, 9/2/86, italics added)

The teacher advisor on this project, who is also head of a high school mathematics department and a geometry teacher, felt that it is important for teachers to look at what students are doing on the Supposer with mathematical as well as pedagogical eyes:

> It's really important that the students think you are seeing conjectures for the first time and considering their responsibility. It makes them think you find it interesting, too, that math isn't something that is all finished being discovered. (R.H., Int. 1)

Another teacher in the group, who is also a department chair, expressed a different sort of connection between his own mathematical interests and his students' work with the Supposer.

> I skipped over parallel lines into triangles *because I was fascinated by them* and wanted to get started. It took me a little away from the curriculum, but it's still tied in. . . .
>
> The kids are noticing that the angles add up to 180 degrees without my telling them. It's hard for me to get used to. But the kids like the lab and feel more comfortable with it. (L.H., Int. 1, italics added)

Because the teachers were working directly on mathematics as well as on the problems of how to teach mathematics with the Supposer, they spent part of their time at Users' Group meetings working at terminals in small groups on geometry problems. More of this time was spent doing the problems than on talking about how to use them in the classroom.

The kinds of problems posed by the Supposer are challenging at different levels, and the teachers obviously enjoyed this opportunity to work on mathematics with other adults. One teacher said that these meetings were a stark contrast to department meetings at his school, where "we never come anywhere near mathematics." He talked about his work with the Supposer Users' Group as an inspiration to go back to school to study more mathematics "and really become a mathematician." (G.S., Int.) Another teacher in the group said that she enjoyed doing the problems on the Supposer herself because:

> There comes a time as a teacher when you have to do something for yourself to keep your mind active. This is just a great opportunity for me. (B.L. meeting, 9/17/86)

Thus teachers recognized that sharpening their own mathematical skills is good preparation for coping with the unpredictability of students' independent explorations on the Supposer.

Who is Responsible if a Learner Takes a Wrong Turn?

The power the Supposer gives students to take off on their own and teach one another made the teachers in this group anxious at the same time that it excited them. At an early meeting of the Supposer Users' Group, one teacher was uneasy about whether the conventions for labeling figures that students developed while using the Supposer would be correct in the terms that might be expected on standardized tests. He also had a deeper worry about the broad course of students' independent inquiry:

> What if kids are doing this off by themselves on the computer, what would happen if they got the wrong idea and went off on a wrong tangent and you weren't there to go with them? (L.H. meeting, 9/17/86)

His anxiety hit a responsive chord in most of the teachers in the group, and as the discussion continued, the staff offered some reassuring comments. One researcher said that the software is designed to help students correct their own mistakes:

> They might just go down a wrong path, but eventually they notice things aren't working and they correct themselves. (D.C. meeting, 9/17/86)

The teacher advisor to the group added:

> It is frustrating and worrisome initially, not knowing what students are doing. The payoff of teaching with the Supposer comes later in the course and you just have to have faith in the early weeks. (R.H. meeting, 9/17/86)

"Having faith" that students are learning what they need to know from the Supposer technology and from one another does not come easily to teachers, because they are responsible to students and parents for the outcome of the experiment. If the teacher takes charge of the agenda, at least he or she can claim that material was covered, even if it was not learned.

The teachers' anxiety about whether students learn what they should exists side by side with their appreciation of the way the Supposer opens a direct line from students to subject matter. One teacher gave up the idea of using the Supposer at a large monitor in front of the classroom (the way she used the blackboard) for teacher- directed lessons. Her students came up with lots of different ideas, which they all wanted to pursue at once.

> I put the problem on the monitor and these kids, granted, knew a lot of geometry. We started some things, started to generate some pictures, and so on. . . . We had fights going on in the classroom. It was a talky group in that class, very verbal, but they were arguing and screaming with one another about the input that I was going to put on the computer. Right then, I said to myself, "We're going to need more than one of these, because certain kids want to take some idea and go with it in their direction and if you don't have enough computers and software to do that, *you are really robbing that student from the thought that he or she wants to continue.*" So immediately after I had exposed a set of students to it, I knew that the only way to teach it was to give them their own individual pieces of software.

> Then we brought the students in here to the computer lab, and they just went crazy. They were all doing their own problems and their own discoveries, and it was wonderful. (P.O., Int., italics added)

Despite her enthusiasm for the students' independent explorations and her appreciation of their importance, this teacher was also quite nervous about letting her students go on the computer right from the beginning of the year. If she had not been receiving regular support from the teacher advisor, she would have begun the year using the Supposer only in teacher-directed lessons with a large monitor at the front of the room:

> After my first experience, I knew that if I were to do the Supposer, I would have wanted to try it this way [with students having their own computers and software], but at this point, I think I would have backed off from that and waited until they knew a lot more geometry. . . . I would have used it more as a teaching tool right now rather than have discovery methods. It's not as good a method of teaching it, but I think that's what I would have done until I was more comfortable with the software. (P.O., Int.)

Her reasons for this hesitation had partly to do with her worries about her knowledge of the software, but they also had to do with the management problems raised by having students going off in all different directions while she was struggling to figure out the mechanics of the technology. Her feelings were shared by the other teachers in the group; they did not often separate their concerns about the classroom management problems associ-ated with the new technology and the more substantial content control issues. This same teacher recounted a particular example of her frustration and compared herself to the teacher advisor who had had more experience teaching with the Supposer:

> When the problem just tells the kids to "generate an isosceles triangle," you've got narrow ones, wide ones, and it's hard because the students are concerned. They're saying "I have a question" and you're going from one real specific problem to another very specific problem. And you as a teacher have all that general information in your head and you're listening to what they're saying and you find yourself feeling very fractured. (P.O., Int. 1)

All these changes in the classroom culture—students learning important material from peers, ambiguity about right and wrong answers, and negotiating the sequence of lessons around student discoveries—mean both more and different kinds of work for teachers who support the kind of inductive inquiry that the Supposer is designed to enable. Even as students enjoy their independent exploration of geometric problems, teachers must guide their activities toward mathematically productive ends. This is both easier and more difficult than getting students to do the problems at the end of each textbook chapter successfully.

The sort of teaching envisioned by the designers of the Supposer materials is what Thomas Green (1971) called *instruction* as opposed to the more commonly found *indoctrination*. The distinction rests on students having *reasons*—both inductive and deductive—for accepting the truths of geometry, rather than accepting them because they are in the book or because they are expounded by a teacher. Having reasons gives students a degree of intellectual and social autonomy that they do not otherwise possess, and it brings the work they do in classrooms closer to the work of the scientist and mathematician (Polya, 1954). But teaching in a way that guides students' inquiry and recognizing that what is taught is not the same as what is learned cannot but make a teacher feel "fractured." It requires a different kind of energy than indoctrinating students to the important facts and skills in a discipline according to a neat and comprehensive agenda. In the words of Robertson Davies (1981):

> To instruct calls for energy, and to remain silent, but watchful and helpful, while students instruct themselves calls for even greater energy. To see someone fall (which will teach him not to fall again) when a word from you

would keep him on his feet but ignorant of an important danger, is one of the tasks of the teacher that calls for special energy, because holding in is much more demanding than crying out. (p. 231)

It also takes more time and a more demanding relationship with students than teaching by telling. Nevertheless, the Supposer teachers in the Laboratory Sites Study, among others, believe it is a worthwhile way to spend their teaching energy. Although all have reservations, each of the teachers said he or she would use these tools again the following year and help other geometry teachers learn to use it as well.

ACKNOWLEDGMENTS

Preparation of this report was supported in part by the Office of Educational Research and Improvement (Contract # OERI 400-83-0041). Opinions expressed herein are not necessarily shared by OERI and do not represent Office policy. The Geometric Supposer was developed at the Education Development Center (Newton, MA) and is published by Sunburst Communications.

REFERENCES

Bowers, C. A. (1987). *The promise of theory: Education and the politics of cultural change.* New York: Teachers College Press.

Brouwer, L. E. J. (1913). Intuitionism & Formalism. American Mathematical Society Bulletin, *20,* 81–96.

Cohen, D. K. (1988). Educational technology and school organization. In R. S. Nickerson & P. Zodhiates (Eds.), *Technology in education: Looking toward 2020* (pp. 8–27). Hillsdale, NJ: Lawrence Erlbaum Associates.

Davis, P. J., & Hersh, R. (1981). *The mathematical experience.* Boston: Houghton-Mifflin.

Davies, R. (1981). *Rebel angels.* Penguin.

Doyle, W. (1985). *Content representations in teachers' definitions of academic work.* Austin, TX: University of Texas at Austin, Research and Development Center for Teacher Education.

Doyle, W., & Carter, K. (1984). Academic tasks in classrooms. *Curriculum Inquiry, 14,* 129–149.

Florio-Ruane, S. (1987). *Teaching as response: The problem of writing conferences.* (Working paper). Department of Teacher Education, Michigan State University, East Lansing, MI.

Goodlad, J. I. (1984). *A place called school: Prospects for the future.* New York: McGraw Hill.

Green, T. F. (1971). *The activities of teaching.* New York: McGraw Hill.

Guskey, T. R. (1986). Staff development & the process of teacher change. *Educational Researcher, 15*(5), 5–12.

Hadamard, J. (1945). *An essay on the psychology of invention in the mathematical field.* Princeton, NJ: Princeton University Press.

Jackson, P. W. (1970). *Life in classrooms.* New York: Holt, Rinehart, & Winston.

Kitcher, P. (1984). *The nature of mathematical knowledge*. New York: Oxford University Press.

Kline, M. (1980). *Mathematics: The loss of certainty*. NY: Oxford University Press.

Lakatos, I. (1976). *Proofs and refutations: The logic of mathematical discovery*. Cambridge: Cambridge University Press.

Morine-Dershimer, G. (1983). Instructional strategy and the "creation" of classroom status. *American Educational Research Journal, 20*, 645–661.

Niven, I. (1987). Can geometry survive in the secondary curriculum? In M. M. Lindquist & A. P. Shuttle (Eds.),*Learning and teaching geometry, K–12* (pp. 37–46). Washington, DC: National Council of Teachers of Mathematics.

Petrie, H. G. (1981). *The dilemma of enquiry and learning*. Chicago: University of Chicago Press.

Polanyi, M. (1960). *Personal knowledge: Towards a post-critical philosophy*. Chicago: University of Chicago Press.

Polya, G. (1954). *Induction and analogy in mathematics: A guide to the art of plausible reasoning*. Princeton, NJ: Princeton University Press.

Powell, A. G., Farrar, E., & Cohen, D. K. (1985). *The shopping mall high school: Winners & losers in the educational marketplace*. Boston: Houghton Mifflin.

Putnam, R. (1987). Structuring and adjusting content for students: A study of live and simulated tutoring of addition. *American Educational Research Journal, 24*, 13–48.

Resnick, L. (1987, April). Learning in school and out. Presidential Address. Paper presented at the annual meeting of American Educational Research Association, Washington, DC.

Romberg, T., & Carpenter, T. (1986). Research on teaching and learning mathematics: Two disciplines of scientific inquiry. In M. C. Wittrock (Ed.), *Handbook of research on teaching* (3rd ed, pp. 850–973). New York: Macmillan.

Russell, B. (1948). *Human knowledge, its scope and limits*. New York: Simon & Schuster.

Schoenfeld, A.H. (1987). On having and using geometric knowledge. In J. Hiebert (Ed.), *Conceptual and procedural knowledge: The case of mathematics* (pp. 225–264). Hillsdale, NJ: Lawrence Erlbaum Associates.

Schoenfeld, A. H. (1988). When good teaching leads to bad results: The disasters of "well taught" mathematics courses. *Educational Psychologist, 23*, 145–166.

Senk, S. (1985). How well do students write geometry proofs? *Mathematics Teacher, 78*, 448–456.

Stephens, M. (1982). *Mathematical knowledge and school work: A case study of the teaching of developing mathematical processes*. (Project Report). Madison, WI: Wisconsin Center for Educational Research.

Thompson, A. G. (1985). Teachers' conceptions of mathematics and the teaching of problem solving. In E. A. Silber (Ed.), *Teaching and learning mathematical problem solving: Multiple research perspectives* (pp. 281–294). Hillsdale, NJ: Lawrence Erlbaum Associates.

Usiskin, Z. (1987). Resolving the continuing dilemmas in school geometry. In M. M. Lindquist & A. P. Shuttle (Eds.),*Learning and teaching geometry, K–12* (pp. 17–32). Washington, DC: National Council of Teachers of Mathematics.

van Gennep, A. (1975). *The rites of passage*. Chicago: University of Chicago Press.

Yerushalmy, M., & Houde, R. (1986). The Geometric Supposer: Promoting thinking and learning. *Mathematics Teacher, 77*, 418–421.

9 How the Supposer Changed My Life: An Autobiography

Richard Houde
Weston, Massachusetts School System

Back in 1983, I think I was the first teacher to work seriously with the Geometric Supposer. Since then I have been an advisor to other teachers. I have also run workshops for teachers and have developed materials dealing with ways to use the Supposer and to teach geometry. I often reflect on how much of all that has happened I might have anticipated.

I don't think I had many conscious expectations back then. I was intrigued with the possibilities the software opened for me as a teacher. I kept trying to learn more and more about it, and one thing led to another. I must say I'm impressed by the way the Geometric Supposer has become a household word in educational circles today. Textbook publishers who want to incorporate the use of computers into their pupil texts look to the Supposer, and researchers enamored of the type of thinking and learning that goes on in that environment are trying to mimic its effects in new pieces of software. The Supposer has achieved a status and notoriety unequaled in computer software designed for use in mathematics classrooms. I feel that it was Judah Schwartz's mission to have the Supposer embraced by the National Council of Teachers of Mathematics (NCTM) and by the larger math education community, and it really is happening now. But that was never my personal mission. Mine was always smaller, just to make the teaching environment better, because I love teaching. The furthest thing from my mind when I first saw the software in 1983 was that I would become such a part of the Supposer story—or that the Supposer would change my life the way it has.

I suppose that one reason I found the Supposer as attractive as I did goes back to the way I was taught mathematics. The course that had the most profound effect on me during my graduate education in mathematics was Harvey Carruth's "Foundations of Mathematics" course at The University of Tennessee (UT). I'll never forget either the course or Harvey. He used no textbook and no notes. Each class consisted of a few definitions and ideas. When it was over, we went home to prove theorems that we then presented in class. We knew we were behaving as working mathematicians. I always dreaded being called on, of course, because you looked bad if you couldn't do the homework. But we moaned and groaned together. Students developed the course under his guidance, learned mathematics, and there was great comraderie.

Let me hasten to add that not all of my own mathematics education had that flavor. I went to Bridgewater State Teachers College and did a semester of student teaching. I remember that my supervising teacher gave me a B; I had all I could do to prepare lessons, keep control, and conduct classes. I left Bridgewater to earn a master's degree at Clark University where I also taught as a graduate teaching assistant. That meant attending lectures and then conducting question-and-answer sessions for 15 students per class. Later I taught for 3 years at Assumption College and then went on to the University of Tennessee where I worked as a graduate teaching assistant for 3 more years.

All of that, however, did very little to prepare me for teaching geometry in high school. When I left UT and came to teach at Weston High School, I received quite a shock! I was a lecturer by training. I expected students to listen to me while I told them what they should know. Needless to say, it didn't work that way with high school students. They responded with intense listlessness to the lectures. They did their work, but their hearts weren't in it. They reacted best when I was able to make the mathematics interesting, when they owned part of the action, when they could work with classmates, and when they could solve their own problems. Increasingly, I found myself searching for ways to make my classes more "interesting," to include students in the action while teaching them what they were supposed to learn. I don't know why I wasn't doing that anyway, given that the best mathematics course I ever took had been the one in which Harvey was an enthusiastic guide and we were willing explorers. Of all the courses I taught, geometry seemed to lend itself most readily to Harvey's approach, because there were plenty of postulates and definitions and plenty of theorems for kids to prove. For 5 years I taught geometry as a rigorous deductive course. My honors students thought it was a really "tough" course. Then the next year I decided to try it Harvey's way, teaching without a book. It was a total bomb. It was so much work to organize, and the kids were lost.

Even though the experiment flopped, it showed me that geometry was a course in which you could easily involve students in conjecturing. I started conducting classes in which I had students close their books. I introduced ideas and had them work with the ideas until we had developed a theorem together. Students copied drawings from the board, measured elements within drawings with rulers, formed conjectures, and tried to prove them. They came to enjoy this format so much that it became almost a ritual for me to try to plan classes with my students as the focus and me as guide and director. Doing things this way, I found that students were actually proving theorems instead of just watching me do it and copying my work to spit back later. We made geometry together and had fun doing it. My colleagues were teaching geometry in the more traditional lecture format, but because we were all teaching the same material, it didn't cause any stirs. I thought my students enjoyed math more my way, but . . . .

It was about this time that the Supposer came along. My introduction to it is as real to me today as it was when it happened in the spring of 1983. Judah Schwartz of MIT had received permission from Gus Sayer, Weston's Assistant Superintendent for Curriculum, to call me about visiting the school to display a piece of computer software he had been developing. During a phone conversation, Judah briefly outlined what the Supposer could do, and when I said our geometry teachers would be interested in such a piece of software, he told me that a graduate student of his would be calling me to set up a time when she could come to display the software. Shortly thereafter, Michal Yerushalmy called, and we set up a series of visits to three classrooms where she observed teachers teach and used the software with pairs of randomly chosen students at a terminal in the back of each room.

During Michal's visit to one of my classes, I noticed that my students seemed to be having a lot of fun with her at the computer. I gave the class something to do, went to the back of the room to see for myself and couldn't believe my eyes. Here were students making drawings, measuring elements within drawings, and making guesses about relationships between elements within drawings. They were having more fun with the software than they had with me for quite some time.

At the end of the period, when Michal asked two students what they thought they had been doing at the computer, one of them responded, "I was supposing!" To this day, I don't know whether the Supposer got its name from that remark, but the memory is so vivid that I want to believe that one of my students named the tool!

After Michal had completed her visits to classrooms, we set up a meeting for her and Judah to talk with all the geometry teachers in the department about using the Supposer in geometry classrooms. Judah began the meeting with two questions: "Why do you like teaching geometry?" and "How do you teach geometry?" The teachers and I were taken aback by the questions, because we thought Judah wanted to talk about computers, not about mathematics and teaching. We sat for 45 minutes answering those two questions, and Judah said he would get back to us after he decided what he wanted to do next. A week later he called to ask who might be interested in meeting further. When I said that I was, he sent Michal back to make plans for the coming year. A mathematics angel had arrived, and I didn't even know it.

I was ready and willing because the Supposer seemed like a tool that could fit beautifully with what I was already doing in class, and it had the plus that students would have more control and could work faster and do more with it. The Supposer had a lot going for it. Computers were the latest thing then, but you didn't have to know a thing about computers to use the Supposer (I classified myself then as a computer illiterate). Also, the Supposer was visual, a bit like computer games, which the kids liked.

My first year with the Supposer in the classroom was exciting. My school was very supportive; they gave me release time to work with Michal Yerushalmy preparing materials, developing teaching strategies, and reviewing student work. They never checked up on what I was doing — at least not that I was ever aware of.

I started out designing problems for students to do. Then Michal would come to observe as students worked on them, and we'd spend hours discussing students' work and writing and revising problems. I really looked forward to Michal's visits, because she was so interested in what I was doing. She freely gave me her ideas, came up with great problems, and put the software onto the school's VAX. For a year, we worked with only six computer terminals. We split the classes in half and ran around trying to be in two places at the same time. Kids really enjoyed being trusted to work without me around. They liked writing up projects, working with each other, trying new things, and having me work with them. Of course, they also loved finding things that I claimed I didn't know about.

One incident I'll always remember happened during an exercise on using the formula $A = .5 \times b \times h$ to find the area of a triangle. Two girls excitedly called me to their terminal and asked, "Why are these two angles equal?" (obtuse triangle with three altitudes). I was taken aback, because I had no idea why the two angles they were pointing to were equal, and because the drawing was not complicated, I felt I should have known. Furthermore, I always made sure that I looked at student homework assignments ahead of time to be sure that I could do every problem, so I wouldn't be embarrassed. So here I was, not knowing why, and put on the spot to answer. When I finally mumbled something like, "I don't know but I'll work on it," the girls responded, "That's okay," and immediately went on to something else. I was shocked! Why weren't they upset with me because I didn't know? Didn't they think that I was supposed to know? They made me feel so comfortable about not knowing that I began to suspect that "Not to know is okay with students as long as you're honest and offer to work on the problem." What they really enjoyed was just having me talk with them about problems. I knew then that teaching with the Supposer could be liberating as well as challenging.

Although I was slowly beginning to learn how to think differently about my class and my students, I still had some reservations. One of my initial fears about using the Supposer was what the parents of my students would think. My fears were heightened by an experience I had 10 years earlier when I used the geometry text, Transformational Geometry. Parents had called the principal asking questions like, "Are we still teaching geometry?" "Where can I find tutors who can teach about transformations?" "Are the kids going to get what they're supposed to get?"

There were so many questions that the principal felt compelled to organize a parent meeting one morning where I had to present what I was doing and explain why. It was pretty unnerving. I felt my audience did not have a good grasp of what mathematics was all about, and I didn't do a good job of explaining what the course was all about. In fact, I created more questions in people's minds than were already there. A couple of parents used the meeting to complain about the mathematics program in general, and some parents who had axes to grind with specific teachers did so. It was a terrible meeting.

The principal called me into his office later that afternoon and said, "Look, we've got to get these parents off our backs. They'll use up all our time. What can we do?" We settled on passing out a second geometry book that had been used the previous year and teaching from both books. The next year, the Transformational Geometry book sat on the shelves and didn't appear at all except in the form of two xeroxed chapters. So, when I began having students use the Supposer in the lab, I waited for the parents' reactions. To my great surprise and pleasure, there were no phone calls, no comments one way or the other. I guess that because kids were using computers and seeming to enjoy it, everything was okay. Computers were the rage in schools then, so I was safe.

In addition to my concern about the reaction of parents, from time to time I had qualms about whether my students were learning enough. But I soon found out that in some ways they could learned more than I ever would have expected. My first inclinations were to use the Supposer for discovery of geometric relationships/ideas, so I gave students discovery problems that were much like the ones I had been using for the previous few years without the Supposer. I had students go to the lab, where I provided a problem for them to do. I asked them to collect data and then make conjectures about what might be true. The problems that I gave them were all from my textbook—things like the sum of the angles in a triangle, the midline theorem, and so on.

Michal thought the problems were okay, but after the first month of work, she began to push her problems at me. They tended to be very open-ended and often involved applications of what students had learned. At first I balked at using them. I didn't know what the kids would do. I thought the problems would be too hard and that my students wouldn't get anything out of them. I was worried, because I wouldn't have solutions for.them. I was afraid the kids would get hopelessly confused, that they would be asked to stretch beyond their capacity.

Finally, one day I relented and told Michal that I would try one. Well, the kids loved it! They came up with a million ideas, the lab was alive and animated. Rich ideas flowed, and I knew then that my perceptions of what kids could do had to change, because this tool gave them the power to express ideas that I had never been able to tap before. I guess that's when I learned that teachers don't always know what students' limits are. If more teachers understood that, they might teach differently.

That was a sort of turning point in my use of the Supposer. I used it in a more open-ended way from then on, albeit with plenty of prodding from Michal. She really pushed me to my limits that year. She was forever trying to stretch my thinking on ways to present geometry to kids using the Supposer. Many times she was impatient for me to do more, but when she sensed I was getting a bit uptight about something, she backed off. Through the Supposer, she asked me to think more about teaching geometry than I had been able to ask myself during 10 years of teaching. The more I worked at it, the more I grew, and the more confident I got.

I think the main thing for me was that teaching with the Supposer was so much fun. My students took a personal interest in their work and asked me to be a part of it. I looked forward to lab periods, because the students often presented unpredictable situations involving new problems that required new and different solutions. For example, one day I asked the students to classify all triangles whose sides are represented by three consecutive integer lengths. After working on the problems for 10 minutes, two students called me to their work station and said, "We can't go any further than 9, 10, 11 for sides of triangles. What should we do now?" I agreed that they could not use the Supposer any longer, because "obviously the Supposer cannot make a triangle with sides whose lengths were 20, 21, and 22 length units." (Screen limitations require that the lengths of lines that are inputted by the user be smaller than 10.) Immediately, from another place in the room, a student who had been listening to our conversation shouted, "That's absolutely false. Just use 2.0, 2.1, and 2.2 for the sides!" I was stunned. This student was using the notion of similar triangles, and I had not even thought of it or presented the concept in class. I praised the student profusely for such an ingenious solution. He certainly had given me an idea to remember for a long time to come.

That was not an isolated incident. There were plenty of such moments.

One time, two students were working on a problem involving similar triangles and called me to their work station, because the Supposer was "computing degrees a little bit off." They were comparing products of appropriate angles rather than comparing their ratios, and round-off errors that did not appear with ratios were now appearing and making them think they had made a mistake. I had never seen students use products of degree measures of angles in this manner, and it took me by such surprise that the students asked, "Did we do something wrong?" I laughed and replied, "Absolutely not." The Supposer had misled them into thinking they had made a mistake. When I asked them to check their work using ratios, everything checked out. Students posed some questions and conjectures that I was never able to answer, prove, or provide counterexamples. I worked with them for awhile, but if no solutions emerged, I would defer them until later. I'm sure that many of their ideas, if carefully analyzed, would have led to theorems that my courses never presented.

When students came up with unexpected ideas like that, it began to affect my thinking about the geometry curriculum I was teaching and was supposed to teach. Wanting my students to use the Supposer forced me more and more to ask why I was teaching particular topics or sections of my text. I knew that lab periods for Supposer work cut into my class time for the presentations that I had always made, so I had to decide what was most important for students to study in the time available. Or, if I decided that everything was still important to do, then I had to think of ways to do it all more efficiently. I used teaching strategies and techniques that I had never tried before. For example, I had students do textbook assignments with no introductions from me (something I had previously shied away from); I reviewed homework every third day rather than every day; I graded Supposer project papers very subjectively (but fairly, the best I could do); I presented lab problems as packages rather than one at a time; I left students alone to complete their work (except that with in-class projects, I would ask to see their work at the end of a period, so that I wouldn't feel guilty that they hadn't done anything!). I scheduled meetings with students before and after school to discuss their work. What made these meetings different was that instead of asking, "How do you do this problem?" students often began with, "Well, this is where we are, here is what we've found. Does it make sense? Are we on the right track? Is this what you want?" The presence of the Supposer forced me into thinking differently about what I taught and how I taught it. The process was invigorating but also emotionally draining and scary at times, because I always wanted to be sure that my students were getting what they were supposed to get.

It did not take long before my work with the Supposer began to take me away from the classroom and into other areas of professional activity. I had been working with Michal in anonymity for about 3 months when Judah

Schwartz called and asked me to make a 1-hour presentation at the Educational Technology Center (ETC) at Harvard as part of ETC's "Targets of Difficulty" series. When I asked him what he wanted me to talk about, he replied, "Oh, just talk about what you've been doing with the Supposer this year." I asked whether there would be an audience, and Judah replied, "Just a few people who work here at ETC." I agreed to speak, and we set a date.

Two weeks later, when I went to my school mailbox, I was shocked to receive a folder containing large cardboard advertisements for my presentation. Seeing my name in bold letters, I remember thinking, "Oh my god, what have I gotten myself into." I considered myself nothing more or less than a schoolteacher doing my job, trying to use computers to teach geometry, and now a group of university people were interested. At that point, my contact with Harvard University had been limited to walking by some of its buildings on Saturday nights out with my wife and friends.

That presentation at ETC is as vivid to me today as it was the day it happened. I remember walking into a room, expecting to see just a few people, and seeing at least 30 strangers. Computer wires were running all over the place, and there was a microphone. For me, it was the works. Judah introduced me to several people before the session started, and he gave me a glowing introduction to the group (I hardly even knew him). A few people asked interesting, probing questions during the talk, and afterwards, others came up to say nice things. It was an incredible high, because not only did people seem to like what I had done with the Supposer, but they also liked what I had to say about teaching and how computers related to it.

This was the first time during 15 years of teaching that I had ever felt that other people thought about teaching as I did. I had received good feedback from students, parents, and school administrators about my teaching over the years, but I never felt it as intensely as I did on that particular day. A similar feeling occurred a few months later when people laughed and nodded in approval during another ETC presentation I gave for school people in the area. I came away from my work that year and from those two presentations with a new confidence that I had something important to say and shouldn't be afraid to say it. So in that sense, yes, my work with the Supposer had a dramatic impact on my professional career. Eventually it led to opportunities I'd never envisioned.

Some people have suggested that teachers and university people live in different worlds, and in a way I found this to be true. I was shocked by their lack of awareness of the function of teaching and its relationships to other aspects of schooling. The more I discussed teaching with university professors, the more I realized that they didn't have a good grasp of what was happening in schools beyond what they saw when they visited classrooms. At first it disturbed me, but after thinking about it for awhile, I realized how impossible it is to live in both worlds. The goals of a university for its staff are not easily compatible with the goals of schools. Given how much universities and schools had to learn about each other, I began to see a place where I fit in. I was a school person with something to say and a soapbox (the Supposer) on which to say it.

Before I knew it, I had gone from being a department chairperson/teacher in a small suburban school system to being a teacher with a regional/national reputation. What I had to say about using the Supposer had given me so much exposure regarding how to use computers that teachers, school administrators, and university professors from all over the country were inviting me to give presentations/workshops. I was even invited to a weekend conference to plan a summer in-service program for teachers using computers to teach mathematics and computer science.

The ironic thing was that I had rarely used computers before my experience with the Supposer, and here I was being invited to give my thoughts about teaching computer science. I had never even taught my school's computer programming course, much less a computer science course. When I told the conference organizers that I was not the person for the job, they were not deterred. "Oh, that's okay," they replied, "we just want you to give us an idea of where teachers are coming from on these issues."

What messages did I have for those outside the classroom — researchers, school administrators, computer people? Judah Schwartz says that, when comparing computer and noncomputer teaching environments, "Teaching with computers may not be easier, but it's far richer." I believe Judah is correct, but his thinking is futuristic because most schools are not equipped to make teaching with computers richer. I tried to give people a teacher's perspective on that.

Ten years ago, a lot of schools climbed on the computer bandwagon because they thought they had to. Computers were the latest thing, and unless your school used them, you weren't keeping up with the times. Unfortunately, what wasn't keeping up with the times was administrators' understanding of how the technology could or should be used. Many schools associated the use of computers with computer programming. Even now, a dozen years later, countless teachers compete with computer programming classes for use of computer labs, and there simply are not enough computer labs to go around. I couldn't use the Supposer circles disk unless I taught topics on circles during the first semester because the school's Apple lab was used every period during the second semester for word processing classes.

I tried to generate some discussion of other problems that arise when using software like the Supposer, for example, the way students sometimes need to work longer than just 45–50 minutes at a time. Often double periods worked best, but they are not available to mathematics teachers. Science classes in my school (and this is true in most schools) had a lock on double periods for labs in the master schedule. If other classes asked for double periods, "the schedule would get messed up." At the moment, computers are causing "messes," and until schools can learn to deal with them, teachers won't find it richer to use computers in their teaching.

Eventually I started helping other teachers learn to use the Supposer. In so doing, I was forced to think about the people who were most likely to "run with" the Supposer and do what it takes to learn to use it effectively in their teaching. I found that those who are like I was when I was first introduced to the Supposer, namely people who are already exploring discovery and inquiry modes of teaching, were most likely to be ready to hear what I had to say. More traditional teachers may stick with it for a while but then return to their old ways, using the Supposer some of the time but never adopting an active inquiry mode. Also, I also found that those who really knew their way around geometry were more comfortable than those for whom the subject was less familiar. In the end, I've come to believe that this is almost a necessity to be comfortable using this tool.

I would say the teachers who made the biggest shifts in their teaching were all people who liked working closely with students. They worked with students after school, and they were interested in the total school life of their students, not just how they were doing in geometry. They had a good understanding of their subject matter, and they were open minded. They were good listeners, soft critics with kids and with each other. They all enjoyed teamwork, and all were seeking something to make their teaching richer, better. They were not afraid of change, even in their personal lives. Their teaching was always changing.

Like me, these teachers worried about things like scheduling lab time, finding time to do all they wanted to do with the Supposer, and still covering everything else they felt they needed to cover. They worried about grading and about how they would be seen by other teachers. They'd ask things like, "Should I invite them (teachers, administrators) in to see what I'm doing, or will it look like I'm showing off?" There can be pride and competitiveness among teachers in a school. The innovators may be more valued by the principal or department head, and that threatens some teachers: "If Mary does this, maybe I will be expected to do it, too."

In the end, though, the most important issue has to do with the differences in kids' learning. Maybe the most significant difference is that there's very little boredom, disinterest, and anger about their time being wasted. I never heard, "Why do I have to know this stuff?" when I used the Supposer. Students see it not only as geometry but also as playing with ideas, learning to communicate. I think they value that. Used to its best advantage, the Supposer is very close to what they see in their other classes. In an English class, they're asked to write a paper, to begin from nothing and create. This tool can be used in that way to create mathematics. In a social studies class, they are encouraged to look at a particular issue from multiple perspectives; with the Supposer, too, they can choose different paths and perspectives to pursue. So it provides a more open-ended environment, much like what they see as part of good teaching in their other classes.

Working in pairs and participating in discussions about their findings in lab sessions, they also learn a lot about communication and collaboration. The paper-and-pencil tests used in Supposer studies measure geometry outcomes, but they miss the other sorts of things teachers value: cooperation, respect, helping. It could be argued that those things are more important; if they learn math, too, so much the better.

Some people say that this more open-ended approach is not equally beneficial for all students. Indeed, it bothers some kids initially, and it's an indictment of education that it especially bothers those of low ability. They have usually been taught in a very linear way, and when they're faced with the Supposer for the first time, it really bothers them that it's so open. One teacher I know was successful at reaching those sorts of kids. She was very patient, good at seeing the details involved for students in their learning and then taking them through the steps she thought were necessary for them. She was willing for them to practice and practice, where I would get frustrated and want them not to take so long.

Sometimes the kids are impatient, too. The question is, how do you stand their impatience. When something goes wrong with the computer for these kids, it's much more of a problem for them than it is for a higher ability student. High ability kids start to problem solve. Low ability students often get mad when things aren't working, so you have to be very patient and help talk them through the problem. If there is a mistake in the directions, high ability students see the mistake, work through it, and then point it out to you. Low ability kids get all mixed up and get totally frustrated. So you have to have teachers with a great deal of patience and teachers who are really skilled at using the tool. I would rather see the Supposer not used than to see kids get frustrated, turned off, angry.

When all is said and done, the greatest strength of the Geometric Supposer and the way in which I have come to teach with it is that kids come to understand that mathematics is relationships between ideas and that it's not set in concrete. The tool allows kids to explore ideas on their own, then come to a teacher or to each other for feedback. The teacher's role is to be sure that everyone learns what's in this year's curriculum, but students enjoy it so much more when they learn it in pursuit of their own ideas. That's the key—their own ideas. That's why it hooks them. That's why it hooked me.

IV PROBLEMS OF IMPLEMENTATION

10

From Recitation to Construction: Teachers Change With New Technologies

Martha Stone Wiske
Harvard Graduate School of Education

Richard Houde
Weston, Massachusettes School System

Mathematics education has been widely criticized for concentrating too much on rote memorization of facts and algorithms and for failing to teach students how to pose and solve problems (National Council of Teachers of Mathematics [NCTM], 1988; National Research Council [NRC], 1985; National Science Board on Precollege Education [NSBC], 1983). Recently, computer technology has been hailed as a tool with the potential to help shift mathematics education away from recitation of ready-made knowledge toward active inquiry and construction of knowledge. Equipped with appropriate software, computers enable users to gather, manipulate, and represent mathematical data in ways that are impractical or impossible with traditional technologies like paper, pencil, and chalkboards. In this way, computers help students and teachers gain access to a broader range of mathematical forms and ideas. Computers also become learning stations where students work independently or in small groups; teachers are then able to guide students' inquiry as they circulate among the stations. (Hawkins & Sheingold, 1986; U.S. Congress, 1988.) Thus, computer technology supports a more constructive, student-centered approach than the traditional teacher-centered recitation format.

Making this tantalizing vision a classroom reality is not easy, however. Purchasing hardware and software does not automatically change classroom practice and curriculum. Close observation of efforts to integrate technology-enhanced guided inquiry into classrooms reveals that this process entails profound shifts in educational goals, practice, curriculum, and classroom roles and structures (Amaral, 1983; Martin, 1987). One must understand the nature and difficulty of making these shifts if one is to provide the resources needed to incorporate new technologies into improved mathematics instruction.

This chapter examines the efforts of a group of secondary school geometry teachers to shift their instruction toward guided inquiry with the use of the Geometric Supposer. The study focuses on the evolution of the teachers' concerns, especially the curricular and pedagogical dilemmas they faced during their second year of working with this innovative approach. Finally, the chapter analyzes several themes in these teachers' experiences that are likely to reappear whenever teachers try to shift from the predominant recitation mode of "teaching as telling" to the widely recommended, but difficult, process of joining students in a process of constructing and critiquing knowledge.

Goals of the Study

The Geometric Supposer (Schwartz & Yerushalmy, 1985–1987) is designed to help teachers and students construct knowledge of geometry inductively, developing conjectures and testing them empirically. The Geometric Supposer's developers hope the software enables teachers and students to build their knowledge of geometry through empirical investigations, recognizing the limits of particular cases as evidence for general truths, and appreciating the need for formal proofs to establish theorems. In short, they hope this innovation, meaning both the technology and ways of using it, facilitates an instructional approach that integrates inductive and deductive reasoning.

This approach to geometry approximates the way geometers work, indeed the way mathematics is made, but it differs radically from the way geometry and other forms of mathematics are usually taught in schools. Most textbooks present geometry as a tight deductive system of theorems built elegantly from an initial set of definitions and postulates. Teachers of secondary school geometry normally organize their course around their textbook. They present topics in the same order as they appear in the text, often believing (Lampert, 1988a) that this sequence both reflects the logical structure of the subject matter and conveys this structure to students in the most coherent way. Teachers commonly present material in class and assign related readings and problems from the textbook as homework. Tests require students to recall definitions and theorems and to use these to produce proofs. The formal two-column proof that many teachers regard as the backbone of their geometry course is, for many students, a fragile construct of partially memorized rules whose relationship to empirical evidence is poorly understood at best. Like most of school mathematics, geometry is usually taught as a body of knowledge to be rehearsed, memorized, and parroted (Sirotnik, 1983). As Judah Schwartz, one author of the Geometric Supposer, is fond of saying, "If English were taught this way, students would be required to memorize passages from Shakespeare, Donne, Emerson, and Hemingway, but never asked to write a word" (Schwartz, 1989).

Understanding the Metacurriculum

An overarching goal of this study is to clarify what is entailed in taking advantage of this new technology to incorporate inductive reasoning into a high school geometry course. This is seen as a step toward helping students understand what mathematics is and how it is made. We call this instructional agenda and approach a metacurriculum, because it aims to teach students *about* the usual curriculum—about how geometric knowledge is constructed and how they can participate in that process. During the course of this study, participants became clearer about what the metacurriculum includes. The clarification was largely implicit, however, and subject to variation across individuals. At the risk of suggesting more clarity and consensus about the metacurriculum than actually existed, we describe it here to orient the reader.

The metacurriculum for this innovation includes several elements. Students are to understand how the processes of inductive and deductive reasoning weave together in making geometry. So, for instance, teachers want students to learn to gather data, to figure out productive ways of recording and displaying data to facilitate analysis, to notice patterns and form conjectures, to verify conjectures with empirical data, to evaluate apparent counterexamples and to appreciate their disconfirmatory power, to view diagrams as exemplars representing a set of cases, and to recognize the limits of particular cases in establishing general truths. To list these aspects of mathematical reasoning may suggest erroneously that the process boils down to a fixed sequence of discrete stratagems. In fact, the process of logical thinking combines examination, conjecture, verification, and communication in an indeterminate sequence. Effective inquiry entails an artful combination of reasoning skills guided by an acquired taste for elegant, powerful ideas.

A second element of the metacurriculum is the recognition that mathematics is the product of human intellect, developed through an arduous but potentially exhilarating process of expending mental energy. Students often believe that mathematics is a collection of right answers waiting to be found by very smart people (Schoenfeld, 1985). This view fails to acknowledge the tentative, evolving nature of the field and undermines a third element of the metacurriculum. This is the realization that students themselves can make and critique mathematical knowledge. They and their teachers can take the risk of trying to figure out things they do not already know, relying on their own judgment to decide whether an idea is important or persuasive.

Helping students develop the confidence, judgment, and skill to participate in arguments about mathematical ideas is an important goal of the metacurriculum.

The participants in this project had not themselves been explicitly taught the metacurriculum nor had they previously articulated their own version of it. Defining the metacurriculum is a process of gradually making implicit understandings explicit, while struggling not to squeeze the life out by pinning it down with false precision. Undoubtedly one source of difficulty in teaching this metacurriculum stems from its implicit, evolving, variously interpreted nature.

Teaching the Metacurriculum

The Geometric Supposer can be used in a variety of ways to support teaching geometry. For example, a teacher might use the Supposer with an overhead projection device to illustrate geometric ideas during a classroom presentation. Alternatively, students might be encouraged to use the software outside classtime as an aid in completing homework assignments. In the project discussed here, teachers were encouraged to hold a portion of their geometry classes in a computer laboratory where students worked, either singly or in pairs, on exercises designed to be explored with the Geometric Supposer. Subsequent class sessions were devoted to discussion of the data and conjectures students developed from their lab exercises. These Supposer-related inquiries in the laboratory and postlab discussions were interspersed with more traditional, text-based presentations by teachers.

Designing and conducting Supposer-based lessons and integrating them into the structure of the traditional deductive high school geometry course was the challenge teachers faced in this project. The goal of the research is to understand how teachers managed this challenge, tracing the evolution of their concerns and focusing especially on the curricular and pedagogical dilemmas they encountered as they attempted to teach the metacurriculum.

Methodology

The five teachers who participated in the project taught in three high schools in Massachusetts.[1] They volunteered to participate in a study conducted by researchers at the Educational Technology Center (ETC of Harvard's Graduate School of Education) to learn about the implementa-

---

[1]The schools were: a small rural high school, a large comprehensive high school in a middle-class suburb, and an alternative school within a large, comprehensive urban high school.

tion of technology-enhanced guided inquiry in the classroom. In the summer of 1986, the teachers attended several meetings where they were introduced to the Geometric Supposer software, given sample problems that they might use with their students, and given opportunities to work through some of the problems. These meetings were led by Richard Houde and Daniel Chazan. Houde, a high school mathematics teacher, had worked with developers of the Geometric Supposer to refine the software, create appropriate problems, and design methods of teaching geometry inductively with this technology. He had taught high school geometry courses with the Supposer for several years and continued to do so while working part time on this research project. Chazan, a former mathematics teacher, had taught previously with the Supposer and had served as an advisor and researcher in a study with other teachers learning to teach with the Supposer. After their initial introduction, the five teachers were given computers, software, and problem sets to take home during the summer. During the 1986–1987 academic year, Richard Houde served as an advisor to the teachers, observing them regularly in their classrooms and meeting with them to plan lessons, prepare materials, and discuss their questions about classroom practice and management. The teachers also met regularly as a group with Houde and Chazan to share problems, ideas, materials, and encouragement for their complicated innovative effort. Their first year experiences are reported elsewhere (Lampert, 1988a; Wiske, Niguidula, & Shepard, 1988).

At the end of the first year in Spring 1987, we decided to follow these teachers as they continued to work with this approach during a second year. Recognizing that the first year of teaching with a complex new technology may be largely taken up with logistical challenges, we anticipated that second year teachers would be able to focus more on the curricular and instructional aspects of this innovation. Throughout the 1987–1988 academic year, Richard Houde continued to observe and consult with teachers at their schools, serving both as advisor and researcher. As an advisor, he helped teachers plan lessons and design and prepare materials. He also observed their classes – both computer laboratory sessions and subsequent discussion sessions – and consulted with teachers about teaching strategies. As a researcher, he prepared detailed notes after each meeting, recording particular events from his classroom observations and summarizing the concerns raised by teachers. Houde and Wiske, a researcher interested in the process of teacher and educational change, met regularly to review Houde's observations, clarifying themes, and relating them to other research on teacher development. As the year progressed, Houde's notes focused on the way the innovation challenged teachers' accustomed curriculum and practice and how teachers dealt with these challenges at many levels of lesson design. Both of us met several times throughout the year with the teachers as a group to discuss teachers' concerns and approaches and to share our emerging analyses with them.

EVOLUTION OF TEACHERS' CONCERNS

The widely cited Stages of Concern model (Hall & Hord, 1987; Hall & Loucks, 1978) describes a sequence of considerations expressed by teachers as they deal with innovations (see Table 10.1). According to this model, teachers initially gather general information about the characteristics of an innovation and consider how it addresses their personal concerns, then focus on the task of managing the new approach in their own settings, and finally progress to assessing its impacts and considering refinements to enhance its effects. Like Hall and Hord, we found that teachers evinced several kinds of concerns at once rather than proceeding in a lock-step fashion through this progression. Nevertheless, this model offers an overall

TABLE 10.1
Stages of Concern about the Innovation

6	REFOCUSING: The focus is on exploration of more universal benefits from the innovation including the possibility of major changes or replacement with a more powerful alternative. Individual has definite ideas about alternatives to the proposed or existing form of the innovation.
5	COLLABORATION: The focus is on coordination and cooperation with others regarding use of the innovation.
4	CONSEQUENCE: Attention focuses on impact of the innovation on student in his or her immediate sphere of influence. The focus is on relevance of the innovation for students, evaluation of student outcomes including performance and competencies, and changes needed to increase student outcomes.
3	MANAGEMENT: Attention is focused on the processes and tasks of using the innovation and the best use of information and resources. Issues related to efficiency, organizing, managing, scheduling, and time demands are utmost.
2	PERSONAL: Individual is uncertain about the demands of the innovation, his or her inadequacy to meet those demands, and his or her role with the innovation. This includes analysis of his or her role in relation to the reward structure of the organization, decision making, and consideration of potential conflicts with existing structures or personal commitment. Financial or status implications of the program for self and colleagues may also be reflected.
1	INFORMATIONAL: A general awareness of the innovation and interest in learning more detail about it is indicated. The person seems to be unworried about himself or herself in relation to the innovation. She or he is interested in substantive aspects of the innovation in a selfless manner such as general characteristics, effects, and requirements for use.
0	AWARENESS: Little concern about or involvement with the innovation is indicated.

Note. See Hall and Hord, 1987, p. 60.

framework that effectively categorizes the kinds of concerns faced by teachers in this study and identifies the sequence in which particular issues tended to preoccupy them. Examining the nature and progression of these concerns clarifies the kinds of resources and assistance teachers need as they incorporate this kind of innovation into their practice.

Personal

Teachers in this project reported they were drawn to the Geometric Supposer innovation for one or more reasons: (a) they were eager to explore the potential of new technologies for mathematics education, (b) they wanted to enliven geometry instruction with more active inquiry, and (c) they wanted to engage students who learned better through manipulation of objects and visual data than through formal, symbolic representations. These overlapping considerations focused on technology, pedagogy, and subject matter, respectively.

The focus of a teacher's initial attraction seemed to shape the teacher's on-going orientation to the project. For example, teachers initially drawn by the computer per se, tended to remain more focused on the technology than on the changes its use implied for teaching and curriculum. Those drawn by the prospect of giving students more opportunity to discover and create knowledge for themselves were attracted to the computer laboratory but slow to recognize the value of the technology for teacher-led demonstrations and lectures. The teachers most interested in helping students see the visual side of mathematics tended to concentrate on extending this aspect of the innovation. Despite these differences in teachers' particular interests and styles, they seemed to move through similar stages of concern.

As Hall and Loucks (1978) predicted, during the first year of work with the Supposer, teachers worried initially about how the innovation would affect them personally. Teachers wondered whether they would have the time, interest, and inclination to deal with the technology, the instructional approach, and the demands of researchers. They questioned whether their participation in the project would help or hinder their work at school. Although these kinds of concerns are common and deserve attention, in this study we focus on the concerns about management and consequences that preoccupied teachers after they began to incorporate the innovation into their practice.

Managerial

In Hall and Hord's model (1987), managerial concerns encompass more than just classroom management or logistical issues. Hall and Hord recognized this stage as including concerns about the best use of materials, time, information, and other resources to carry out the innovation in one's own setting. We viewed these concerns even more broadly. Like Lampert (1985), we saw teachers balancing multiple, often conflicting agendas as they made myriad decisions about designing and conducting their lessons. In managing to teach, they faced a set of considerations at various levels of lesson architecture, such as designing exercises and problems sets for students, managing interactions with students during a lesson, planning a sequence of lessons to address a particular topic, and mapping the overall structure of the course syllabus. At every level, teachers confronted questions about how to integrate the new technology and inquiry approach into their accustomed curriculum and practice.

Particular examples illustrate the nature of teachers' concerns and the complexity of dealing with them. Descriptions of the advisor's interventions reveal the kinds of assistance that teachers may need as they work an innovation like this into their practice.

Designing Problem Sets and Exercises.   The selection and presentation of problems is a crucial aspect of the guided inquiry approach to teaching. Teachers in this project were offered many sets of problems designed to be investigated with the Geometric Supposer. The problems instructed students to make a geometric construction (e.g., a triangle with medians drawn to each side) and to investigate the geometric relationships among elements of the construction. In selecting, modifying, and presenting problems to their students, teachers took a range of considerations into account. Problems must (a) address appropriate subject matter about geometry, (b) provide enough guidance about how to investigate the problem yet leave room for students to make intellectual leaps, (c) be arranged on the page so that students can record diagrams or other data, and (d) be worded clearly and accurately so that students are not confused. One typographical error, such as labeling an angle ACB rather than ABC, could create major confusion. (See Chazan, Yerushalmy, and Gordon in this volume for a more detailed discussion of the characteristics of good problems.)

In designing and presenting a problem to the class, the teacher makes multiple judgment calls based on educational goals, preferred teaching style, and student needs. For example, one teacher assigned a problem to be investigated in the computer lab that required students to reflect points over the sides of a triangle, then gather data and make conjectures about a range of relationships among elements of the resulting figure. She wanted students to then prove one or more of their conjectures as a homework assignment. The problems that arose illustrate the interplay of judgments. First, some students did not understand the term *reflect*. Second, some students did not know how to record their data in a systematic way that facilitated making conjectures. When the advisor recommended that the teacher suggest a format for collecting the data, the teacher responded that she thought the students would learn more by discovering the need for a system and inventing one on their own. Clearly, the decision required a judgment about how much structure to provide, given multiple agendas and perhaps alternative pedagogical approaches. Finally, several students were not familiar enough with the geometry raised by the problem to figure out which conjectures they might be able to prove. Addressing multiple goals, in ways both consistent with one's pedagogical preferences and tailored to students' level of knowledge and skill, is a tricky business.

Managing Teacher–Student Interactions.   When teachers lecture to a class, they confront relatively few decisions about managing interactions with students. Shifting to a guided inquiry approach, which invites students to generate and share ideas, greatly increases the number of occasions when a teacher must decide how to respond. On such occasions, teachers must make choices shaped by multiple agendas. The teacher's goals might include: (a) teaching certain subject matter about geometry, (b) developing students' abilities to conduct and critique inductive reasoning, or (c) fostering students' confidence and skill as members of a productive intellectual community. For example, the teacher might want students to learn that the sum of a triangle's interior angles equals 180 degrees, that verifying a conjecture with several cases is not the same thing as proving the conjecture, and that an idea need not be correct to be worth expressing. Another goal might be helping students develop and express their own ideas, particularly if the teacher believes that students learn best by making sense of their own observations and that in order to do this in school they must overcome a heavily reinforced belief that their role is simply to memorize the methods the teacher gives them.

The complexities of balancing multiple instructional goals were particularly apparent in this project when the teachers led discussions of the conjectures students had made regarding a problem they had investigated with the Geometric Supposer in the computer lab. As the advisor watched teachers lead discussions, he often found himself thinking, "What a missed opportunity!" Sometimes this happened when a student offered a conjecture that the advisor recognized as related to the teacher's content agenda, but the teacher responded, "We won't be getting to that until next month." To see the connection, the advisor had in mind a broad mental map of the content domain indicating multiple paths among topics, whereas the teacher seemed to map the subject as a fixed linear sequence of topics. Sometimes the advisor perceived a missed opportunity when a student's comment related to his meta-agenda (e.g., teaching students how to reason inductively), but the teacher attended only to the geometry content of the remark. In these cases, it was often difficult to tell whether the teacher simply did not understand or care about the advisor's metacurriculum, was too preoccupied with the demands of a new approach to notice the opportunity, or consciously chose to attend to a different agenda in fashioning a response.

Clearly, leading such a session is a complicated affair. The discussion easily loses coherence unless a teacher keeps track of many agendas at once. To help simplify the process, the advisor developed a strategy that he called *the three-board technique.* On one chalkboard he wrote down students conjectures as they called them out. By writing them in the students' words he credited their ideas and spared himself the cognitive demand of translating them into more standard vocabulary. When no new conjectures were forthcoming, he shifted to the second board where he rewrote the students' conjectures, grouping them into categories and translating them into language that led toward the points he wanted to make. During this process he explained how the conjectures related to each other, modeled the process of analyzing and evaluating conjectures, and wondered aloud whether any of the conjectures could be proved. He used the third board to work out proofs for selected conjectures. He found this technique useful in balancing attention to both content and process and in synthesizing students' ideas with his own agenda.[2]

Lesson Design.   This innovation challenges teachers on several fronts at once, thereby necessitating a redesign of lesson architecture at several levels. The innovation involves integrating a new technology into the teaching and learning process, shifting the pedagogical approach from a primarily teacher-centered lecture mode to a more student-centered and problem-focused inquiry mode, and weaving a new inductive reasoning curriculum into the standard deductive curriculum. Teachers find themselves rethinking the structure of their lessons, the sequence of lessons within a particular topic, and the overall syllabus of their courses.

In designing lessons, teachers first need to consider overall teaching format. They can choose to teach a topic in the regular classroom through teacher-led lecture, demonstration, or discussion. They can also teach it in a computer laboratory where they decide when to address the whole class and when to circulate among stations to guide students' working independently. Or they can approach a topic through a homework assignment that either introduces concepts to be examined later during class or reviews material already discussed.

The Geometric Supposer technology is amenable to a variety of lesson formats. Used with a large monitor or display screen, the Supposer serves

---

[2]See Lampert (1988b) for a more extensive discussion of the factors that constrain teachers' efforts to connect students' ideas with their own agendas and of some strategies they employ to accomplish this difficult feat.

as a dynamic blackboard, augmenting a teacher-led presentation or discussion with the whole class. Several teachers, who had used the Supposer only in the laboratory where students worked with the software directly, found using the Supposer in front of the class a bit awkward at first. They had to become fluent with the new technology before its advantages outweighed those of the accustomed technology of chalkboard, compass, and straight-edge.

Computer laboratory sessions offer the advantage of engaging students in active inquiry, but they require both teachers and students to learn new skills and practice new roles. Teachers found that students learned to use the software fairly quickly but took longer to learn how to read and interpret a problem set, collaborate on making constructions, make observations, gather visual and numerical data, record their findings, and form conjectures. Teachers gradually learned how to introduce a problem, walking a line between explaining so much they eliminated the need for inquiry and leaving students too confused to work productively on their own. Although the laboratory-based lesson format offers many advantages, it is sometimes a very time-consuming way to cover a topic. Teachers had to learn to be selective about the lessons they chose to teach through computer-based inquiry in order not to slight important topics in their syllabus.

Selecting homework assignments and weaving them into the course is also problematic. Sometimes teachers assigned homework that either introduced or followed up exercises students investigated in the computer laboratory. Designing homework to follow lab sessions was tricky if students did not all proceed with lab work at the same pace. Collecting, grading, and incorporating these assignments into class discussions was a challenge. Faced with these challenges, teachers frequently took the more familiar path of assigning textbook problems as homework. These problems were often structured and worded in a way that made them difficult to integrate with the inductive approach to the lab material, however.

Course Architecture. This discussion of issues in lesson design reveals another set of dilemmas at the level of course architecture. The inductive approach to geometry with the Supposer sometimes prompts teachers to rearrange the sequence in which they presented certain topics and even calls into question their accustomed sequence of units within the course. Two examples help illustrate this point.

1. The Supposer's measure menus allow students to measure easily the sizes of angles, lengths of segments, and areas of shapes, but most textbook-based geometry syllabi do not examine the topic of area until the fourth or fifth month of the school year. Teachers in this project faced a dilemma: teach a unit on area at the very beginning of the school year and

thus open rich opportunities for students to investigate area relationships or tell students to ignore the Supposer's area options until the textbook chapter on area had been formally studied. Most teachers opted for the former choice and modified their curricula accordingly.

2. The geometry textbooks used by teachers in this project present chapters on quadrilaterals followed by chapters on similarity. After teachers had students investigate quadrilateral problems with the Supposer during the first year of the project, however, they discovered that the richness of their quadrilateral units might be significantly enhanced if students first studied similarity. Thus, during the second year of the project, two teachers revised their previous year's curricular sequences and taught units on similarity before units on quadrilaterals.

Making decisions at this level of course architecture is an aspect of the management concerns generated by this innovation. Given the range and depth of these concerns, it is little wonder that teachers struggled with them throughout this study.

Consequences

As teachers faced and coped with personal and management concerns, they gradually began to worry more about the consequences of this innovative approach. Their concerns settled on several aspects of their multi-faceted responsibilities: students' learning of the traditional course content as measured by standard achievement tests, teachers' coverage of the traditional course materials as laid out in the textbook and perhaps in required curriculum guides, and students' learning of the new metacurriculum, that is, learning how to reason inductively and to understand and participate in the process of making mathematics.

These concerns imbued the dilemmas described earlier with particular urgency. Deciding how to respond to a student remark, selecting problems, and designing lesson architecture all involved tradeoffs among sometimes conflicting priorities. Three themes recurred in teachers' discussions of the consequences of this innovation: time, assessment, and authority.

Time.   Time is the engine that runs life in most secondary schools. The day is segmented into periods signaled over the loudspeaker system. Both teachers and students carry little schedules marked off in a grid that determines their activities during each period, 5 days a week. Except in the rare cases when teachers can schedule a double period, they cannot continue an activity past the end of the period. Such a rigid schedule is much better suited to a teacher-controlled lesson than to a student-centered, inquiry-oriented one. Once students become engrossed in working on a problem, the teacher loses control over the focus and pace of their thinking. A student may have just caught the scent of a powerful proof when the teacher gives the 5-minute warning before the bell rings. Teachers in this project often remarked that standard periods were too short for computer lab sessions. Students often needed more time to take their seats and arrange their materials, study the exercise enough to understand it, then try on several lines of inquiry, examine their findings, and decide which conjecture to pursue.

The larger blocks of time into which the school year is divided also conflict with the rhythm of the inquiry-oriented approach used in this project. Teachers were accustomed to devoting a certain number of weeks to a predetermined set of topics: for example, a week for parallel lines, followed by 3 weeks on congruence, then three weeks for quadrilaterals. Especially in one school involved in this study, where a year of geometry was intertwined with a year of algebra in a 2-year course sequence, the schedule of topics was elaborately set. Teaching with the Supposer made teachers want to reduce or expand the amount of time they devoted to some topics and reconsider the sequence in which they could be taught most effectively. Such juggling was complicated by the framework of the predetermined school year, including scheduled events like vacations, field trips, and exams.

Finally, teachers remarked on the difficulty of finding time anywhere in their week, let alone during the school day, to prepare for this innovation. Teaching this way required time for a host of activities. Teachers had to invent or modify exercise sheets and then try out problems themselves as a way of proofreading the sheets and anticipating students' reactions. They needed time to design the lesson architecture described earlier, orchestrating an effective combination of lesson formats. They needed time to think, for example, after leading a discussion, about the points students had raised and decide how they might weave them into a later class or pursue them if they came up another time. They needed time to grade student papers that included disparate drawings and arguments rather than standardized short answers.

Assessment. Assessment is another recurring theme in teachers' discussion of the consequences of this innovation. Teachers wondered what their students were learning, how to make this determination, and how to conduct assessments in a way that reinforced their purposes in the course. With respect to computer-based assignments, teachers needed to articulate criteria for assessing student work. As they became clearer about the skills and knowledge they wanted students to master, they became better able to design tests that helped reveal and support such mastery.

During the year discussed here, teachers used three types of lab tests reflecting progressively more advanced stages of development they wanted students to achieve with the Supposer during the course of a school year. During stage one, which usually occurred during the first 2 months of the year, teachers administered tests that required students only to state conjectures and exhibit data to support them. Teachers were primarily concerned that students learn how to use the Supposer to gather empirical evidence and placed little emphasis on asking students to write logical arguments to support their conjectures. As the year progressed and students learned more about the meaning of proof, teachers required students to write proofs for their conjectures (stage two). Some teachers insisted that students report all their data, state their conjectures, and write just one or two proofs whereas other teachers simply asked students to state conjectures. Teachers were continually forced during this stage to decide how much emphasis to place on proof in computer lab-based testing situations. During the third and final stage, teachers de-emphasized or omitted the need for reporting empirical data and asked students to concentrate on using the Supposer to verify their ideas and develop logical arguments or proofs to defend them. No two teachers ever administered exactly the same test, but all led their students through these stages.

Teachers also needed to develop strategies for grading Supposer-based assignments. They found themselves buried in papers that required much more thought and commentary than they had time to provide. With a mounting backlog, they sometimes gave up trying to discuss lab assignments with the class or even skipped reading some papers. The advisor recommended that they grade only portions of each paper, devoting thoughtful attention to selected problems rather than superficial treatment to the entire assignment.

Weighing student mastery of the new curriculum in relation to mastery of the old curriculum constitutes another dilemma. During the first year, students in one school figured out they could make good enough grades on their computer lab assignments to pass the course, even if they failed the examinations. The teachers found this unacceptable, especially because the examinations more nearly mirrored the material included on standardized achievement tests that other mathematics teachers would expect students to have learned in a geometry course. In the second year, they redesigned their grading system to better reflect their course goals.

The lack of appropriate assessment instruments and strategies both reflected and hampered the teachers' ability to articulate and legitimize the new curriculum. The advisor offered to help teachers design Supposer-based tests. He recognized that such tests accomplished several purposes: (a) they helped teachers specify the aims of this curriculum and demonstrate their commitment to it, (b) they helped students chart their own progress, and (c) they enabled teachers to monitor and demonstrate what students had learned.

Authority. Finally, teachers' deliberations about the consequences of this innovation reveal that it had occasioned a shift in authority in the geometry classroom. The basis of authority broadened from the textbook and the teacher's interpretation of the standard curriculum to encompass the judgment of an intellectual community made up of the teacher and students. Like paradigm shifts in the history of ideas, this change was gradual, multifaceted, and marked by fits and starts and reversions to the old ways.

The basis for authority shifted in several ways. One was that teachers took on more authority for exercising their own judgment about how geometry should be taught, rivaling the textbook and curriculum guide as shapers of these decisions. Teachers wavered as they took on this role, but the progression was clear in several cases.

For example, during the first year of the project, one teacher taught a unit on concurrency that closely followed the dictates of his textbook. He taught students how to copy segments and angles and construct angle bisectors, altitudes, and perpendicular bisectors of line segments with compasses and straightedges. He presented lessons and assigned homework exercises that followed the text's recommended guidelines. Although he had students use the Supposer to do a lab assignment, his manner of teaching the unit did not change significantly. Midway through the second year of the project, this teacher told the advisor he was unhappy with his previous approach and intended to teach concurrency using the Supposer as the primary technology and his text only for selected exercises. His new unit included sets of problems that students investigated in the computer lab, followed by classroom discussions of these exercises. Homework exercises emerged from lab work and class discussions. The teacher's agenda and students' findings shaped the unit whereas the textbook served merely as a reference.

Another teacher radically changed her methods for teaching elementary geometry concepts. She abandoned her former approach of assigning pages in the textbook that instructed students in basic definitions and substituted a series of computer-based problems that helped students discover similar concepts. She led discussions about students' lab results to summarize the important understandings she wanted students to remember and used the textbook problems to reinforce lab work.

A second kind of shift occurred as students exercised more authority as makers and critiquers of knowledge rather than passive receivers and reciters of knowledge made by others. The Supposer supported them in this process by enabling them to work from empirical evidence. With the Supposer, they could check whether their conjectures held true for multiple cases, thus investigating the limits of generality of a pattern or relationship. The tool helped to put empirical verification within reach and, for some students, seemed to help them recognize the limits of empirical evidence. As a member of the class accumulated examples confirming a conjecture, students challenged, "Prove it!" The ready access to empirical evidence helped students gain confidence in their conjectures, and, in some cases, apparently helped students develop a more sophisticated intolerance for the particular case as a basis for proof.

A third type of shift in authority stemmed from the structure of the Supposer. Its menu and facilities place the software in a position to rival the textbook as a curriculum authority. For example, the Supposer Circles disk menu includes the word *inversion,* a fascinating topic rarely taught in traditional high school geometry courses. The Supposer makes this topic readily accessible. One of the teachers experimented with this option, following the Supposer's directions but was unable to discover the meaning of the term. The advisor shared some knowledge of the topic and responded to the teacher's request for suggestions about an exercise to culminate her unit on circles. He suggested that she assign some Supposer-based problems involving inversion. The teacher became so interested in the topic that with the advisor she designed a set of lab problems on inversion for her students to investigate.

Refocusing

Hall and Hord (1987) asserted that once teachers figure out how to manage an innovative approach and think through its consequences for teaching and learning, their concerns often turn toward rethinking the innovation itself. In this process, they seek out opportunities to collaborate with colleagues in revising or extending the innovation. In this study, we find that teachers dealt with this range of concerns but did not address them on a lock-step linear sequence.

At the end of the first year of the project, several of the participating teachers decided to introduce the Supposer and inquiry-oriented geometry to their colleagues. In three schools, they used their own positions and their system's idiosyncratic norms and structures to encourage the spread of the innovation beyond their own classrooms. Their efforts are described in Shepard and Wiske (1988). During this process, the teachers opted to balance dependence on their own wisdom and resources with support and guidance from ETC researchers and their fellow teachers on the project. In many respects, their way of dealing with the innovation paralleled the guided inquiry process they carried out with their students. The teachers appeared to learn best when guidance from the research and development team was combined with opportunities for them to invent and extend ideas on their own and to examine their experiences with fellow learners confronting similar challenges.

As teachers supported the spread of the innovation within their own schools, they also reconsidered how to modify and extend the innovation. Some of the adjustments resulted from wrestling with concerns about management and consequences, reconsidering goals, and finding ways to retune problems, strategies, and techniques to address these goals more successfully. Other adjustments grew out of the experience of introducing the innovation to other teachers and recognizing the range of interpretations that might be made to accommodate various student needs, teaching styles, and course syllabi. Debates continued throughout the year among the teachers and ETC staff about, for example, appropriate ways to modify Supposer-based and inquiry-oriented lessons to suit students of varying academic achievement levels. Teachers also recognized that their colleagues varied in their pedagogical preferences and instructional goals. Whereas one teacher was deeply committed to letting students discover ideas on their own, another instinctively directed students so that they learned the textbook definitions. As the veteran teachers became advisors to their colleagues, they experienced the dilemmas their own advisor had faced in balancing his advice with respect for his fellow professionals' goals, preferences, and expertise.

DILEMMAS OF GUIDED INQUIRY IN THE CLASSROOM

As discussed earlier in the chapter, the instructional goals of this innovation include teaching students how to reason inductively and helping them understand and participate in the process of making mathematics. The instructional approach includes guidance from teachers as students investigate problems, work to make sense of their findings, and formulate arguments and proofs regarding their results. The examples provided in the preceding section illustrate the multiple challenges teachers face in teaching this curriculum through a guided-inquiry approach.

This type of innovation requires most teachers to make a fundamental paradigm shift. Most teachers operate within a recitation paradigm, assuming that knowledge is specifiable, that the teacher's role is to transmit information, and that the students' role is to absorb, remember, and repeat what they are taught. Teaching for understanding through guided inquiry reflects a constructivist paradigm, assuming that knowledge is personal and problematic, that the teacher's role is to help students build on their own ideas to construct understanding, and that the students' role is to participate actively in making knowledge not just to memorize what they are told. In shifting from one paradigm to the other, teachers do not suddenly and totally transform their knowledge, behaviors, and beliefs. They confront myriad decisions and dilemmas, choosing among alternative approaches.

Curriculum Dilemmas

Berlak and Berlak (1981) described these dilemmas of teaching in ways that illuminate the choices faced by the geometry teachers in this study. In rethinking educational goals, teachers must decide what is worthwhile to teach. Among the curriculum dilemmas they face are those that I now discuss.

Knowledge as Content Versus Knowledge as Process.   Should teachers concentrate on teaching facts, concepts, and theories, or should they help students experience and understand the process of thinking, reasoning, and critiquing ideas? Should geometry teachers focus on Euclidean geometry theorems and their use in solving real-world problems? Or should they emphasize that geometry is the study of ideas whose relationships are determined by a rigorous, axiomatic, deductive system leading to formal proofs?

Many school systems in effect favor teaching the content of Euclidean geometry by endorsing either locally developed or nationally standardized tests that focus almost entirely on this material. Meanwhile, many geometry teachers believe that the power of a geometry course lies in its ability to hone students' logical thinking skills. This project promotes an approach that places more emphasis on learning to reason, but the process encompasses inductive reasoning as well as the deductive reasoning that geometry teachers usually emphasize. Teachers in the project varied in their judgments about the proper balance of geometry content, deductive reasoning, and inductive reasoning. Their judgments depended on their own teaching preferences, their assessment of their students' ability, and the priorities of their school system.

Personal Knowledge Versus Public Knowledge.   Should teachers concentrate on transmitting to students the information in their textbooks and the knowledge the teacher possesses? Or should they focus more on helping students make sense of their own ideas and build their own personal understanding? This dilemma arises from questions about the basis of intellectual authority in the classroom. How much ought teachers to rely on the textbook or curriculum guide or other codification of the geometry to be taught rather than look to their own judgments about what to teach or build on students' ideas? The answer lies at the heart of teachers' decisions about balancing their guidance with opportunities for the students to pursue their own inquiries.

Pedagogical Dilemmas

Along with curricular dilemmas, teachers face poignant pedagogical dilemmas. Of those mentioned by Berlak and Berlak (1981), some appear particularly salient for teachers in this project, which we now discuss.

Learning is Social Versus Learning is Individual. Is learning a private matter between child and text or child and teacher or is it a more social affair whereby understanding is developed through argument, collaboration, and corroboration with other people?

Teachers in this project wondered whether students learned well and efficiently when they helped each other analyze exercises. They were also concerned about assessing students' individual learning and felt obligated to structure at least some assignments as individual rather than collaborative projects.

Teacher Control Versus Student Control of Time, Operations, and Standards. Should teachers direct the classroom agenda and schedule or allow students to control the focus and pace of their learning? Should teachers prescribe how and in what order students learn their lessons, or should students be encouraged to invent and discover their own approaches? Should teachers determine the standards for intellectual and social performance, or should students participate in deciding what, for instance, is a persuasive argument, which of several conjectures is worth trying to prove, or whether a remark is worth making to the whole class?

If teaching a course is conceived as building a community of scholars who share responsibility for teaching and learning, then students must be helped and allowed to take more control in the classroom. Teachers in this project found it difficult to decide when to relinquish control. They also puzzled over ways to help students develop the judgment, self-discipline, and confidence to exert such control responsibly.

Resolutions

Teachers' efforts to manage these dilemmas appear to reflect their preferred teaching styles, their assessments of their students' level of ability and learning needs, and the norms and values of their schools systems.[3] In addition, teachers' views and choices seem to change as they become more familiar with the innovation and more adept at weaving guided inquiry into their accustomed practice.

The advisor often noticed opportunities when teachers resolved some of these dilemmas. For example, he noticed opportunities when teachers developed students' inductive reasoning skills by modeling, labeling, and

---

[3]See Shepard & Wiske (1988) for a fuller discussion of the ways school structures and values shape teachers' ways of dealing with this kind of innovation. They suggested that in schools where students are expected to do what the teacher tells them and teachers are expected to do what the administration decides, both teachers and students are disinclined to exercise the kinds of intellectual authority that a guided-inquiry approach calls for. By the same token, this approach seems to be encouraged by school systems that expect teachers be active learners and to participate in decisions about curriculum, assessment, and school administration.

reinforcing these skills during class. Using terms like *conjecture, verify,* and *prove* consistently and carefully established a form of discourse in the classroom that emphasized and legitimized a set of activities. In this way, teachers attended to their inductive reasoning agenda without always taking time in class for explicit instruction on this topic.

Other opportunities arose when students made conjectures or asked questions related to the teacher's' agenda. Recognizing and seizing these opportunities depended on the teacher having certain knowledge, skills, and beliefs. As Lampert (1988b) noted, connecting students' ideas with the teacher's agenda is a complicated endeavor. The teacher must see the connection between the students' ideas and his or her own lesson plan. This requires the teacher to have in mind a map of the subject matter domain in which topics are connected by multiple links rather than laid out in the single linear sequence that textbook chapters and curriculum guides suggest. To build on students' ideas also requires the teacher to revise his or her lesson plan on the spot, taking up an idea or an activity that was not scheduled. Achieving this flexible spontaneity without sacrificing coherence is particularly difficult when the teacher is first using a new technology or approach. As the innovation becomes more familiar, the teacher may free up the mental energy to hear students' ideas more clearly and to discern connections to his or her own agenda. Making such connections also requires the teacher to respect and trust students' ideas as legitimate grist for the intellectual mill of the classroom. These beliefs are easier to espouse as both students and teachers become more accustomed to being active participants in constructing knowledge (Lampert, 1988a). Such connections reduce or resolve the problem of choosing between poles of the dilemmas described earlier.

Our findings suggest that as teachers become more knowledgeable about the goals of the curriculum associated with this innovation and develop more materials and strategies for teaching this curriculum, they are more able to resolve or at least manage some of the curricular and pedagogical dilemmas it poses. This is not to say that the dilemmas disappear entirely. Although teachers learn to recognize and use opportunities to integrate the old curriculum with the new, they still have to make difficult choices.

CONCLUSIONS

Computer technology is a powerful support for teaching through guided inquiry, but this approach still depends on teachers, who often find it extremely difficult to carry out in classrooms. The recitation paradigm is reinforced by curriculum guides, textbooks, and tests that direct teachers to cover a prescribed sequence of many topics and that assess how well students retrieve this material on demand. The recitation paradigm leads to a didactic instructional approach that is much better suited to teaching whole classes, many periods a day, on tightly structured schedules. As a rarely examined, only partially articulated, pervasive educational philosophy, the recitation paradigm shapes both teachers' and students' assumptions about what they should do and expect of each other in the classroom. Even more broadly, this paradigm is reflected in school policies and procedures that favor discipline and central authority over individual initiative and invention. The entrenched recitation paradigm reinforces deeply rooted beliefs and patterns of behavior in schools. The construction paradigm and the process of guided inquiry pose major intellectual, emotional, and moral challenges as well as technological and practical ones for teachers in classrooms.

This chapter attempts to map the dimensions of these challenges in order to clarify the kinds of support that teachers need as they face them. Our study demonstrates that incorporating technology-enhanced guided inquiry into their practice is a protracted process for teachers. The process raises a predictable sequence of concerns for teachers that calls for varied and evolving forms of implementation assistance. Initial concerns focus on personal issues such as learning to use the technology and finding the time and other resources in their lives to tackle the innovation. Once embarked on the new approach, teachers face a range of concerns about managing the incorporation of the innovation into accustomed curriculum and practice. These concerns arise at many levels, from the design of exercises and teaching materials to the management of class discussions to the structure of curriculum units and course syllabi. As teachers find ways of incorporating the new instructional approach into their repertoire, they face concerns about impact and tradeoffs. For teachers in this project these concerns focused on questions about time, about effective means of assessing the impact of the innovation, and about a new basis for intellectual authority in the classroom encompassing the teacher, the students, and the software. Eventually, teachers turn to reassessing the innovation itself, rethinking how they wish to use it, and attempting to spread it to their colleagues. In the course of supporting colleagues to extend the innovation, teachers readdress issues of management and consequences in light of their deepening understanding of the innovation.

As teachers deal with these evolving concerns, they need a range of implementation assistance. Initial training in the use of the software and exposure to sample problems has to be supplemented with ongoing consultation. As they work through managerial concerns, teachers need assistance both from an experienced advisor and from each other. The advisor and their fellow innovators help them to think through the innovation at all levels of lesson architecture and to develop exercises, lessons, curriculum units, and tests. The advisor also observes the way they put their plans into effect and offers feedback and suggestions.

The support of colleagues engaged in the same innovative effort helps teachers identify and deal with the logistical, curricular, and pedagogical dilemmas they face and the emotional strains these create. They confront choices about the balance of attention to teaching geometry content versus teaching thinking skills, to covering the standard curriculum versus developing students' abilities to reason inductively. They also face pedagogical dilemmas regarding the appropriate balance of teacher control versus student control over the focus, pace, and assessment of instruction.

Teachers' responses to these choices reflect their preferred teaching styles, their assessments of students' needs, and the prevailing priorities and expectations of their school systems regarding curriculum and teacher–student roles. Teachers' reaction to these apparent choices change as they become more experienced in weaving a guided-inquiry approach into their standard courses. As teachers become clearer about the goals of the innovation and more adept at integrating the innovative methods into their practice, they find more ways to integrate the old and new approaches rather than choosing between them.

If our supposition is correct that incorporating guided inquiry into standard secondary school courses requires a fundamental shift in educational paradigm, we should expect that most teachers will need the same sort of extended, multifaceted assistance that teachers in this study received. If the innovation entails not merely learning how to use a new technology to do the same work in the same ways as usual but a change in educational goals and in deeply rooted behaviors and beliefs, then making the change requires considerable time, thought, courage, and practice. Our study suggests that teachers need help to plan, prepare, and think through the management, consequences, and extensions of such innovations. This help appears to be most useful if it combines assistance from experienced advisors with opportunities for collegial exchange among fellow innovators. Such a combination may be thought of as the equivalent of guided inquiry in implementation assistance. From this perspective, the form of the implementation assistance serves to model and engage teachers in a process like the one they are trying to create with their students. If teachers are to share authority with their students in constructing understanding, the process of supporting this shift must include a similar sharing between leaders and learners.

REFERENCES

Amaral, M. (1983). Classrooms and computers as instructional settings. *Theory into Practice, 22*(Autumn), 260–270.

Berlak, H., & Berlak, A. (1981). *Dilemmas of schooling: Teaching and social change.* London: Methuen.

Hall, G. E., & Hord, S. M. (1987). *Changes in schools: Facilitating the process.* Albany, NY: State University of New York Press.

Hall, G. E., & Loucks, S. F. (1978). Teacher concerns as a basis for facilitating and personalizing staff development. *Teachers College Record, 80*(1), 36–53.

Hawkins, J., & Sheingold, K. (1986). The beginning of a story: Computers and the organization of learning in classrooms. In J. A. Culbertson & L. L. Cunningham (Eds.), *Microcomputers and education: 85th Yearbook of the National Society for the Study of Education* (pp. 93–108). Chicago: University of Chicago Press.

Lampert, M. (1985). How do teachers manage to teach? *Harvard Educational Review, 55*(2), 178–194.

Lampert, M. (1988a). *Teachers' thinking about students' thinking about geometry: The effects of new teaching tools* (Tech. Rep. No. TR88-1). Cambridge, MA: Harvard University, Educational Technology Center.

Lampert, M. (1988b). *Teaching that connects students' inquiry with curricular agendas in schools* (Tech. Rep. No. TR88-1). Cambridge, MA: Harvard Graduate School of Education, Educational Technology Center.

Martin, L. M. W. (1987). Teachers' adoption of multimedia technologies for science and mathematics instruction. In R. D. Pea & K. Sheingold (Eds.), *Mirrors of Mind.* (pp. 67–81). Norwood, NJ: Ablex.

National Council of Teachers of Mathematics Commission on Standards for School Mathematics. (1988, October). *The curriculum and evaluation standards for school mathematics.* Reston, VA: National Council of Teachers of Mathematics.

National Research Council Committee on Research in Mathematics, Science, and Technology Education. (1985). *Mathematics, science, and technology education: A research agenda.* Washington, DC: National Academy Press.

National Science Board Commission on Precollege Education in Mathematics, Science, and Technology. (1983). *Educating Americans for the 21st century.* Washington, DC: National Science Foundation.

Schoenfeld, A. H. (1985). *Mathematical problem solving.* Orlando, FL: Academic Press.

Schwartz, J. L. (1989). Intellectual mirrors: A step in the direction of making schools in knowledge-making places. *Harvard Educational Review, 59*(1), 51–61.

Schwartz, J., & Yerushalmy, M. (1985-1988). *The Geometric Supposer.* Pleasantville, NY: Sunburst.

Shepard, J. W., & Wiske, M. S. (1988). *Extending technological innovations in schools: Three case studies and analysis.* Tech. Rep. No. 88-29. Cambridge, MA: Harvard University, Educational Technology Center.

Sirotnik, K. (1983). What you see is what you get: Consistency, persistence, and mediocrity in classrooms. *Harvard Educational Review, 53*(1), 16–31.

U.S. Congress, Office of Technology Assessment. (1988). *Power on! New tools for teaching and learning* (OTA-SET-379). Washington, DC: U.S. Government Printing Office.

Wiske, M. S., Niguidula D., & Shepard, J. W. (1988). *Collaborative research goes to school: Guided inquiry with computers in classrooms* (Tech. Rep. No. TR88-3). Cambridge, MA: Harvard University, Educational Technology Center.

Yerushalmy, M., Chazan, D., & Gordon, M. (1988). *Posing problems: One aspect of bringing inquiry into classrooms* (Tech. Rep. No. TR88-21). Cambridge, MA: Harvard University, Educational Technology Center.

11 Geometric Supposer Urban Network

Grace Kelemanik
Mark Driscoll
Education Development Center

> The network has forced me to question everything I do in a constructive manner. I'm never complacent and am always asking myself if there is a better way of doing things.
>
> Phyllis, participant in the Geometric Supposer Urban Network

The Geometric Supposer software and the Urban Mathematics Collaboratives (UMC) Project grew up together in the late 1980s. On the surface, the two have little in common, but UMC teachers like Phyllis find the Supposer to be an effective tool for pursuing the goals of the collaboratives.

The UMC Project, with funding from the Ford Foundation (1987), operates in 14 cities across the country to develop new models of professionalism among mathematics teachers. It challenges teachers to explore the terrain of their subject matter and to question old assumptions about their professional roles and the limits on their power and influence.

For a group of teachers from several collaboratives, the challenge to experiment and grow professionally became concrete when they embraced the Geometric Supposer, a software environment that encourages users to see geometry teaching and learning in new ways. These teachers have since gone on to explore solutions to other problems—for example, design of tests, textbooks, and staff development. This chapter discusses the role of the Supposer in facilitating their exploration and innovation.

THE URBAN MATHEMATICS COLLABORATIVES

Within the UMC Project, each collaborative is primarily a venture, making it possible for mathematics teachers to take advantage of local resources

217

and opportunities. Nevertheless, as the collaboratives have developed their programs, two common element have characterized their pursuit of reform:

The programs are rooted in a commitment to collegial sharing among teachers, and

Staff development is driven more by teacher questions and concerns than is the norm in mathematics education.

Documentation of the UMC Project shows that the collaboratives succeed in encouraging consistent sharing and questioning among participating teachers (Webb, 1989). But whether sharing and questioning become catalysts for lasting change in teacher professionalism depends on how much they empower teachers and give them voice. In our opinion, one development is especially desirable in order for this to happen: sharing and questioning should evolve into networking based on more reflective classroom practice.

At Education Development Center (EDC; Newton, MA), we support the collaboratives with an Urban Mathematics Collaboratives Technical Assistance Project, also funded by the Ford Foundation. Like most technical assistance projects, ours includes a wide range of support activities. We devote much of our planning and support to activities we hope will lead to networking among the collaboratives' teachers.

Hence, when interest in the Geometric Supposer blossomed among a group of UMC teachers several years ago, we saw in this innovative tool — considered an engine for changing the way learners approach mathematics — a possible engine for changing the way mathematics teachers view and experience their profession. Like the UMC Project, the Geometric Supposer has to do with breaking away from old assumptions and raising questions about teacher roles. It seemed like fertile territory in which to explore and encourage networking based on reflective practice among UMC teachers.

Our assistance has taken several forms. We have provided Supposer training in individual UMC cities; we have supported UMC teachers to attend Supposer workshops and to observe Supposer-using teachers, sometimes in other cities; and we have invited a small number of users in Philadelphia and Los Angeles to participate in an electronic conference addressing innovation in the teaching of geometry. This pilot project is called the Geometric Supposer Urban Network (GSUN), which we at EDC moderate, using the Common Ground telecommunications software.

In general, we find what managers of other electronic conferencing systems have found: it is a very difficult task to sustain regular, substantive discussions among users. A couple of unanswered questions or ignored requests discourage even the most motivated participant. Nevertheless, using Phyllis and the other GSUN participants as examples, we illustrate how well the Geometric Supposer serves the UMC goal of stimulating networking based on reflective practice among urban mathematics teachers.

URBAN TEACHERS — URBAN PROBLEMS

In most urban school districts, systemic conditions impede the development among teachers of networking and reflective practice. Large mathematics departments within schools and centralized decision-making processes conspire to isolate teachers from each other and to prevent them from involving themselves in decisions that affect their professional lives.

Knowledge acquisition among urban teachers usually depends on the decision-making mechanisms within large bureaucracies. As Donald Schon (1983) pointed out:

> [Urban public schools] are built around a special view of privileged knowledge, its communication and its acquisition. But they also conform to the outlines of a bureaucratic system. The school presents itself as governed by a system of objectively determinable formal rules and procedures which are administered through a hierarchy. (p. 331)

Bureaucratic views of knowledge as privileged and governed by objective, formal rules are faulty on several grounds. For one, they misrepresent the knowledge that good teachers use in their work, which is often based on what Schon called *reflection-in-action;* for another, they serve to isolate teachers from important decision-making processes in urban school districts. Isolation is especially damaging when teachers want to adopt innovations like the Geometric Supposer, because the district's formal rules and procedures are not designed to support their innovative efforts.

The isolation of urban teachers is widespread. The 1988 Carnegie Foundation report, *An Imperiled Generation,* finds that urban teachers are "three times as likely as their counterparts in non-urban districts to feel uninvolved in setting goals or selecting books or materials. They are twice as apt to feel they have no control over how classroom time is used or course content selected." In his book, *The Empowerment of Teachers,* Gene Maeroff (1988) stated that "Being so isolated that they get little feedback, teachers end up dwelling on the limitations of the job and their shortcomings. Bringing teachers into closer contact with one another is a key to moving closer to empowerment" (p. 24).

The experiences of two GSUN participants, Phyllis and Pat, are typical of urban teachers who want to be innovative, to grow professionally, and to move closer to empowerment. Phyllis has spent the last 8 years of her 20-year career teaching at a magnet school for the sciences in Philadelphia. Pat has spent the last 10 of her nearly 20-year career teaching mathematics at a vocational technical school, also in Philadelphia. The two settings are quite different. Phyllis's school is equipped with one Macintosh lab and three Apple II labs, whereas Pat's school has one computer lab with 20

Apple IIs. Student SAT scores at the magnet school are consistently above the state and national averages, and almost all graduates go on to college. At the votech school, 90% of Pat's students will never see an elementary functions course, let alone study calculus.

Despite their different circumstances, these two women's professional lives have striking similarities. Both are advocates for a piece of software they believe can change the way students learn geometry but, as Phyllis says, their departments see as a "luxury and not a device where students can learn more material than they can in class." Both initially worked in isolation as they took the risks necessary to incorporate this new technology into their classrooms. Both were mindful that they would be held accountable as they deviated from the norm in their schools and districts. And both became active members of the Geometric Supposer Urban Network.

For advocates of the Geometric Supposer, isolation is heightened by the resistance of colleagues. Phyllis' interest in using the software with her class was not shared by the rest of the faculty at her school. The general feeling (even shared by Phyllis initially) was that there wasn't enough time to get through the mathematics curriculum using a piece of software that encouraged a guided discovery approach to learning and teaching geometry. The job of the mathematics teacher at the magnet school was to prepare students for calculus, beginning in the ninth grade. Phyllis summarized her colleagues' resistance: "We have to cover the whole text plus area and volume, and we can't spend time letting kids explore and try to make conjectures."

Nevertheless, Phyllis began to see the Supposer as an asset in this race against time. She designed her labs to teach her students to come up with their own definitions and descriptions of geometric terms and objects. After spending a session in the lab, her students came to class ready to discuss knowledge that complemented what was in the textbook, and she was the discussion leader.

Phyllis

I was convinced that if I used the Supposer I could change the teaching of geometry, at least in my own classroom, to represent a geometry that stressed an organization according to concept rather than according to Euclid.

The Supposer enables the students to learn material independent of me; it frees them up to question and then provides a structure that they may use to answer their own questions.

Pat's advocacy of the Geometric Supposer developed after 3 years in which the software sat on a shelf in her department. She had bought the Supposer software as part of a grant she wrote in collaboration with two of her colleagues at the high school, for a project designed to keep their students abreast of the cutting edge of technology.

The grant was constraining in that it offered limited funding for staff development and expected the recipient to teach herself how to use a piece of software without outside training or the availability of published support materials, all while maintaining a full teaching load. Because of the constraints and lack of outside support, Pat resisted using the Supposer, until she got the needed support and encouragement through the Urban Mathematics Collaborative Project several years later.

In his book, Maeroff (1988) noted how the isolation and alienation that teachers feel affect their interactions with each other. He observed that teachers generally do not share achievements or knowledge, even in department meetings:

> Teachers, separated as they are in their classrooms, normally have limited time to share and compare ideas. Professional growth is bound to be impaired in a setting where practitioners (teachers) do not see their colleagues practice their profession and hardly ever teach each other techniques. (p. 23)

For Pat, one of the biggest obstacles to overcome with regard to teacher training was learning how to help other teachers without being perceived as too overbearing. Phyllis, having functioned in an isolated environment for over 20 years, also resisted interacting with her colleagues. As she put it when she first started using the software, "I'm an independent bird and would like to see, on my own, in what different ways the Supposer can be useful."

Both Phyllis and Pat were able to end their Geometric Supposer isolation when they got involved in the Philadelphia Mathematics Collaborative. The collaborative provided Phyllis with training, support materials, and the software itself. Pat credits the collaborative with helping her become a "Supposer advocate" by providing a network through which she could see her ideas validated and know that she was on the right track with her use of the Supposer.

NETWORKING IN GSUN

If the profession of teaching mathematics is to change substantially in urban settings, where rigid views of professional knowledge stand in the way of innovation, then networking among teachers is an important precondition. With that conjecture in mind, we began the Geometric Supposer Urban Network as an electronic conference in the fall of 1987 and continued it through the summer of 1989. Although the frequency of use varies from teacher to teacher, it is fair to say that about 10 teachers in Los Angeles and Philadelphia along with a couple of EDC staff members constitute the GSUN core. There are usually at least three or four entries per week.

Conversations on GSUN that foster networking fall into two categories:

Questions and suggestions about using the Geometric Supposer.
Questions and reflections about extending the innovative practices derived from using the Geometric Supposer.

Here are examples of each, in the participants' own words. The quotes are a sampling from each category and, in most cases, represent only part of the participants' messages.

Using the Supposer

One strand of conversation in this category concerns questions of how and when to use the several Supposer programs in a course:

Alan (Los Angeles) 1/21/88

I am finding the Sunburst geometry book to be just about the right level for my students. . . . I use the Triangles problem book as a problem source, then modify the assignment to fit the needs at hand. . . . Students develop their own definitions derived from their findings using the Supposer. I feel this procedure accelerates acquisition of new vocabulary (a definite problem in my predominantly Hispanic school).

Tom (Los Angeles) 3/14/88

At a math conference recently, I saw a presentation whose theme was, basically, one computer with 33 kids. The presenter begins each Supposer lesson with an overhead transparency that says: I Suppose . . . followed by the conjecture of the day.

Sue (Philadelphia) 5/25/88

Have any of you out there used the Presupposer and, if so, at what level, and how? Can you recommend places in the curriculum to use it, or activities that have worked for you?

(in response) Tom (Los Angeles) 5/27/88

I think that now that I have the Presupposer I will use it during the first three introductory chapters of my text. I think it could be used for everything we cover before triangles (angles, pairs of angles, parallel lines).

Chip (Los Angeles) 1/26/89

Does anyone know how you can label a point that is determined by the intersection of two circles when using the Presupposer? [Several responses were sent.]

Another strand of conversation concerns matching the use of the software with particular student needs:

Sue (Los Angeles) 6/6/88

I have had my classes make the conjectures at home many times and have been very frustrated with the results. It is on my list of things not to do next year.

Eva (Los Angeles) 6/24/88

Thank you for responding to (my question on) easing the frustration of many students in the open-ended question situation. They really want to be told exactly which options to pick, what to measure, and what their conjectures should be. I want to guide them, but not to the extent of doing it all for them. I will try your suggestions of more specific directions and checking diagrams before getting started.

Eva (Los Angeles) 11/15/88

How do you meet the needs of students who use less than a class period to complete the lab, and those who need the whole period and can use it productively? [Several responses were sent, pointing to a different structure for conjectures and for pairing students.]

Pat (Philadelphia) 11/28/88

The biggest problem I'm having is getting (the students) away from asking "Is this right?" and always looking to me for the "right answer." I never realized how deeply ingrained this attitude toward learning is.

Extending the Supposer

Two strands of networking conversation are concerned with extending innovative practices derived from using the Geometric Supposer. The first concerns teacher ideas about reaching topics ostensibly not reachable with the Supposer, as the following discussion about volume illustrates:

Phyllis (Philadelphia) 4/13/88

(After a discussion of her students' difficulties in visualizing) I wish there was a Supposer for volume.

(in response) Sue (Los Angeles) 5/2/88

We just supplemented the Supposer text with the Cylinder and Cone section from the Harcourt, Brace, Jovanovich text. Last year, before the Supposer, I had each student create a model of a prism and pyramid with congruent bases.

. . . At the beginning of the year, I used material from a book by Rancucci called *Seeing Shapes* to develop their visual perception.

(continuing the discussion) Chip (Los Angeles) 5/12/88

Regarding solids, I was really pleased to see the feelings expressed by so many others about the obviously lack of Solid geometry in the Supposer. (In my class) we supplemented with a lot of building of three-dimensional things. . . . We built with straws and pipecleaners, rolled newspapers and string.

Similarly, participants expressed a need to expand the networking to other software:

Phyllis (Philadelphia) 6/12/88

A thought just occurred to me. Since we are all apparently using software other than the Supposer, wouldn't it be nice to share knowledge of usable software throughout the network. The next time I get on the horn, I will list all the software we use in the math department, plus a list of software I was able to preview at a local college's resource center.

The second strand of conversation extends into broader issues, with the teachers reflecting on topics such as assessing the impact of using the Supposer:

Chip (Los Angeles) 9/21/88

Many of you told me (at the NCTM Annual Meeting) in Chicago . . . that the real test of how the original class did was not the final test (where we averaged 5 percent lower than the other geometry classes), but in how well the information would be remembered. A senior from last year came back to tell me yesterday that on his college math test he was placed in college algebra, but he passed out of geometry completely. Thanks for your faith and support.

Phyllis (Philadelphia) 1/30/89

My honors geometry class of last year is now the honors alg2/trig class of this year; their teacher is amazed at not only their body of knowledge as they seemed to have absorbed all of the algebra, geometry, and analytic geometry of last year, but she is astounded by their self-confidence and their ability to question. She attributes much of this to the Supposer use and indicates the class thinks of things she would never consider. She also intends to use the Supposer the next time she teaches geometry.

Other topics include the value of current textbooks (with comments similar to other Supposer users, reported by Lampert, 1988):

Phyllis (Philadelphia) 5/17/89

Are textbooks worth reading? If you read ours, you could get the distinct feeling that mathematics in general and geometry in particular are like cooking. You dish up the right recipe and out comes the volume of a cone for dinner. What are textbooks good for?

(in response) Pat (Philadelphia) 5/17/89

Discovery is great, but we certainly don't want to bother reinventing the wheel every day. I use the text this way: After the students have worked in the lab and written a conjecture in their own words, then I refer them to their text. The theorems are much more readable (reading level is a concern here) and understandable.

and the essence of good teacher training:

Phyllis (Philadelphia) 3/1/89

My student teacher wrote her first labs today on circles; they're not like mine at all and they're terrific. When we discussed the unit and how to do this I found myself struggling to articulate procedures that I have internalized to the point where I don't even think about what I'm doing. In this articulation lies the clue to training teachers in Supposer use.

EFFECTS OF NETWORKING

Participation in the GSUN network has begun to change the teacher's professional lives and to foster professional growth. Both Phyllis and Pat, for example, have successfully reached out to colleagues in their respective departments to increase the number of teachers using the Geometric Supposer. Referring to this effort, Phyllis remarked, "We can do things despite the system , . . . because it is large a teacher can slip through the cracks and crevices to get what she wants." But, referring to the need to expand the base of support, she added, "There is power in numbers."

Phyllis and Pat are becoming professional leaders beyond their schools. They have negotiated visits to observe each other and their respective labs. Together, they have led staff development workshops for the district, and Phyllis has been asked to train the district math supervisors in the use of the Geometric Supposer.

Pat and Phyllis have also had an impact beyond Philadelphia. Both women have traveled to other states to give Geometric Supposer workshops, to lead teacher training, and to speak at national conferences. In the fall of 1989, they made presentations on the Supposer at the UMC's annual science and technology conference.

CONCLUSION

Change such as that inspired by Geometric Supposer spreads gradually and seems to develop best when teachers control the process of change. The Geometric Supposer Urban Network exists to allow teachers to strengthen that control.

The teaching profession—mathematics teaching, in particular—has given teachers scant room to reflect on their own professional knowledge. In his book, *The Reflective Practitioner*, Donald Schon (1983)made the point that the best professionals know far more than what researchers and other technical experts tell them ought to be in their body of professional knowledge. This is especially true in professions where "the scope of technical expertise is limited by situations of uncertainty, instability, uniqueness, and conflict" (p. 345), and where the best professionals must rely less on formulas learned in graduate school than on a reflective practice that is often improvisational in nature.

In general, urban teachers are discouraged from exploring or nurturing such reflective practice. However, the evolving GSUN network demonstrates that using the Geometric Supposer requires teachers to reflect on and to improvise in their professional practice more than is ordinarily required. GSUN, in turn, makes it possible for them to share their reflections. The results, we believe, are enriched professional lives for participating teachers.

REFERENCES

Carnegie Foundation for the Advancement of Teaching. (1988). *An imperiled generation: Saving urban schools* (Carnegie Foundation Special Report). Princeton, NJ: Author.

Ford Foundation. (1987). . . . *And gladly teach.* New York: Author.

Lampert, M. (1988). *Teachers' thinking about students' thinking about geometry: The effects of new teaching tools* (Tech. Rep.). Cambridge, MA: Harvard Graduate School of Education, Educational Technology Center.

Maeroff, G. I. (1988). *The empowerment of teachers: Overcoming the crisis of confidence.* New York: Columbia University, Teachers College Press.

Schon, D. A. (1983). *The reflective practitioner: How professionals think in action.* New York: Basic.

Webb, N. (1989). *The urban mathematics collaboratives project: Report to the Ford Foundation on the 1987–1988 school year* (Program Report 89-1). Madison, WI: Wisconsin Center for Education Research.

12 What is the Supposer a Case Of?

Myles Gordon
Education Development Center, Inc.

First student: "In class, it's like 'This is how it is!'"

Second student: "In lab, it's like 'How is it?'"

I see a lot of the way I learn in using the Supposer. . . . You learn from your observations. . . . I like learning from experience or from seeing what other people have done. That's what it is. You're doing the stuff yourself, so you're rediscovering stuff. It's really your own learning.

A COHERENT CALL FOR CHANGE AND A MODEL OF AN ANSWER

Amidst the clamor for education reform, the most coherent proposals have come from the mathematics education community.

The federal government, foundations, corporations, professional organizations of mathematicians and math educators, and universities—all agree that mathematics education as practiced in most United States schools is not meeting anyone's needs. They further agree that our inability to promote effective learning of mathematics for all students is a dangerous state of affairs. It limits the participation of a large portion of the population in the economic, political, and social mainstream of American life; it places the United States economy at a severe competitive disadvantage; and, some would say, it threatens the very security of the country.

What is the Problem?

The National Council of Teachers of Mathematics (NCTM), in its recently released curriculum and evaluation standards document, put the problem quite simply: "What a student learns depends to a great degree on how he or she has learned it" (1989, p. 5).

If what one reaps depends on both what and how one sows, then we get every bit of mathematics learning that we deserve. Throughout elementary and secondary schooling, students are expected to go through only the motions of mathematics, and perhaps more so than in other subjects, as John Goodlad (1984) found, what goes on in the mathematics classroom is teacher lecture and student recitation. It should come as no surprise then that what passes for learning in mathematics is the predigested mechanics of symbol manipulation. Students come away with a meager understanding of mathematical concepts and no first-hand experience of the power and excitement of mathematics.

Is There an Alternative?

Again, the NCTM (1989) provided a useful definition of mathematical literacy, embodied in five goals for students in mathematics education:

1. Learning to Value Mathematics
2. Becoming Confident in One's Own Ability
3. Becoming a Mathematical Problem Solver
4. Learning to Communicate Mathematically
5. Learning to Reason Mathematically

If this is "what" students should be learning, then where can we find the appropriate "how"?

Consensus is also emerging on that question, building on research findings in cognitive science on the nature of knowledge and knowledge making. These findings suggest what is often referred to as *a constructivist approach:* "A close consideration of recent research on mathematical cognition suggests that in mathematics as in reading, successful learners understand the task to be one of constructing meaning, of doing interpretive work rather than routine manipulations" (Resnick, 1987, p. 12).

This approach is echoed in the blueprints for reform. The NCTM (1989) emphasized that "'knowing' mathematics is 'doing' mathematics" (p. 7); the Mathematical Sciences Education Board (MSEB) of the National Research Council, in its report *Everybody Counts* (1989), pointed out that "students learn mathematics well only when they construct their own mathematical understanding" (p. 58).

If the verbs *lecture* and *recite* characterize most current mathematics instruction, the constructivist approach calls for a new set of verbs to characterize what ought to happen in the classroom. In the words of the National Research Council's MSEB (1989), if students are "to understand what they learn, they must enact for themselves verbs that permeate the mathematics curriculum: 'examine,' 'represent,' 'transform,' 'solve,' 'apply,' 'prove,' 'communicate'" (pp. 58–59).

Moreover, this new approach calls for a shift in the perception that the learning of mathematics is an activity students ought to engage in only as isolated individuals. The National Research Council's MSEB (1989) called for "genuine give-and-take in the mathematics classroom, both among students and between students and teachers. . . . This happens most readily when students work in groups, engage in discussion, make presentations, and in other ways take charge of their own learning" (p. 59). The NCTM (1989) argued that "instruction should . . . include opportunities for appropriate project work; group and individual assignments; discussion between teacher and students and among students . . . " (p. 10).

In many ways the experience of thousands of students and teachers over the past several years with the Geometric Supposer is consonant with the proposed new approach to mathematics education. In fact, I argue that software like the Supposer, along with a rich collection of open-ended projects and problems approached through a pedagogy of guided inquiry, is a model of how educators can make real the vision that the NCTM and the MSEB have espoused.

My argument about the relevance of the Supposer to mathematics education reform hinges on the findings of a year-long study of Supposer use in three Boston-area schools that I conducted with Michal Yerushalmy and Daniel Chazan (Yerushalmy, Chazan, & Gordon, 1987) and more than a dozen other research studies done on the Supposer over the past 5 years. These include studies of student learning, teacher attitudes and behaviors, school contexts, and implementation. I review these findings to support the contention that the Supposer experience serves as a model for the national reform of mathematics education. Much of the work I refer to was carried out by the authors of earlier chapters in this volume and is reported by them in their chapters and elsewhere in the research literature.

Not all of the research yields answers. Sometimes it brings to light new questions or questions whose importance was not fully appreciated. I try to discuss some of these findings as well.

Finally, beyond the argument that the Supposer experience serves as a model for national reform in mathematics education, lies the question of education reform in general. I also consider whether the Supposer experience affords any insight into that broader question.

SOME REMARKS ABOUT GUIDED INQUIRY

In the mid-1980s, those of us involved in the development of the Supposer and in the first research studies found ourselves learning mathematics in the domain of geometry in a new and exciting way. In reflecting on this experience, we realized that a new style of learning calls for a new style of teaching. Working with the Supposer, we evolved a pedagogic strategy that we call *guided inquiry* that contrasts sharply with much of current practice in the mathematics classroom.

> [In guided inquiry,] the content of the curriculum is the same as [that in] a standard geometry course. . . . [However,] rather than focusing only on deductive reasoning and proof, the guided-inquiry approach calls for students to integrate inductive reasoning and empirical work with conceptual work in solving problems and devising proofs. . . . While new material is often introduced by teacher lecture . . . , guided inquiry emphasizes laboratory work and class discussion in which students take a more active and responsible role in the learning process. (Yerushalmy et al., 1987, p. 7)

In the computer laboratory, students investigate problems designed to introduce, reinforce, or bring to light ideas, axioms, or theorems from the curriculum. Working with the Supposer, students, usually in pairs, investigate the problem, make constructions, and record numerical and visual data. From these data, they are typically asked to generate conjectures and then to support their conjectures with arguments and proof. Returning to the classroom, discussion periods focus on the sharing of student data, conjectures, and supporting arguments, building collective understanding from individual investigations.

Clearly there is a high degree of overlap between the process of guided inquiry as described here and the vision of a new mathematics education put forward by the NCTM and the MSEB.

Although it is logically possible to separate the use of the Supposer from a pedagogy of guided inquiry, all of the studies I call upon look at guided-inquiry classrooms. If, on the basis of these studies, one wishes to make an argument about a model for mathematics education reform, then the Supposer experience in conjunction with a pedagogy of guided inquiry must be taken as the kernel of the model.

THE GOOD NEWS FROM THE RESEARCH

Findings About Students

The findings about student behavior with the Supposer can be sorted into four categories: mathematical behaviors, attitudes, geometry content, and learning behaviors. Before I summarize each category, let me point out that these behaviors were seen in a wide range of students, at all ability levels, and in a variety of school systems. This is not to say that all the behaviors were seen all the time in all students. Nor is it to say that the behaviors were a direct consequence of using the Supposer. I report only that I saw these behaviors occurring frequently, often in students who were not regarded by their school systems and their teachers as mathematically able.

Mathematical Behaviors. I found that students are able to:

- Discern patterns in both numerical and visual data.
- Make conjectures.
- Make generalizations from numerical data, visual data, and formal statements.
- Construct definitions, axioms, and theorems.
- Construct arguments, both formal and informal, and distinguish between the two.
- Move from the intuitive to the formal and back.
- Use diagrams and understand which features of a diagram are specific to a particular diagram and which are not.
- Reorganize visual fields.
- Offer counterexamples.
- Build on existing knowledge.

Attitudes. I found that students display curiosity, no doubt long dormant, and willingness to explore. In sharp contrast to the normal course of events in mathematics classrooms, students seem willing to take intellectual risks. They also seem willing to make mistakes, a particularly uncommon occurrence when mathematics is thought of as a domain in which there are unique right answers. Above all, they seem to value new ideas and to recognize that there are occasions when they themselves are the originators of such ideas.

Geometry Content. Students in Supposer classes learn as much geometry as the students in traditional classes do, as indicated by their performance on department geometry examinations. In addition, they seem to develop an interest in and an ability to explore geometric ideas not normally encountered in the standard curriculum. They are able to consider generalizations across polygons. They use constructions as an aid in proof. In short, they become geometers—nimble ones for the secondary school setting.

An example illustrates students' ventures beyond the commonplace and their ability to generalize. A geometric construct encountered early in the study of triangles is the median, a line drawn from the vertex of a triangle to the midpoint of its opposite side (see Fig. 12.1). In most geometry texts,

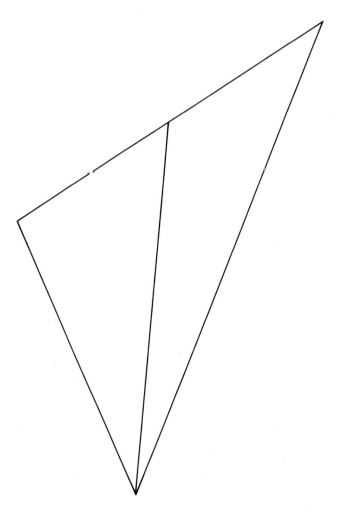

FIG. 12.1. A Median in a Triangle.

the standard definition states that the median bisects the length of the opposite side. While exploring this construction with the Geometric Supposer, students discovered that the median also bisects the area of the triangle (i.e., divides it into two triangles of equal area). The students tested this conjecture to see if it held for all triangles, saw that it did, and proceeded to investigate a proof as well. In some classes, students went on to consider whether this might be the basis of a definition of a median in a quadrilateral or even an n-gon, because there is no definitive opposite side in a quadrilateral.

Learning Behaviors. Perhaps the most desirable outcome of the Supposer experience for many students is the growth of intellectual independence. They learn both to carry out independent investigations and to collaborate with one another when necessary. They learn to value their own ideas and those of others. This leads to a growing ability to communicate about mathematics and to integrate individual and group learning. Above all, they assume an increasing amount of responsibility for the making and transmitting of knowledge in the classroom.

Findings About Teachers

The research findings on teachers can be sorted in much the same way as the student findings into four categories: mathematical behaviors, attitudes, geometry content, and teaching behaviors. As in the case of the students, not all the findings apply to all of the teachers all of the time. Nonetheless, I made the observations reported here across a wide range of teachers in a variety of schools, working with students of widely ranging abilities.

Mathematical Behaviors. The most extraordinary observation about teachers' mathematical behavior in Supposer classrooms is the degree to which teachers started to do mathematics instead of simply teaching the subject. I believe that this modeling of desired behavior influenced the students in these teachers' classes in a strongly positive way (in fact, I found it to be one of the most important and powerful teaching strategies).

This doing of mathematics takes several forms. In addition to working collaboratively with students on still unsolved problems, many of the Supposer teachers began to collaborate with fellow teachers in thinking about and making mathematics. To the extent that such collaboration occurs, it reflects two promising directions for professional development: (a) teachers seeing themselves as active members of the mathematics community, and (b) ongoing collegial exchange as an alternative to the injection of outside expertise as the key source for continuing professional growth.

Finally, many teachers reported excitement, liberation, and invigoration with the use of open-ended problems and with the utterance—with dignity and pride—of the words, "I don't know."

Attitudes. Among the attitude changes in teachers is a growing willingness to explore new technologies and their potential for enhancing the teaching and learning of mathematics. Often teachers are eager to enliven the teaching of the subject. Implicit in this attitude is a belief that lack of positive student response to the subject might be due, at least in part, to dull material presented in dull ways and in ways that are ineffective for some students.

In addition, teachers working with the Supposer and guided inquiry display an uncommon eagerness to discern the varying learning styles of their students and to find ways to modify their teaching to address these varying styles.

Geometry Content.   The most remarkable finding in this category is that many of the Supposer teachers realize that the scope and sequence of the traditional geometry course is not sacred. It is possible to think about a wide variety of routes through even quite traditional material.

Further, many of the Supposer teachers came to a new understanding of the intertwined roles of theorem formulating and theorem proving. In traditional geometry classrooms, theorems originating in antiquity arrive via the text, and students set out to prove these theorems that they assume to be true. The emphasis in such classrooms is clearly on proof, to the neglect of the equally important mathematical act of formulating the theorem to be proven. In Supposer classrooms, this imbalance is redressed in some measure. Over time many Supposer teachers learned how to perform an intricate and difficult intellectual minuet, moving with grace from inductive to deductive thinking and back.

Teaching Behaviors.   Clearly, Supposer teachers struggle to integrate technology into the curriculum, and to some extent they succeed. But there are more important changes in the behaviors of these teachers. Many of them learned to let go, to give up their role as the only authority in the classroom. They learned to acknowledge the value of students' ideas and to respond to them. In classrooms where little inquiry typically occurred, where collaboration might have been viewed as cheating, and where discussion was a rarity, Supposer teachers learned to support student inquiry, to foster collaboration among students, and to moderate the vigorous discussions that inevitably followed sessions in the computer lab.

In sum, teachers are able to go well beyond teacher talk and to support students well beyond recitation and mechanics. They not only learn how to support student inquiry, but, in many cases, they become inquirers themselves. As such, they become both members of and managers of a learning community.

I recognize that this is an unrelievedly positive report of both student and teacher findings. Needless to say, the news is not all good. There were, and are, many problems not yet overcome. Indeed, there are many whose dimensions I am only now coming to appreciate. I now turn to that part of the Geometric Supposer story.

THE OTHER NEWS FROM THE RESEARCH

The first and by far the most important of the other findings is that even with extensive, varied, and often individualized support, implementing the Supposer and guided inquiry is not easy. In one implementation project, roving advisors visited schools and worked with teachers as they tried to incorporate the Supposer into their curriculum and to modify their teaching styles in the direction of guided inquiry. In addition, more experienced teachers and members of the research team met with teachers in monthly seminars and provided a great deal of informal coaching. Computers were made available to teachers so that they could work on problems by themselves and plan lessons away from the pressures of school. Extensive written materials in the form of projects and problems were made available for teachers to use. And still it wasn't easy!

The difficulties derive from the changed and expanded demands on teachers, the dilemmas that confront teachers, and the deep shifts in thinking about themselves and their subject that face teachers who attempt to implement this new approach to mathematics education.

Demands

Working with the Supposer in a guided-inquiry mode takes more time and effort than traditional teaching and a different kind of effort as well. In part, the greater time demands come from the need to deal with technology in the classroom. As computers come to permeate every facet of our society, this problem is likely to diminish in importance, but for the moment it remains a difficulty.

A second kind of increased demand comes from the heavy emphasis on the deductive and formal aspects of the subject in the way most teachers have learned and taught. They are asked to shift their perspective on the subject and to begin to value and incorporate into their teaching inductive modes of thinking. Moreover, they are asked to consider seriously the idea that the sequence of topics that is covered in the traditional geometry course, either the one they previously taught or the one they were taught, is far more arbitrary than they thought. In fact the sequence is set, in very large measure, by the text in use. If the pedagogic style becomes one of guided inquiry, then at any given time, quite different topics are likely to come up for exploration and discussion.

I believe that the heart of the complaint about greater demands lies in the uncertainty teachers experience when they are not in a position to know precisely what issues, constructions, theorems, or even topics their students will raise. Teachers feel that if they are going to be responsive in this sort of open-ended inquiry environment, then they must be ready to respond to a range of potential questions that is far less predictable than is the case in a traditional classroom. Under these circumstances they need more time to prepare and review for class.

Open-ended problems need to be explored, conjectures considered, and possible proofs identified before class. Grading homework and quizzes based on open-ended problems is the mathematical equivalent of dealing with a stack of essays: all are prompted by the same question, but each one requires careful consideration and a unique response. With time, no doubt, teachers will build up a repertoire of problems and strategies, and this effort will diminish, but it will never be as mechanical as correcting two-column proofs or as intellectually empty as checking student responses, year after year, against the answer key in the teacher's edition.

A thoughtful teacher in one of the studies had a successful year with the Supposer but then became disappointed with her students' performance and level of understanding the following year. Finally, she realized the source of her disappointment: guided inquiry gave her a far better understanding of what her students didn't know or understand. It made their lack of knowledge more apparent. With this better information, she found herself driven to develop new approaches to address students' misconceptions and concerns.

Among the most difficult issues for many teachers to rethink is assessment. How does one keep track of who knows what when different students are pursuing different paths? How does one judge performance? Can one quantify the kind of mathematical process knowledge that is at least as important as the factual knowledge of geometry? How does one weigh a bold conjecture in relation to an airtight proof?

In time, the insistent quality of some of these increased demands receded. The technology began simply to be present as a classroom tool, in much the same way as the chalkboard or a shelf of reference books. Grading strategies emerged and were refined. Habits of classroom management developed. Students increasingly became accustomed to their new roles and responsibilities in the classroom.

Dilemmas

The constructivist approach to knowledge not only places new demands on teachers but also forces them to confront a series of new dilemmas.

The essence of this series of dilemmas is well captured in the work of Magdalene Lampert (see chapter 8, this volume) who points out the basic conflict between "What can I help these students learn?" and "What am I supposed to teach?" Let me spell out some of the implications of this conflict.

Teachers who adopt a constructivist approach often find it necessary to question the way they think about the very subject they are teaching. If the specific set of topics and the sequence in which they are covered is no longer completely prescribed, teachers begin to ask, "What is the purpose of teaching this material?" When they face the fact that not everyone in the class learns the same material, they must address the questions, "What is the essence of this subject?" and "Are there things about geometry that everyone should know?"

The pedagogical counterpart to this subject matter dilemma is the question of "how much structure?" On one hand, there must be sufficient guidance so that the process of inquiry is productive and fruitful and yields substantive mathematics. On the other hand, too much structure makes a mockery of inquiry and reduces classroom activity to the ceremonial rituals of traditional mathematics instruction. Should students completely reinvent geometry (see Healy, chapter 5, this volume) or should inquiry, if desirable at all, be merely a motivator?

A second kind of dilemma arises because a constructivist approach is the enemy of coverage. Inquiry is time consuming and may not fit neatly into the 50-minute time bundles in which the school day comes packaged. If one commits oneself to taking students' ideas seriously and to following the implications and consequences of at least some of them, then life in the classroom becomes unpredictable, full of side trips and possible dead ends.

A constructivist approach is also at odds with the notion of problems that have unique correct answers. There are such problems. They are, however, not the real problems of adult life. Nor, for that matter, are they the real problems of the disciplines learned and taught in schools. If schools allow students to inquire, they are unlikely to pursue problems that have unique correct answers. The problem of assessment then demands delicacy, because correctness can no longer be the measure of how much and how well a student has learned the subject.

Many teachers who have adopted a constructivist approach in their teaching find themselves questioning their own identities as teachers. They begin to ask, "What does it mean to be a good teacher?" For some, the once adequate response of "making it through the lesson or the textbook" no longer suffices. It can be unsettling when students leave the class after a lesson, a lab, or a week with no crisp sense of closure, completeness, or accomplishment. Teachers often begin to recast the question of what it means to be a good teacher so that it becomes, "Am I giving the students what they need?" This brings the teachers back to the dilemma mentioned earlier, "What do students need from geometry?"

The teachers are not the only ones confronted with these dilemmas. Coverage is not solely a concern of teachers. Students in guided-inquiry classrooms often compare their progress through the textbook, if they have one, with that of their peers in traditional classes and ask, "Are we behind?" Some report feeling different from their friends and unable to share homework.

Because schools tend to transmit information rather than support the acquisition of knowledge, and because students tend to internalize a notion of intellectual authority inherent in teacher and text, they often feel at a loss to establish "truth." Many students from traditional classes find the shift in their roles that accompanies guided inquiry disconcerting and the lack of single correct answers disorienting. Students ask, "How do we know if it's right?" about some newly devised conjecture that emerges from the class. Only when they realize that knowledge is not the private preserve of teachers and textbook writers do they internalize the essential message of guided inquiry.

Some students are also relieved about what is to come when they move on to the next year's mathematics class. They look forward to algebra class, where they will "just learn like we did before. Right from the book and have the teacher teach." A return to normalcy.

Shifts in Thinking

The kinds of intellectual and psychological adjustments that many teachers and students have to make in order to become comfortable with a pedagogy of guided inquiry and with curricular materials like the Geometric Supposer are not minor changes, even for the best of teachers and students. The nature and extent of these changes contrasts with the kinds of changes often asked of those in schools to make. The adoption of a new text or the addition of a new topic or even a new course to the curriculum does not engender the same questioning of fundamental assumptions. Teachers and students are asked to face a range of profound questions about every aspect of learning and teaching in schools. This means violating norms, shifting paradigms, and making a cultural transition. It is little wonder the process seems difficult.

THE IMPLICATIONS

What, then, is learned from the overall Supposer experience?

First, technology serves as a catalyst for change, but it can't carry the day. Technology—with appropriate software, with appropriate materials, with an appropriate pedagogy, and with appropriate support for the learning community that is the classroom—can catalyze change. Specifically, technology plays a role in empowering students to acquire knowledge on their own and to develop the concomitant sense of intellectual independence that is the hallmark of a successful education. Furthermore, technology helps teachers to become sufficiently self-confident and self-assured that they willingly abdicate their role as supreme intellectual authority and share such authority with those who earn it. Needless to say, these changes require working out a vastly different set of roles, rules, and relationships among teachers, students, texts, and subject matter. I hasten to emphasize that the technology, although necessary, is not sufficient. It is at best a tool. And like any tool, it can be abused and used in ways that mock its potential. I saw Supposer classrooms in which a whole class was led through an "inquiry," keystroke by keystroke.

Second, teachers are central to the constructivist approach and must be supported. To take advantage of the constructivist approach to learning and teaching with technology, teachers must be supported with adequate time and appropriate mechanisms for study and preparation and with appropriate curricular materials. One must question whether the existing school structures allow for the kind of collegial interaction among teachers that is necessary for the success of this approach to education.

Moreover, teachers must be helped to cope with the new and increased demands placed on them and to wrestle with the dilemmas that they will inevitably confront.

Teachers by themselves, though, constitute neither the problem nor the solution. It is both unfair and naive to place the responsibility and burden of embracing and implementing such fundamental change solely on the shoulders of teachers. Classrooms and teachers do not exist in a vacuum. Rather, what happens in the classroom is the product of a much broader teaching and learning system that exists beyond as well as within the walls of schools. For changes to occur, one must be prepared to undertake what Jerrold Zacharias, M.I.T. professor, progenitor of school curriculum reform, and mentor to me and to many in the curriculum improvement business, called a *proper systems engineering job.*

What would it take? Like the MSEB and NCTM, one needs to think about all the actors—from students and parents right on through communities and states to the President of the United States—who need to be engaged and about all the tasks and problems, from curriculum and testing to equity and research, that must be tackled to make school reform a reality. We need to get our restructuring act together. Reforms like those of MSEB and NCTM, calling for restructuring content and instruction, must be integrated with reforms calling for the restructuring of schools and of the ways time and people in school buildings are organized and with the reforms calling for restructuring the teaching profession. One needs to take seriously the notion of Elmore and McLaughlin (1988) that successful reform and innovation require an understanding of the interaction of policy, administration, and practice. One needs to heed Cohen's warning that inquiry-oriented instruction runs counter to "an old and deeply rooted scholastic inheritance" in which "teaching is telling, learning is accumulation, and knowledge is facts, strung together by rules of procedure" (1988, p. 256).

> Ordinary sources of knowledge are at least as powerful an influence on children's learning as their school instruction. And in large parts of America, this ordinary knowledge is quite traditional and closely tied to the instructional practices that inquiry-oriented approaches to reform have sought to replace. (p. 263)

Clearly teachers and students, technology and texts are not sufficient. There is no choice but to undertake it all. The price is high, but the price of not doing so is higher still.

WHAT IS THE GEOMETRIC SUPPOSER A CASE OF?

Let me conclude with an observation. Nowhere in the previous section on the implications of what has been learned is the word mathematics mentioned. That is neither an oversight nor a coincidence. What has been learned from the Supposer experience about reforming mathematics education can and must apply more broadly to education in general. Like technology and teachers, neither geometry by itself nor even mathematics by itself is up to the task.

There is a need for questioning, intellectually independent students in all subject areas. There is also a need for flexible teachers in every discipline, who can be both members of and managers of learning communities. There is a need for schools to become knowledge-making places across the curriculum.

One confronts the same problems in all subject areas and at all levels of education. There are new and extended demands on teachers. There are dilemmas to face. There is a need to rethink roles and responsibilities for both students and teachers. And there are systemic questions to consider.

The Supposer experience is not a clear model for how to bring about such change in education across the board, but the experience does shed light on the challenge and the opportunity.

ACKNOWLEDGMENTS

I would like to acknowledge the encouragement and editorial support of Judah Schwartz in the writing of this chapter. I also wish to acknowledge the contributions of the authors of the research on which this chapter draws, including Pat Butler, Daniel Chazan, Mark Driscoll, Chip Healy, Richard Houde, Grace Kelemanik, Magdalene Lampert, Judah Schwartz, Beth Wilson, Martha Wiske, and Michal Yerushalmy.

REFERENCES

Cohen, D. K. (1988). Educational technology and school organization. In R. S. Nickerson & P. P. Zodhiates (Eds.), *Technology in education: Working toward 2020* (pp. 231-264). Hillsdale, NJ: Lawrence Erlbaum Associates.

Elmore, R. F., & McLaughlin, M. W. (1988). Steady work: Policy, practice, and the reform of American education (Report No. R-3574-NIE/RC). Santa Monica: Rand.

Goodlad, J. (1984). *A place called school.* New York: McGraw-Hill.

National Council of Teachers of Mathematics. (1989). *Curriculum and evaluation standards for school mathematics.* Reston, VA: Author.

National Research Council. (1989). *Everybody counts: A report to the nation on the future of mathematics education.* Washington, DC: National Academy Press.

Resnick, L. B. (1987). *Education and learning to think.* Washington, DC: National Academy Press.

Schwartz, J. L., & Yerushalmy, M. (1985-1988). *The Geometric Supposer.* Pleasantville, NY: Sunburst.

Yerushalmy, M., Chazan, D., & Gordon, M. (1987). *Guided inquiry and technology: A yearlong study of children and teachers using the "Geometric Supposer"* (Tech. Rep. No. 90-8). Newton, MA: Education Development Center, Center for Learning, Teaching, and Technology.

APPENDIX: A GUIDE TO THE GEOMETRIC SUPPOSER

The purpose of this appendix is twofold. For those readers who are acquainted with the Geometric Supposer, this appendix will refresh their memory as to the way the program looks and the way it operates. Those readers who have never had an opportunity to use any of the Supposer programs will find it useful to read this appendix as a brief introduction in order to help them make better sense of much of the discussion in the book.

THE ESSENTIAL IDEA OF THE SUPPOSER

There is a problem facing both the teacher and the learner of geometry. We need to work with diagrams when we deal with spatial matters. Any diagrams we make are, of necessity, specific. But the geometry we wish to teach and to learn deals not with specific spatial forms, but rather with classes of forms. The essential idea of all the Supposer programs is to enable the user to make constructions on specific forms and to be able to explore the consequences of those constructions on those forms as well as on a wide variety of other members of the same class of forms.

The ability to explore the consequences of one's actions on a variety of forms, all belonging to the same class, is, we believe, a necessary precursor to the making and exploring of conjectures, which, in turn is a necessary ingredient in the development of a deep and creative understanding of mathematics.

There are three Geometric Supposer programs. They are devoted respec tively to the study of triangles, quadrilaterals, and circles. There is also an introductory program entitled the Geometric Presupposer, which we do not discuss here.

THE TOP LEVEL MENU

All of the Geometric Supposer programs have the following top level menu:

DRAW
    allows the user to make a variety of constructions on the shapes that are present on the screen

LABEL
    allows the user to label a point that may result from previous actions, for example, intersections

ERASE
    allows the user to erase elements of prior constructions

MEASURE
    allows the user to make measurements of angles, lengths, and areas

SCALE
    allows the user to rescale a construction

REPEAT
    allows the user to repeat the present construction on another member of the same class of shapes

NEW SHAPE
    allows the user to start over with a totally new shape

QUIT
    allows the user to leave the program

THE SUBMENUS

Some of the options on the top level menu need no further discussion. Some of them, however, do require further elucidation.

New Shape

In order to begin to use any of the programs, the user must either choose or construct a shape. Here are the possible shapes available in each of the programs under the *New Shape* option.

TRIANGLES
  Acute
    Scalene
    Isosceles
    Equilateral
  Right
    Scalene
    Isosceles
  Obtuse
    Scalene
    Isosceles
  Construct your own triangle
    by SIDE SIDE SIDE
    by SIDE ANGLE SIDE
    by ANGLE SIDE ANGLE

QUADRILATERALS
  Parallelograms
    Random parallelogram
    Rectangle
    Rhombus
    Square
  Trapezoid
    Random trapezoid
    Isosceles trapezoid
    Right angle trapezoid
  Kites
  Quadrilaterals inscribable in or circumscribable by circles
  Construct your own quadrilateral
    by sides and angles
    by ratio of diagonal lengths & nature of their intersection

CIRCLES
  One circle
  Two circles
    Intersecting circles
      any intersecting circles
      orthogonal intersecting circles
    Tangent circles
      externally tangent
      internally tangent
    Separate circles
      external
      internal

concentric
Construct your own circle or circles

Draw

The most likely thing a user of the program would do at this point to make some constructions. Here is a list of the primitive constructions in each of the programs.

TRIANGLES
Segment
Circle
    circumscribing given shape
    inscribed in given shape
    specified by center and radius
Median
Altitude
Parallel
Perpendicular
Angle bisector
Perpendicular bisector
Midsegment
Extension

QUADRILATERALS
Segment
Circle
    circumscribing given shape
    inscribed in given shape
    specified by center and radius
Parallel
Perpendicular
Angle bisector
Perpendicular bisector
Midsegment
Extension

CIRCLES
Lines
    Segment
    Extension
    Parallel
    Perpendicular
    Angle bisector

    Perpendicular bisector
  Lines related to Circles
    Tangent through a point
    Common external tangents
    Common internal tangents
    External line
    Secant
    Chord
  Circles
    by specifying center and radius

Label

In the Triangles and the Quadrilaterals programs, this option allows the user to label the intersections of lines. It also allows the user to subdivide segments into subsegments of equal length and reflect points in lines. Finally, it allows users to place points at random inside, outside, or on the boundary of a shape that the user specifies.

In the Circles program, this option also permits the inversion of a point in a circle.

Repeat

This option allows the user to repeat the current construction on another shape in the same class. Thus, a construction carried out initially on a rectangle can be repeated on a trapezoid or a kite. The user has the option of repeating constructions on new shapes or on shapes that were used previously. More recent versions of the Supposer allow the user to repeat constructions on shapes that are derived from the current shape by deformation.

A NOTE ABOUT THE GEOMETRIC SUPERSUPPOSER

Development of the Supposer software environments has continued and, at the time of this writing, a new program called the Geometric Supersupposer has appeared. It incorporates the features of all of the Supposer programs, and many new ones as well, in one program. The Supersupposer was developed primarily for two reasons. First, the advance of technology made it possible to eliminate many of the logistical difficulties brought about by having the content spread out over three (or four, counting the Presupposer) programs. The second and by far more important reason is to respond to the lessons learned from watching students and teachers do geometry in these environments for several years.

Author Index

Boldface numbers denote chapters in which references are cited.

Subject Index